The University of Alberta Press

TONY ROBINSON-SMITH

The Dragon Run

Two Canadians,
Ten Bhutanese,
One Stray Dog

Published by

The University of Alberta Press
Ring House 2
Edmonton, Alberta, Canada T6G 2E1
www.uap.ualberta.ca

Copyright © 2017 Tony Robinson-Smith

LIBRARY AND ARCHIVES CANADA
CATALOGUING IN PUBLICATION

Robinson-Smith, Tony, 1964– , author
     The dragon run : two Canadians,
ten Bhutanese, one stray dog / Tony
Robinson-Smith.

(Wayfarer)
Issued in print and electronic formats.
ISBN 978-1-77212-300-5 (softcover).—
ISBN 978-1-77212-349-4 (EPUB).—
ISBN 978-1-77212-350-0 (Kindle).—
ISBN 978-1-77212-351-7 (PDF)

     1. Robinson-Smith, Tony, 1964-.
2. College teachers—Bhutan—Biography.
3. College teachers—Canada—Biography.
4. Running races—Bhutan. 5. Fund
raising—Bhutan. 6. Education—Bhutan.
7. Bhutan—Social conditions—21stcentury.
I. Title. II. Series: Wayfarer (Edmonton,
Alta.)

DS491.4 R63 2017   954.98
C2017-904144-4
C2017-904145-2

First edition, first printing, 2017.
First printed and bound in Canada by
Houghton Boston Printers, Saskatoon,
Saskatchewan.

Substantive editing by Kimmy Beach.
Copyediting and proofreading by
Meaghan Craven.
Map by Wendy Johnson.

The University of Alberta Press is committed
to protecting our natural environment.
As part of our efforts, this book is printed
on Enviro Paper: it contains 100% post-
consumer recycled fibres and is acid- and
chlorine-free.

The University of Alberta Press gratefully
acknowledges the support received for its
publishing program from the Government
of Canada, the Canada Council for the Arts,
and the Government of Alberta through the
Alberta Media Fund.

To Her Majesty the Queen Mother Ashi Dorji Wangmo Wangchuck and the Tarayana Foundation

Contents

Map

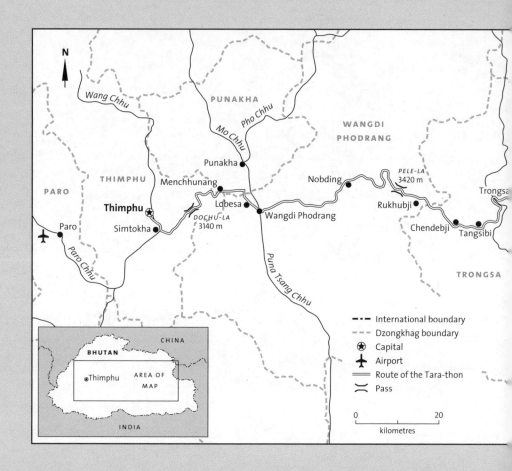

N

Wang Chhu

PUNAKHA

Pho Chhu

Mo Chhu

WANGDI
PHODRANG

THIMPHU

Punakha

Menchhunang

PELE-LA
3420 m

Nobding

Trongsa

PARO

Thimphu

Lobesa

Rukhubji

Paro

Simtokha

DOCHU-LA
3140 m

Wangdi Phodrang

Chendebji

Tangsibi

Puna Tsang Chhu

TRONGSA

CHINA

BHUTAN

Thimphu

AREA OF
MAP

INDIA

International boundary

Dzongkhag boundary

Capital

Airport

Route of the Tara-thon

Pass

0   20
kilometres

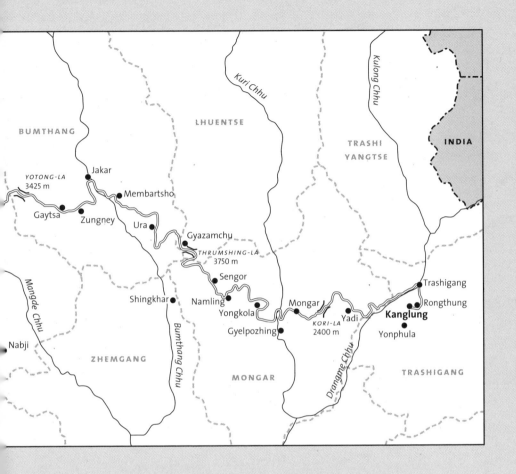

With the blessings of the Trashigang Lam Neten, 10 students and two lecturers of Sherubtse College hit the east–west highway yesterday in a 600 kilometre marathon from Kanglung to Thimphu to raise funds for poor Bhutanese children.

Final year economics student, Ugyen Lhendup, said he and his friends had covered more than 3,000 kilometres during practice. "We're confident," he said.

The boys, however, dread the stretch across the 3,650 metre high Thrumshing La between Bumthang and Mongar. The climb and the cold were expected to pose a challenge.

"But it's a once in a lifetime opportunity to help unfortunate children avail education," said Sonam Wangdi, a II year English honours student.

—KUENSEL, December 22, 2007

1

1 Lama's Blessing

Day 1 Itinerary

9:00 A.M.	*Runners, lecturers, and school children gather on college playing field*
9:15 A.M.	*Arrival of dignitaries (Lam Neten, Khenpo, Dasho Dzongdag, Dasho Drangpon, director of Sherubtse College)*
9:20 A.M.	*Welcome address by Rongthung Sangay, event coordinator*
9:25 A.M.	*Speech by Tony Robinson-Smith, project leader*
9:30 A.M.	*Presentation of Team Tara-thon by Tony Robinson-Smith*
9:35 A.M.	*Blessing of the event by Lam Neten*
9:45 A.M.	*Presentation of the morning activities by Nadya Ladouceur, project leader*
9:50 A.M.	*First activity: short story writing and drawing on the theme of "Helping Others" in auditorium*
10:45 A.M.	*Second activity: warm-up for the run*
11:00 A.M.	*Official start of the Tara-thon: Dasho Dzongdag and Dasho Drangpon flag the runners off; children and lecturers join until Rongthung village*
11:30 A.M.	*Refreshments served at Rongthung Community Primary School; children disperse; runners continue to Trashigang*

FROM A BUDDHIST PERSPECTIVE, December 21, 2007, begins auspiciously. The horoscope in last week's *Kuensel* assured me it would be "a good day to conduct thruesel," and Lam Neten has driven up from Trashigang Dzong specially. The Khenpo, abbot of the local shedra, has come to assist. I am a little concerned that the paper also said it was "not a good day to venture on long journey" but recall it saying in February, when the lunar year began, that "the symbolic good direction is north and south. While starting new ventures or an important task, the datho recommends facing in one of these two directions." We are running west across the Dragon

Kingdom, but we start our new venture auspiciously by heading north today to Trashigang.

From an earthly perspective, however, our departure day, although pleasantly warm and dry, does not start out very promisingly. "A hundred shouting school kids will descend the mountain with us," I wrote in my first entry on our Tara-thon blog two days ago. My wife Nadya and I had decided earlier in the year that a run for education should involve as many children as possible. We would drop in on all the schools along the way; speak on the value of education, sports, and volunteerism; have the students draw or write about acts of kindness; and get teachers and students to run a few kilometres with us. I sent letters to district education officers (DEOs) across the kingdom, asking them to alert the schools in their dzongkhags. Nadya visited Kanglung Primary School and talked to the head teacher, and Mr. Sangay contacted the primary school in his home village five kilometres down the mountain. As a result of our preparations, at 9:30 A.M., Nadya is ready on the playing field with paper, pens, crayons, and a whistle. No school children, shouting or otherwise. An hour later, she is still there alone. We are also short of the two dashos, the dzongkhag administrator, and the judge from Trashigang.

"Today marks the beginning of a great event," I say, not so sure now that it does. It is already eleven o'clock, and we have not had the lama's benediction yet. We are expected at Rongthung Primary School in half an hour. We have retreated to a square of worn grass with a jacaranda tree just inside the college entrance. Nadya and Mr. Sangay are at my side, and our student runners, driver, and cook stand behind. Our audience is the college administrators, five Bhutanese lecturers, and four monks sitting on plastic chairs. Team Tara-thon almost outnumbers the well-wishers. I hardly need raise my voice. Sherubtse College is dead now exams are over.

"We have given the name 'Tara-thon' to our fundraiser, a word combining Tarayana with marathon..."

We are lucky to be running for the Tarayana Foundation. At the start of the year, the executive committee rejected our proposal, saying that the foundation was interested "more in advocacy than charity," which we took to mean "helping the vulnerable...help themselves," as declared in the leaflet Aum Chime, the secretary general, had given us. Fortunately, Her Majesty the Queen interceded on our behalf, saying that our project was a worthy initiative. After that, things started falling into place. In June Aum Chime promised to get Tara-thon T-shirts printed and sent me a list of schools with Tarayana clubs. In July I sent her a month's salary to help with expenses and to confirm our commitment to the project. I wrote to the new director of Sherubtse and asked to borrow the twenty-five-seater college bus for the winter. Mr. Sangay came on board in August to handle logistics. ("I think you will need someone to say kuzu zangpo to official and make arrangement.") In September Nadya made a press kit for the media and gave a presentation on our run during morning assembly. She invited students either to run part of the way with us or volunteer to be sponsorship collectors. In November we got news that the minister of education had authorized the release of funds to the DEOs of the six dzongkhags we would cross "to provide assistance and support for the Tara-thon program."

"...and our team hopes, through the funds it raises, to give as many village children as possible the chance to attend school."

We had our first team meeting for runners in the fall, shortly after Nadya's presentation in assembly. Thirty-four students attended: thirty-two male and two female. I recognized three foot-ballers, one a player on the national team. Twenty-nine of the thirty-four wanted to run all the way to Thimphu (pronounced *Tim-poo*). Recollecting Sherubtse's Annual Spring Marathon, I had a vision of students in football kit and flip-flops sprinting down the hill from Kanglung, barging each other off the road, some taking shortcuts across farmers' fields, one clutching his side and trying to wave down a passing Tata truck for a ride. Nadya and I talked soberly for twenty minutes about the potential health risks of running up and down mountains, the responsibilities of the organizers, and the reputations of the college and Tarayana. And this would be a run, we stressed, not a walk...and a run to raise money, not a run to win cash prizes as in the college race. Only those who were both physically capable and committed to our cause would be accepted on the team. A three-day running trial would determine the first, an interview the second.

"...Ugyen Younten, first year, English and environmental studies; Sherab Jamtscho, third year, commerce; Tharchen, second year, life science..."

The ten runners we have selected step forward in turn and take deep bows, throwing their arms to the ground as I read out their names. They are a mixed bunch: two third-years, four second-years, four first, studying a range of subjects. With the exception of Ugyen Lhendup and Tharchen, Nadya and I barely know them. Ugyen finished third in the college marathon of 2006. We discovered this year that he was the nephew of Tshering Wangdi, a colleague in the English Department. "He has been running marathon since junior high school and won many prize," Tshering assured us when we asked him whether Ugyen was up to running across the country. "He always commits to whatever he set out to do." Dr. Jagar Dorji, the former director of the college, recommended Tharchen as he had taken a leading role in his "Clean Bhutan Campaign" last winter, a drive across the kingdom to pick up roadside litter. Whether he was any good at running, Dr. Jagar could not say. "When PE teacher made us run at school," Tharchen informed me when we went out for a jog around campus together, "I was always last to finish."

Sonam Wangdi is an amiable footballer who took one of my English classes in the spring; Ugyen Younten, a lanky orphan from a village near Thimphu; "Tiger" (Yenten Jamtscho), a bubbly twenty-one-year-old, who broke stones as a child to afford his schooling; and "Tee" (Tshering Dorji), an earnest twenty-two-year-old studying science. Tee's training partner is Wangchuk Rabten, another science student, who, with spectacles and goatee, resembles more a junior professor than a student. Sonam Gyalpo is a thin-faced first-year, lucky to be on the team as he only did one day of the trial run, and Dendup is a beefy-looking second-year taking English and fond of wearing a red baseball cap when he runs. The shiest member of our team is Sherab, who whispered to me in his interview, "If I could successed this project, it will be my life long achievement."

I end my speech with a round of thanks—to the minister of education, to Tarayana, to Sherubtse, to Lotus Tours for the bus— and then the college director, Singye Namgyel, comes forward to say a few words. He is a soft-spoken, thoughtful man in his mid-fifties who, over the past months, has encouraged us to consider what we are doing with care. Have we thought about a police escort, especially through the towns? What happens if someone collapses or gets injured? How will we look after the money we collect? After he has shaken everyone's hand and wished us tashi delek, he gives us a cheque for 7,000 Bhutanese ngultrums (BTN). He will look out for us when he drives to Thimphu in a couple of weeks' time. This brings donations from the Sherubtse community to BTN 48,164 (about 1,284 Canadian dollars), a good start—although we are on home turf, and Nadya explained the concept of sponsorship in assembly. Whether strangers will understand what we are doing and respond as generously is another matter. I am hoping the DEOs have spread the word and that Mr. Sangay will call ahead and advise officials.

Lam Neten leads the way to the main gate, orange robe swishing left and right behind him, a little wooden drum with string clappers knocking in his hand, a splash of sunlight on his shaven crown. Nadya and I have gotten to know him a bit as the Trashigang monk body owns real estate in Kanglung. He has dropped by our bungalow for tea a couple of times and sent monks to fix our electrics or plumbing. We stop just inside the gate, form a line in front of him, take off our caps, and bow our heads. For several minutes, the lama chants words of Choekey into the sky, his voice gravelly and sonorous. I imagine him putting in a good word for us: *Sakyamuni, Guru Rinpoche, Gods of mountain pass and rocky ravine, smile on these crazy mortals for the next month. Keep them safe from earthquakes, landslides, blizzards, drunk drivers, and spiteful spirits.* A teenage monk brings a mirror and a bronze jug with a peacock feather sticking out the top and pours a thin, wavy line of holy water at our feet. Then another and another. It seems he is drawing a diagram of the mountains we will cross. Next, the lama takes a handful of rice from a bowl held by another monk and tosses it over us. He does this with his right hand while sounding the damaru in his left and reciting more prayers. Out of the corner of my eye, I see the two men from Bhutan Broadcasting Service filming the ceremony. A journalist from *Kuensel* crouches and takes photographs.

"Holy water is offering to good spirits for success of our mission," Mr. Sangay whispers in my ear. "Mirror send our prayer back to us. Rice purify our bad deeds."

"And what do the words mean?"

"All beings should support as a whole, universal." I look at him, puzzled. "If good luck come to Mr. Tony, then this good luck will go from him to other beings. If good spirit good to us, we in turn good to other." It was Mr. Sangay who insisted we have thruesel before beginning our Tara-thon.

The blessing ends when the Khenpo ties a small pouch of prayers on a bit of string around our necks and puts a white silk scarf called a tashi kaddah over each runner's head. I am nervous. No one has attempted this before. Nearly six hundred kilometres and five mountain ranges separate us from the capital. I am not so worried about myself or about Nadya, but what happens if one of the students gets hypothermia? In their baggy shorts and ill-fitting Tara-thon T-shirts, they seem woefully frail, skinny legs goosepimpling in the bitter winter wind. I pray these young men are reincarnated mountain goats, inclined in their past lives to race up and down mountains for pleasure. I hope our cause has put fire in their blood. Her Majesty will not be impressed if she sees ten of her subjects, future leaders of the realm, staggering into Thimphu on bloody feet. She would surely regret giving us permission to run for her foundation.

For some reason, we skip the warm-up on our itinerary but, at Ugyen Lhendup's insistence, circumambulate the lhakhang in front of the college, spinning the squeaky tin prayer wheels embedded in its walls as we go. For the two chilips from Canada, this is the final act before saying goodbye to Sherubtse College and to Kanglung. No one flags us off, but the lecturers and monks, and some of the shop-keepers, yell encouragement. Knowing I won't find him, I look about for Dr. Jagar. Without him, Nadya and I could not have staged this event. Without him, I would not have gotten a contract to teach in Bhutan. Running down the mountain and seeing for the last time a crude representation of Guru Rinpoche painted on a rock at a bend in the road, I think back to our first crossing of the kingdom with the former director and how, in a ceremony at his home village, we propitiated the gods for an auspicious start.

The whole of the Bootan territory presents a succession of the most lofty and rugged mountains on the surface of the globe. Their stupendous size almost precludes the possibility of obtaining a position sufficiently commanding upon them, to afford a bird's eye view of the general direction, for they are separated only by the narrow beds of roaring torrents, which rush over huge boulders of primitive rock with resistless violence...the consequence is, that the traveller appears to be shut out on every side from the rest of the world, and it is only when winding round some spur from the minor ranges, that he obtains an occasional glimpse of the more distant peaks and ridges which bound the view of the deep dell at his feet, where some restless river is urging its way to the sea.

—CAPTAIN R. BOILEAU PEMBERTON,
Report on Bootan, 1839

2 | Precious Teacher

ALMOST TWO YEARS BEFORE, Nadya and I were in the back of a Land Cruiser, heading the other way on the east–west highway. In my bag, I had a signed contract from the Royal Government of Bhutan, ten passport photographs, a medical certificate declaring that I was of sound health, a work permit, a permit to travel across the kingdom, a police report from Fredericton declaring that I had been a law-abiding citizen there, a "Certificate of Character and Good Conduct" that was supposed to be signed by a senior government officer but was in fact signed by a former colleague at the University of New Brunswick, and an "Oath of Secrecy" that I would sign in front of witnesses when we arrived at Sherubtse College. In signing the contract, I had promised not to engage in "harmful practices which may have a sinister inspect on the society." My wife did not have a work contract and would be my "dependent" until she found a job. We also had a Lonely Planet guide, pepper spray, a tent and sleeping bags, pills for indigestion, two pairs of running shoes each, fabric plasters, a copy of *Gulliver's Travels*, Salim Ali's *Field Guide to the Birds of the Eastern Himalayas* (bought in Thimphu), and a bag of mandarins (bought en route). Dr. Jagar Dorji was at the wheel.

"Where in the world you go in opposite directions to reach same place?"

Swinging hard around yet another hairpin bend in the road, dodging a brown cow with a bell on its neck, he looked in the rear-view mirror for a response from the back. Taking us under his wing from our arrival in the country, he had sent his son to pick us up from the airport and an alumnus from the Royal University of Bhutan to show us around Thimphu. While I was still in Canada, he had put me in touch with the "English in-charge" at Sherubtse; I now knew that I would be teaching eighteenth- and nineteenth-century English literature to third-year students. With his bristly black-and-white hair and sturdy build, Dr. Jagar looked to me more like a retired boxer than the director of the university's largest college, but I knew he had a master's degree in geography education from England and a PHD in education from Australia. His wife sat beside him, looking equally robust with sun-scorched cheeks and a farmer's hands. Muttering "Om mani padme hum" and feeding prayer beads through her fingers for most of the nine hours of our journey, she now focused her attention on a small jam jar sandwiched between her knees. Extracting a dollop of lime paste and smearing it over a green leaf, Zangmo dropped an areca nut into the centre, rolled the leaf up, and stuffed it in her husband's cheek. Soon, he, too, would have a red mouth. Nadya and I shared the back seat with Dr. Jagar's ten-year-old nephew, Pema, who had already succumbed to motion sickness. We piled against the left door as the Land Cruiser lurched.

"North Pole?" I grunted, a fresh wave of nausea washing over me.

"Bhutan!" hollered Dr. Jagar triumphantly.

It was February 11, 2006, and we were bound for Kanglung, a village halfway up a mountain on the other side of the kingdom, where Sherubtse (meaning "Peak of Learning") was located. It would take us, apparently, three or four days to get there. I knew from the map in my guidebook that the village was about as far east of Thimphu as it was possible to go without finding ourselves in the Indian state of Arunachal Pradesh, but the distance was only two hundred kilometres as the crow flies. Yet, we had started out from the capital at eight that morning, and we were little more than a third of the way there. I noticed that symbols on the map that resembled bridges represented the reason for our slow progress. The "bridges" were actually mountain passes, "la" in Dzongkha, and we had crossed two of six: Dochu-La at 3140 metres and Pele-La at 3420 metres. There is no mistaking when you arrive at a la. Apart from the obvious fact that you stop going uphill and start going down, there are hundreds of prayer flags marking the spot. These are red, blue, yellow, white, or green with prayers printed on them in black and are either strung up the sides of six-metre bamboo poles or suspended over the road like pocket handkerchiefs on washing lines.

"Do monks come and put up all these flags?" Nadya had asked Dr. Jagar at Dochu-La.

"Anyone can put up a prayer flag. People who want good fortune in their lives, or God's protection, or someone died and they want his spirit to be cleaned, or a family member is ill, or they have to do something important and they want God's help."

"Some of the flags need to be replaced," I observed. "Look, those over there are coming apart." One chain of flags had come loose and wrapped itself around three poles. Each flag was a fraction of its original size, more a hairy tongue now than a flag, grey with age and trailing long filaments that danced in the wind.

"That is as it should be," said our new acquaintance. "The wind slowly breaks them, and that releases the prayers."

There were also chortens, white pillars the size of telephone boxes with orange belts around their waists and matching "hats" resembling squashed pyramids. Corpulent gold Buddhas gazed beatifically from trefoil windows in their sides. Chortens came in three styles, Dr. Jagar told us, Bhutanese, Tibetan, and Nepali, and they contained carved holy sticks called sokshing or sometimes the bones of a dead lama, endowing them with spiritual life force. There were 108 of them (an auspicious number in Buddhism) at Dochu-La, rising in three tiers on a grassy island and looking like surpliced choirboys. Cars had to drive around them clockwise once or three times (twice would bring ill luck). We got out of the Land Cruiser and walked around, a chill wind raking our legs, and I wondered whether Dr. Jagar was cold, knees exposed beneath his gho, the national dress resembling a heavy bathrobe. The tempera-ture was close to 0°C, and banks of snow lined the road. In Thimphu, a thousand metres below, it had been twenty.

"Om mani padme hum."

Every half hour, Zangmo wound down the window and spat out the remains of the doma (I had been puzzled by the red splats on Norzin Lam, the main drag in Thimphu). Sometimes the doctor joined his wife in reciting the prayer: "Praise to the jewel in the lotus." The jewel was Chenresig, guardian of the Buddhist faith, he told us, and chanting his mantra helped believers cleanse themselves of sin and gain liberation from unenlightened existence. Our new

Chorten beside a rice field. *Drawing by author.*

friends ran the words together, and I found them quite soothing to hear. But every now and then, it became "Omaaaaneeepemehuʋ uʋ!" when the driver took a corner too quickly and the vehicle leaned over the knee-high concrete posts separating us from an unbroken descent to certain death.

Travel on a steep, twisting road cut into a mountainside that is little more than a single lane wide and that reveals itself in thirty-metre sections is hair-raising, especially up near the passes. Fortunately, there was barely any traffic. When a car does come from the other direction, you must slow down to a walking pace and breathe in as you pass. When it is a truck, you stop and hope you are on the inside where you can hug the rock face and sit tight. Sometimes we had to reverse to find a bit of grass to pull onto to let trucks by. Thankfully, none were larger than dumper trucks. When you encounter a cow on the road, you wind down the window and say "kuzu zangpo," it would seem, and then gently nudge forward until it steps aside. At times there were large boulders on the road to negotiate or dents where boulders had thumped the road and bounced off. We travelled at an average of thirty kilometres an hour, Dr. Jagar sounding the horn at blind corners. I saw no road signs warning of hazards, only the Buddhist mantra, painted repeatedly on the rocks in flowing Sanskrit letters.

| Our halt for the night was at Tangsibi, Dr. Jagar's home village. In the last of the daylight, we walked up a dirt path to a two-storey house with mud-brick walls and a tin roof. Two cows were out front, roped to a stake; a rhododendron bush bursting with crimson flowers was at the side. Dangling from the eaves, a foot-long wooden phallus spun gently in the wind. A woman with flushed cheeks and a baby strapped to her back stood in the doorway. This was Jangchub Dolma, Dr. Jagar's niece. In a dazzling orange kira, the female equivalent of the gho, and an iridescent green silk waistcoat, she seemed to be wearing her best clothes. After exchanging a few words with her uncle, she led us up steep wooden stairs to a room lit by a flickering light bulb and into the company of some fifty Bhutanese, all squatting on the floor around an empty bench. We were clearly intruding on some kind of special event. The village chief's birthday perhaps? A surprise homecoming for Jagar Dorji? Registering not the least surprise and beckoning us to follow, our leader made for the bench. The deep-throated rumble of horns was coming from the room next door.

Jangchub brought ngaja, sweet milk tea, and I looked around the room. Our arrival had certainly put a stop to conversation. An old man with deep furrows in his cheeks and the sinewy legs of a distance runner was staring at us. By the look of his feet, the soles crusted with dirt, the toenails fractured and gnarled, he had no use for shoes. A woman rocking an infant to sleep in her lap eyed us furtively and looked away when I returned her gaze. Four boys sitting with their legs crossed and their ghos peeled down to their waists leered before getting slapped by a matronly woman with thick arms. Feeling a little overwhelmed, I looked up at two posters on the wall, one of an Indian actress, plastered in makeup and with a ring in her bellybutton, reclining erotically on a couch, the other a pictorial map of Tibet with photographs of the principal monasteries. The attention of the crowd turned when a man entered the room with a ladle and a pot resembling a large paint tin. As he circulated, everyone dug into the front of their ghos or kiras for a cup.

A woman burst through the door of the adjoining room with three bowls stacked high with food. Dr. Jagar introduced us. I could see little family resemblance. His sister Norbu was about forty-five with wide-set eyes and Zangmo's doma-stained smile. Like her daughter, she appeared decked out in her finest garments: a violet kira, clasped at the shoulder with a silver brooch, and a shiny black waistcoat. She set the bowls down on a knee-high table in front of us, and Nadya and I mumbled, "Kadrinche." In Thimphu, we had eaten mainly Chinese and Indian food, only two or three Bhutanese dishes: beef with radish, pork with rice noodles, and emadatse, the national dish of chili peppers and melted cheese. The meal before us now was new: half a pomegranate, a putrefying mandarin with one side caved in, several raw chili peppers, a plug of meat with a generous rind of fat drooping off it, a raw spring onion with a cake of soil in its roots, some vanilla cream biscuits, bubble gum in plastic wrappers, and, topping the heap, a curl of butter as big as my ear. These items rested on a bed of rice crackers. Couldn't we have dal from the paint tin like everyone else? I had a keen appetite after the day's drive but waited for the doctor to begin.

The horns sounded again, dying-elephant blasts that made the cups on the wood floor jump. The door to the adjoining room was ajar now, but I couldn't see much: a row of guttering candles, something wrapped in embroidered fabric hanging from the ceiling. Judging by the fierce tiger painted on the door and the three snarling wooden heads suspended over it, this was a room to be respected. The steady *tok-tokking* of a drum and the chant of several voices now poured from the room. The door opened further, and I caught a glimpse of a Buddha with a shining face, pinched eyes, and pierced earlobes.

Dr. Jagar looked at us and smiled. "Do you want to go in?"

The four monks in the room took not the slightest notice as we entered. They were sitting cross-legged behind low tables, their eyes glued to stacks of paper covered in curly script. One beat a drum like an enormous lollipop using a stick the shape of a question mark while a second clapped cymbals. All four nodded their bodies forward and back as they chanted. They faced statues of three deities at an altar against the far wall. I could not see them clearly by the light of fifty butter lamps battling a draught from the door, but the middle one was familiar. Guru Rinpoche, I knew from reading, had brought Buddhism to Bhutan in the eighth century and travelled around the country converting rulers, subduing local spirits, and hiding records of his teachings in caves. Followers considered Sakyamuni the first of a line of Buddhas, and Guru Rinpoche was recognized here as the second. Devotees prostrated themselves before the "Precious Teacher," listened to sacred texts in his presence, and performed rituals to gain enlightenment. In front of his image, there were nine cups of holy water and food offerings like those I had assumed were dinner.

A sudden caterwauling made me jump. When lowering myself to the floor, I hadn't noticed the two monks nearest me switch from six-foot horns to short, bronze clarinets. The sound was deafening: no recognizable tune, no synchronization. The pair played expressionlessly and with little effort. Then, as abruptly as it had begun, the wailing ended. A man wearing khaki army fatigues beneath his gho and an orange shawl draped over one shoulder walked around the circle of onlookers with a jug, giving blessings. We drank a little of the holy water he poured into our palms and, like everyone else, slicked back our hair with the rest. He came around again, this time with wine, and then a third time with a bowl of pellets resembling musket shot. I took two and sniffed them. They were soft like bread dough.

"When we eat these," Dr. Jagar whispered, "God dissolves into our body. Then you wish for all the sentient beings, animals, birds, insects that leap in sky, on earth, under earth, even germs." He rolled one between his fingers and put it carefully on his tongue. "You wish well for all things. You wish suffering ends and taken up to higher life."

Smoke wormed out of incense sticks on either side of the gods, thickening the air in the room and making my eyes water. I began to feel heady and tired...the long day on the road, the rush of new information...the chanting of the monks. My ears were ringing from the clarinets. The outlines of people became furry. More deep-throated bellows from the horns. Maybe someone got married or died. The lay monk circled again, giving each of us a cup of ara and a handful of rice. Just a single drum now, a pulsing beat echoing in the little room. Like the others, I set the cup down in front of my legs and waited. The monk drummed on for two minutes then stopped and picked up a bell. Grains of rice were bouncing off my head like hail before I understood what I was supposed to do. With each ring, fling the rice in a broad arc across the room at the people sitting opposite.

"Tashi, tashi gayemba," intoned the monks. "Tashi chepadaa. Chepadaa, gomosori."

Silence. A woman in a green kira, eyes shut tight, swayed back and forth; a young man with head bowed mumbled into his gho. I looked at the rice grains littering the floor. A minute passed. Dr. Jagar raised his cup and drank the liquor. The others in the circle followed suit, relief visible on their faces. A period of trial had ended perhaps...a new day was soon to dawn. For Nadya and me, Chevy trucks, Tim Hortons, winter blizzards, beef burgers, and hockey were behind us...an isolated college deep in the Himalayas and a year in Druk Yul, the Land of the Thunder Dragon, lay ahead. Each bend in the road we went around, each mountain pass we crossed committed us further. What would happen over on the other side of the kingdom was anyone's guess, but I felt privileged to have a contract to lecture for the Royal University of Bhutan. Tourists had to pay a tariff of USD 250 *per day* to visit this tiny Himalayan

kingdom. Through UNB, which had forged an unlikely relation-
ship with RUB, I had got to meet Nancy Strickland, manager of the
Canadian Cooperation Office in Thimphu, on one of her returns to
Fredericton. Nancy had forwarded my CV to the Royal Civil Service
Commission and put me in touch with Dr. Jagar. It so happened that
Sherubtse College, which was taking on more students than ever in
2006, was in need of extra staff.

I looked at my wife and wondered what she was thinking, then
I looked at Guru Rinpoche and tried to make out his face through
the smoke. With his curly moustache, downturned eyebrows, and
head tilted to one side, he seemed amused.

Dr. Jagar leaned over and peered in my cup. "If there is no rice in
your cup, Tony," he chuckled, "your year is off to bad start!"

| On the third day, we crossed Thrumshing-La, at 3750 metres the
highest point on the lateral road crossing Bhutan. Dr. Jagar slid down
his window and tipped ara onto the road from a bottle he kept next
to the gearstick: an offering, he said, to the gods of the pass. We
descended cautiously as there was snow on the road. Frosty rhododendron leaves looked like collapsed propellers, pine needles
wrapped in ice and coated in snow like dead men's fingers. With the
bends in the road appearing suddenly, Dr. Jagar's driving became
erratic. Zangmo braced herself in the front seat, prayer beads
discarded, jam jar tucked away in her kira, her chanting squeakier.
In the back, we rolled from side to side. Pema opened the door and
relieved himself of the yak porridge he had gobbled for breakfast at
a wood shack on the other side of the pass. In a soft voice, Nadya said
she wasn't feeling good. I gripped the door handle and stuffed Lay's
chips in my mouth to keep my stomach from rebelling. I had this
idea that if we did fly over the edge, I should fling open the door and
exit the vehicle immediately to have any chance of surviving.

"Om mani padme ho-ah!" Jagar swerved. A squawking flash of
blue and red dashed out from under the wheels and sprinted into
a gully, before stopping on one leg to eye us with disgust. "You see

Outraged blood pheasant. Drawing by author.

that? What do you call that in English?" He laughed. I gulped and
promised to look it up later in the bird book.

It took us the full day to cover the remaining 230 kilometres to
Kanglung, including a visit to a friend of Zangmo's in Mongar for
ngaja and cookies. Up, up, up long z's pinned to the mountain sides,
engine churning, looking out for chortens and prayer flags on poles,
pulling our coats around our shoulders at the snowline. Then down,
down, down, swinging around corners, blaring the horn, ears popping,
clutching our stomachs. We looked forward to the warm air in the
valleys and watched the thermometer on the dash rise every couple
of minutes. One succession of tortuous switchbacks was called the
Yadi Loops. I wondered how it would be to run up the Yadi Loops.

I realized I had no idea where we were going or which way was east. I was lost, swallowed by the Himalayas. When we were in the bottom of a valley, I would peer through the windshield at a cleft in the mountains up ahead, surely the gateway to the next valley. Then the Land Cruiser would do a 180, and a new array of inter-locking options presented itself. But it was not just the mountains that threw me off; it was the trees. There were few clear views until we reached a pass, only brief glimpses between trunks and through leaves, and this of another wooded slope opposite. In this respect, Bhutan was very like Maritime Canada. Then there was the wood smoke. My view from the plane ten days before was of clear-edged ridges cutting ragged holes in pure white cloud. The air had seemed so pristine. Now, the mountains nearby were smudged and the more distant ones lost in haze—hardly the Shangri-larian image I had seen in books. I craned my neck to the side and gazed up at a line of fires climbing a ridge. Blooms of brown smoke formed giant mushrooms.

"Slash-and-burn month," Dr. Jagar said. "Farmers are clearing the trees to plant new crops."

It was dark and there was no power when we arrived in Kanglung. Candles flickered in people's windows. The Land Cruiser's head-lights picked out curls of barbed wire straying from a fence made of roughly hacked branches. We jogged down a rough track of mud and stones, squeezing past a cow tied to a tree, and parked on a strip of grass in front of an iron gate obscured by stinging nettles. Dr. Jagar got out of the vehicle and shone a flashlight on a rudimentary stone bungalow. Five stray dogs, one with an eye missing, were snapping at his legs. Armed with my pepper spray, I joined him. The roof of the building was also making a racket, part of it scrolling off like old bark. A stiff breeze from the valley was making the loose section clatter. Nadya came around from the other side of the Land Cruiser, and Dr. Jagar turned to us.

"This," he yelled, "is your home for the year! Welcome to Kanglung."

Thanks to its small population and relatively fertile land, Bhutan has never had to face the insurmountable problems that beset some of its neighbours. Its problems are human in scale and can be worked out, a factor which contributes to the optimism and enthusiasm of those involved in the development process. King Jigme Singye Wangchuck sets an example by devoting much of his time to travelling about the country, visiting districts and making sure that programmes are being carried out to everyone's satisfaction.

In 1961, the present King's father initiated the first five-year plan of development. Top priority was given in the first two five-year plans to the building of roads...

—FRANÇOISE POMMARET,
"A Cautious Road to Development," in *Bhutan*, 1990

3

"Long Distance Dozen"

AS WE JOG DOWN THE NARROW ROAD from Kanglung, around two tight U-bends, past a farm with a barking black dog, and over a steel Bailey bridge, I think of how hard it must have been to build the first highways. Dr. Jagar told us he saw road crews when he was growing up, blasting the rock with dynamite, straining to budge boulders using crowbars, and clearing debris with spades or their bare hands. Just hacking a way through the tangle of forest must have been a godforsaken task. I imagine sun-darkened labourers like those who have been doing the building work at Sherubtse: bootless, helmetless, covered in cuts, and coated in dust. Formed in 1960 to construct and maintain roads of strategic value in the border areas, the Border Roads Organisation (BRO) of India executed the work, calling on the Royal Government to contribute to the labour force. A decade and a half later, Project Dantak had cut 1500 kilometres of roads through the Bhutanese Himalayas at a cost of seven hundred lives. The kingdom now has about eight thousand kilometres of road, five thousand of this paved. Construction of the east–west highway from Trashigang to Thimphu began in 1965 and took ten years to complete. The average width of the east–west highway is 3.8 metres.

"Run on horse-power, not on run-power," advises the BRO on a concrete tablet near the bridge, a message to motorists who like to coast downhill with their engines switched off to save gas. Half-asleep on long training runs, I was, at times, rudely awakened by cars gliding silently around bends, their drivers hurriedly hitting the brakes when they spotted me. We have put a banner on the front of our bus saying, "Slow Down—Runners Behind," but we know we will each have to watch out for reckless drivers. The bus cannot cover our tails.

Beyond the bridge, a man in a smart, ochre gho stands beside a bucket of diluted orange juice and some plastic cups. Behind him is a steep mud path leading to Rongthung Primary School. I shake the man's hand, decline a drink, as the water is unboiled, and apologize for being late. He looks at me puzzled. Late? Late for what? No one has been waiting for us, except him. It is winter break. The

"Slow down—Runners Behind." The Tara-thon bus. Drawing by author.

school is closed, and the children have all gone back to their villages. Of course they have, yes. I thank the teacher for turning out, and jog away with the same feeling of foreboding I had in Kanglung.

The highway swings left, right, left, and down around lone farmhouses. I hear only two sounds, the chuckle of a stream following the road to my right and the clang of a bell belonging to a foraging cow somewhere off to my left. Looking ahead to the next bend, then back over my shoulder at the last, I realize I am alone. An hour ago, we were Team Tara-thon, dressed in identical "Run for the Kids" T-shirts, united in our mission, boldly setting forth to conquer mountains. Now we are strung out along the road. Not that I am surprised. Running is not a team sport. Everyone has a different pace, and it is especially easy in this creased land to suddenly find oneself alone. We will probably run much of the way to Thimphu alone or in pairs, becoming a team only when we enter towns, visit schools, or stop to camp.

Right now, I have no objection to being alone as I am not feeling much like a conqueror of mountains. The final months of college were hectic and exhausting. The launch of the new English curriculum last year meant more classes to teach and new exams to set, administer, and mark; meetings followed the marking to cross-check results. Then there was the business of terminating our contracts and getting severance pay: a raft of documents to complete and repeated visits to the admin officer and the accountant. A barrage of logistics related to the Tara-thon centred as much on getting the small army of sponsorship collectors organized and authorized as selecting and preparing the runners. And we needed Immigration to issue road permits for us to cross the kingdom and Tarayana to sponsor our visa extensions. Our days began in the dark with two-hour training runs. With two weeks to go, we learned that the college bus would not be available after all: it had a busted rear axle. We knew of no others on this side of the kingdom. Could Aum Chime send a replacement from Thimphu perhaps?

Half a kilometre lower than Kanglung, the foliage at the side of the road thickens and becomes more luxuriant. Now there are fewer conifers, more oak, alder, birch, sal, ficus, and banana. The slender, arching branches with pinnate leaves of one species remind me of moth antennae. The temperature rises gradually, and I remove my tashi kaddah and stick it in my shorts, wondering as I do whether this is disrespectful or unlucky. It unravels behind me as I run and flaps like a prayer flag in the updraft from the valley. Feeling thirsty, I look for the bus. There are several jerry cans of purified water on board. In the commotion of departure, I have neither drunk properly nor worked out with Mr. Sangay how often the bus will stop. A BRO marker tells me I have done fifteen kilometres of running, and my left knee has begun to complain. I sigh and feel like kicking myself for not including more "downhill first" runs in my training.

I turn a corner and see the bus parked beside an orchard, Mr. Sangay standing on the road with his arms folded. Eight of the students are devouring papaya and mandarins. There are some red faces and bulging eyes, but they all seem fine despite the late night. This is another reason I am tired. Nadya and I had the team over for dinner so everyone could make friends and meet Kezang and Ngawang, our driver and cook. A long telephone interview with Kuzoo FM meant we didn't get around to eating until eleven o'clock.

A man of about fifty comes barrelling down a stone staircase across from the orchard. It is the dzongdag, and we have stopped outside his house.

"Ah, Tony! There you are! What have you done with your wife, hey?" Dasho Minjur Dorji is a short, spectacled man with a jolly manner and limitless energy. We have seen him at big events at Sherubtse, most recently when the Je Khenpo, the chief abbot of the kingdom, came to Kanglung to consecrate 108 chortens newly built around the shedra.

"Is she tail-end Charlie?"

"Um, yes, Sir...quite possibly." I would like to offer some witty remark in return but cannot think of one.

"It's a good job you're doing. Keep it up, keep it up!" He shakes hands with each of the students in turn and gives me an envelope with a cheque inside. "Sorry I could not be there for your send-off. I have been travelling around the dzongkhag campaigning." I nod and smile. His bonhomie has given me a boost. Like Dr. Jagar, Dasho Minjur has quit work and hopes to serve in the new government.

It was about this time last year that the fourth Druk Gyalpo (Precious Ruler of the Dragon People) announced to the nation that, after thirty-three years of rule, he was stepping down as head of state and that the nation would become a parliamentary democracy in 2008. It was time for Bhutan to enter the modern era. Bhutanese would have to go to the polls and elect their own government. The newly formed Election Commission of Bhutan issued every citizen with a voter photo identity card, distributed a thirty-page voter guide explaining what an election is and how to vote, delimited constituencies, and, in its Bhutan Electoral Education and Training Strategy, sent 188 electoral instructors out to all households. There were two rounds of mock elections in the spring, in which people voted for imaginary parties given different colours: Druk Red for industrial development, Druk Blue for a "free and fair society," Druk Green promoting environmentally friendly development, and Druk Yellow preserving tradition and culture. Druk Yellow won both rounds hands down (46 of the 47 constituencies in the second) as yellow is the royal colour. "A political party will not be allowed to have a party logo or symbol that is associated with national or religious colours," a frustrated Dasho Kunzang Wangdi, the election commissioner, warned afterwards.

Two main political parties have emerged: the People's Democratic Party, led by Sangay Ngedup, former prime minister and brother of the four queens; and Druk Phuensum Tshogpa (Land of Blissful Harmony), led by Jigmi Y. Thinley, former minister of home and cultural affairs. Both leaders had to resign from the Royal Government in order to enter politics. Their manifestos aim to reassure the Bhutanese, who love the king and are happy for him to make decisions on their behalf, that all will be well come the New Year. "By gifting us democracy, our Monarchs have not forsaken us. As the Sovereign of our nation and the symbol of our unity they will be everpresent, reassuring us of their continued guidance and benevolence," insists the PDP. "We shall always uphold the sacred institution of the Monarchy and the person of His Majesty the King with the highest of reverence and allegiance as the fountainhead of justice and the symbol of our nation's sovereignty and unity," guarantees the DPT.

Newspapers report that voters, especially in rural areas, remain worried about the future and "confused" about colours, parties, and voting procedure. The crown prince, Jigme Khesar Namgyel Wangchuck, has been on tour, answering questions and attempting to put people's minds at rest. He attended the first mock election in Dunkhar in the far north, the ancestral home of the Wangchucks. "Where villagers seemed hesitant and apprehensive, His Royal Highness urged them to seize this opportunity to play their part in a historic moment in Bhutan," *Kuensel* reported. They must get involved in the electoral process and choose the right leaders. I recall him giving a rallying cry similar in tone to graduates at Sherubtse's eleventh biennial convocation in April: "The future depends on you...Shall we sit and dream or work hard and reap the benefits?" The general election will be held in March next year.

| Ten future leaders of the realm race ahead of me into town. Trashigang (meaning "fortress of the auspicious mountain") is an elegant seventeenth-century dzong, perched on a narrow promontory four hundred metres above the Drangme Chhu, and eighty timber houses packed into a tight ravine behind. It is one of the older urban centres in eastern Bhutan and is home to about 2,500 people. It has a hospital, three schools, a police station, a bus station, a bank, six hotels, and a bakery. The town has grown rapidly over the past decade and is seeing an increasing number of tourists, but it still lacks certain basic amenities. In its ninth five-year plan, the government has promised a waste disposal service, street lights, a sewage treatment plant, public toilets, and a crematorium. (Bhutanese do not bury their dead but burn them on pyres, a custom becoming more and more difficult to carry out as settlement size increases.) The Danish International Development Agency has agreed to support these initiatives.

"See down there next to the river? That's where the new sewage plant is going," Dasho Minjur told us when we first visited in the fall of 2006, pointing at a flat spot beside the Mithidang Chhu, the river flowing through town. "People, they go to toilet in river, throw all their litters, old dal, and whatnot in river. Everything goes in river! Maybe that's why it gets little bit angry!"

The Mithidang Chhu has turned monster on three occasions (1936, 1962, and 1994) and swept houses and people down the mountain in monsoon season. Fourteen people died in the last flash flood. Trashigang is also to get riverbank retention walls and a storm-water drainage system.

I do not look out for signs of these improvements as I jog into town. I am groggy from the heat. Trashigang is eight hundred metres lower than Kanglung and 10°C warmer. I am also distracted by the reception. There is a gang of twenty teenagers holding a four-metre-long banner at the final bend, all cheering uproariously. Their banner says, "Safe Journey" and "by Trashigang MSS and the Community." I wave and shout, "Kadrinche!" enormously relieved that the "shouting school kids" have at last materialized.

Trashigang Dzong: "Fortress of the auspicious mountain." Drawing by author.

Two minutes later, I enter the town square to a round of applause. Shopkeepers are standing in front of their shops; townsfolk have gathered on all sides. I see another banner, as big as the last, saying, "Tara-thon—Race for Health, Education, and Compassion," strung up in front of a restaurant, and a third, "Tara-thon 2008—Education for All" with the Tarayana logo, suspended from the third-floor balcony of a hotel. I never expected anything like this. We have caused a stir. I grin and wonder, as I slow to a trot, whether or not I should wave.

The assistant DEO, a woman in a grey half-kira and blue waist-coat, looking as capable and authoritative as Aum Chime, shakes my hand and introduces me to the vice-principal of Trashigang Middle Secondary School. A girl in a kira brings me a cup of ngaja on a tray, and I see behind her how the dzongkhag has used the funds sent by the minister of education. There are baskets of cakes, biscuits, and momos (steamed dumplings), flasks of ngaja and suja (butter tea), bottled water, and boxes of fruit juice on two tables, refreshments as good as at any road race back home. If the students are tired, they do not show it. They are chattering and laughing, talking with everyone,

Trashigang Middle Secondary School welcomes Team Tara-thon.

riding high on the moment. When Nadya arrives, we line up and receive tashi kaddah, this time from the assistant DEO. I have the feeling I will be returning to Canada with a lot of silk scarves.

We spend the rest of the day and our first night at the school, a nest of concrete and wood huts built on the hill above town. The several hundred students who attend the school are in either Grade IX or Grade X, meaning they are fifteen or sixteen years old. For most Bhutanese, school begins at the age of six. After a year of pre-primary (PP), children spend six in primary school (Grades I to VI), and then, at age thirteen, move to secondary. This is divided into lower, middle, and higher, students doing two years at each. At the end of middle secondary, they can continue at school, opt to go for vocational training at one of the six institutes in the country, or else enter the labour force. At eighteen (Grade XII), those who pass their exams can go on to college. The government has done a remarkable job of creating a general education system over the last half-century. Before the first 5-year plan (1961–1966), there were only 11 schools in the kingdom and 400 students. Now there are 502 schools and 152,194 students, plus 16 colleges and institutes with an enrolment of 4,630. Thirty-seven of the schools are middle-secondary and Trashigang MSS is one of the original 11.[1]

The vice-principal escorts us along a swept concrete footpath to the schoolyard, and I notice messages nailed to the trunks of eucalyptus trees on the way: "Cleanliness is next to godliness" and "Think globally, act locally." I know that, as well as doing subjects like mathematics, geography, history, English, and Dzongkha, students study four subjects under the heading Health, Physical Education, and Personal Development, one of which is Moral and Value Education.

"Being fit and healthy is important, but we also have to take care of those less fortunate than ourselves, and that is essential. If we all care for and help each other, we will be able to live happily together. The theme of our project is 'Helping Others,' and we'd like you to write..."

My speech is to a younger audience this time: ten boys and nine girls, wearing jeans, sweatshirts, and sneakers. Either they are dressed for a run or school uniform (gho and kira) is not required during winter recess. I look around the circle of faces. It may be that the afternoon sun is in their eyes, but they seem a little bemused. I have the feeling I am preaching to the converted. Do I really need to remind Bhutanese students that helping others is a good idea? When dignitaries like the king or the chief abbot or the district administrator visited Sherubtse, everyone would pitch in and sweep the campus, put out furniture, and make food. When asked to present on "The Vanity of Human Wishes" or "Tintern Abbey," the study groups in my third-year class would show up with a single script and take turns reading bits of it out. "All for one," said the third speaker cheerfully when I asked him if everyone in the group had worked independently on some of the lines. "And one for all!" chorused his group in response.

Nadya takes over, handing out paper and pencils to the students, and they readily take to the task of writing a story on our theme. We have decided to collect stories and drawings from all the schools we visit along the way and get Tarayana to award prizes for the best when we reach Thimphu, even make a book out of them. I wander

Mr. Rongthung Sangay, event coordinator for the Tara-thon.

off with our event coordinator, for whom coming to Trashigang Middle Secondary is a nostalgic experience. He graduated from the school in 1967 when he was seventeen—exactly forty years ago— and he wishes me to take a picture of him standing in front of his old classroom.

Rongthung Sangay is a barrel-chested Bhutanese with a straight back and a head like a boulder: smooth, shiny, solid, and screwed directly to the shoulders, a line of whitening hair prickling the top. After eighteen years of service as director of sports at Sherubtse College, he has just handed in his notice. Nadya and I have got to know him quite well over the past two years as we competed in several of the sports events he organized and had tea round his house a couple of times.

"I admitted in this school in 1960," he tells me. "When I join, there was no subject but the basic education and all in Hindi medium. When Father Mackey come, he stop Hindi medium and start English medium. I remember he used to teach the wholesome education to student."

"Wholesome education?"

"He make timetable that, every day, all should play some game or any other physical activities, so his student are good in studies and in sports. I learn many thing from school, and there were great respect from the people since there were only few school in country. What Father Mackey taught me is that the modernization was just entering into Bhutan. He told me that we have to maintain own culture, which he found it was very rich culture as in Bhutan. Father Mackey used to say life is hard and we have struggle, but we must be good citizen of the nation."

I recall the photograph of the Jesuit priest hanging on the wall in the director's office at Sherubtse. The third king invited Father William Mackey to Bhutan in the 1960s to lay the foundations for an education system (until then, the kingdom had only monastic schools and about twenty primary schools). Asked to find a suitable site for a high school in the less-populated east, he chose Kanglung because it was neither too hot nor too cold, and there was enough flat ground for a playing field. Sport, the priest believed, was an essential part of education. According to Dr. Jagar, Father Mackey used to have students leap through flaming hoops on the playing field at the new school. The school became Sherubtse Junior College in 1976, a college attached to Delhi University in 1983, and one of eight colleges belonging to the Royal University of Bhutan in 2003. While the high school was being built, Father Mackey taught at Trashigang Elementary School (now the Middle Secondary). A thirteen-year-old boy's passion for sport—especially soccer—clearly did not escape the priest's attention.

"He always keep good eye on me." Mr. Sangay chuckles at the memory. "One time, he say, 'Sangay, you always kicking that football ball around. Don't forget your studies. If you study hard as you play football, you become intellectual!'"

I think of "All for the Love of the Ball," an article in the newspaper that Mr. Sangay showed us earlier in the year. "Long time back, when things were different than what they are today," it began, "pigs held special significance for rural boys in Bhutan."

The moment a pig was slaughtered, little boys gathered around in excitement. They would not be anticipating a hearty pork meal but would be eyeing the raw pig bladder.

Rongthung Sangay was one such boy for whom the pig bladder was always a prized possession, since the bladder made a perfect substitute for a football. Thus, Rongthung Sangay grew up fooling himself with the notion that a rag-stuffed pig bladder would someday make him a great soccer player in the country...

After graduating from high school, he joined the Royal Bodyguard. As it turned out, he was not fooling himself.

"After few year in Bodyguard, I get good luck and play for national football team," he told us. "Team become first official Bhutan side in 1974 with name 'Druk 11.' Druk mean Thunder Dragon, and we have black shirt with gold dragon on back. His Majesty Fourth King was our goalkeeper. When we train together, we careful not to score too many goal!"

On his wall at home, he has a photograph of the team. The king is standing in the back row, wearing a golf shirt, looking about nineteen or twenty years old and utterly remote from the picture of the patriarch in golden robes with four wives that graces every office, restaurant, and store across the realm. I understand that football really took off in Bhutan when the king started playing.

The biggest event on the sports calendar at Sherubtse was the Monsoon Football Tournament. The first year Nadya and I were at the college, the finalists were the Campus 11 Alligators and the D.H. 111 Day Scholars. It seemed like everyone from the college and the village turned out to watch. Lecturers and deans sat on plastic chairs and drank tea in the wooden pavilion beside the playing field, and students sat in the bleachers beside them. Shopkeepers, farmers, mothers with babies, kids from the local primary school, and monks from the shedra yelled from the sidelines or jumped up and down behind the goals. As the playing field was a grassless quagmire after weeks of torrential rain, mud flew in every direction, most spectacularly when the players performed sliding tackles. The ball, by contrast, refused to fly very far in any direction, despite the players' best efforts to kick it hard and give it lift. The game deteriorated into a mad free-for-all in the Day Scholars' goal mouth with Mr. Sangay, who was refereeing the match, blowing his whistle repeatedly. Plastered in mud from head to foot, the students battled on until the final whistle. Nadya and I were impressed with their determination, and, I thought at the time, were he still alive, Father Mackey would have been, too.

| After a night stretched out on the floor of a classroom, we are back in the town square at 9 A.M. The team goes in search of donations from the shops, hotels, and dzong, and we collect BTN 11,885 for our cause (including the district administrator's contribution). We also go shopping for supplies, as Mongar, the next town of any size, is ninety-two kilometres away. Last night over dinner, Tharchen offered to be team leader and help us organize duties like shopping and collecting donations. I wondered if this might not sit well with our two more senior students, but Mr. Sangay approved. This initiative does not overly surprise us. It was Tharchen, together with Ugyen Lhendup, who came to Nadya's office in August and suggested that we present our project to the college in morning assembly. Tharchen helped with preparations in the final weeks, recollecting his experiences travelling across the country on Dr. Jagar's litter campaign. ("We must check the college tents are okay, Ma'am." "We should have banners on the bus, Sar." "We need big box to put donations.") Donations collected by the team will go to the team leader, and he will give them to Nadya. It will be up to the team leader to find out from the cook what provisions we need, make a shopping list, and then come to me for cash. Nadya and I have agreed to cover all expenses.

Day 2 begins with tea, cake, and biscuits, the two girls who staffed the tables yesterday now circulating with flasks and baskets. We had rice, chana, and ngaja for breakfast at the school, and I wouldn't usually eat or drink tea just before a run, but I do so now out of courtesy. I have a feeling a lot of runner's lore is going to go out the window over the next month. As Nadya does warm-up exercises with the middle-schoolers, I give a battered prayer wheel in the middle of the square a good spin. Sitting on a concrete dais under a roof, it not only serves as a roundabout for cars but also as a gathering point for farmers who come from the surrounding villages to sell their vegetables. On previous visits, Nadya and I have seen swarthy women with doma-reddened mouths sitting cross-legged in front of cucumbers, saag (Bhutanese spinach), tengma, and ginger. Highland Brokpa tribesmen and women bring yosha, a foul-smelling fermented yak cheese good for emadatse, sold stitched up in leather pouches. The villagers sleep a night or two huddled around the wheel and buy salt, cooking oil, kerosene, and dried fish before returning to their villages.

We are on our way again after Tharchen, Tee, and Tiger have loaded potatoes, cabbages, chickpeas, cheese, milk powder, dried chilies, and snacks on board the bus (lentils and rice we have already, leftovers Mr. Sangay managed to scrounge from Sherubtse mess). The vice-principal of Trashigang MSS flags us off, although there is a look of confusion on his face when Mr. Sangay asks him to do so. He does not have a flag. He scratches his chin and thinks for a moment then faces the runners and hollers, "GO!" and claps his hands. For the first two kilometres, the "Long Distance Dozen," as *Kuensel* has chosen to call us in the morning paper, are joined by a short-distance two dozen: eighteen school children, two teachers, the school cook, two villagers, and a stray dog. Milk tea slopping about in my stomach, I leave last with the school cook, a diminutive southern Bhutanese called Suleiman, who tells me he has never run before in his life. We descend to a fork in the road and stop there for more tea, cake, and cookies, served by two more girls behind tables. This is where we shake a lot of hands, say a lot of kadrinches, and bid Trashigang a final goodbye. It takes me another two kilometres before I realize that one Trashiganger has remained with us.

"HIC-CURP." The temperature climbs as we descend to the valley floor. Nadya and "the boys," as she now calls them, have gone ahead, and I am tail-end Charlie.

I think of Tashi, the frail greengrocer who owned a tiny store near us in Kanglung. He was often ill, his most recent ailment being an odd belching hiccup. "I've had it four days now, Sar. HIC-CURP! It never leave me in peace...from when I open my eye in morning to when I go to sleep at night. Doctor HIC-CURP! he say I must, HIC, eat no more chili CURPers!"

Bhutanese eat a staggering number of chilies: long, fiery, red ones, grown locally in the summertime (often seen drying on people's roofs), and short, even fierier, green specimens from India in winter. Mostly, the peppers are cooked and added to other food, but I have watched Bhutanese take raw peppers, dip them in salt, and crunch them up whole (without bursting into tears or reaching for a fire extinguisher). The health benefits of setting light to every meal are questionable. On the one hand, chili peppers are rich in vitamins, probably scour the digestive tract of parasites, and warm up the body (as doma does); on the other, they can cause heartburn, stomach inflammation, even cancers. I have not seen much of Tashi this year. His last words to me were, "I would like to run with you, Sar, but I am not able." I am not feeling so able myself. My stomach is churning. Too many chilies in last night's curry, far too many teas this morning. I have to keep stopping for a pee. And my knee is troubling me again. After a half-marathon of downhill yesterday, the last thing it needs is ten kilometres of more downhill today. I also have mild sunburn. I did not think I would need to use sunscreen. I should know by now that the sun is stronger in the mountains.

A bottle-green river that I know as a glistening earthworm from Kanglung starts to make itself audible, and I am soon at the army checkpoint at the end of a ninety-metre iron bridge. Our journey west begins on the other side of the Drangme Chhu. The bus has parked in front of the checkpoint, but only Nadya remains with it. The others have carried on. Mr. Sangay knows of a spot where we might camp, eight or nine kilometres farther. I get a drink and a packet of chips to calm my stomach and then disappear into the bushes for my fourth leak of the morning. An engine growls to life. It takes me several critical seconds to react.

"The road permits. Shit!" Nadya and I can go no farther without presenting them.

When the soldiers on duty step out of their cabin to see what all the racket is about, they see two mad chilips (one with red knees and a burned neck) jumping up and down, frantically waving their arms over their heads and shouting, "HEY! HEY!" at a bus picking up speed on the other side of the river.

Only middle class romantics with full bellies talk about returning to a "state of nature" in which, as a 17th century philosopher reminded us, the typical life is "poor, nasty, brutish and short." It had fallen to the King, my guide and his kind to make a conscious choice of what Bhutan should become. Had I been born in Bhutan, wouldn't I too have strived for these very changes? Why should Bhutan or any other country live in medieval ignorance; quaint, colourful and attractive to tourists, but actually drab, underdeveloped and soul destructive? My guide's generation were marching forward out of the medieval past, determined on change. I could only hope that somehow the best of the old would mingle with the new.

—LT. GENERAL E.A. VAS,
The Dragon Kingdom: Journeys through Bhutan, 1986

4 | Birth of an Idea

THE IDEA OF RUNNING across the Dragon Kingdom came to
me on the final leg of our journey from Canada in 2006, the flight
from Bangkok to Paro with Druk Air. There was an article in the
in-flight magazine called "Pedalling through Paradise" about three
Bhutanese who had cycled from Samdrup Jongkhar in the southeast to Phuentsholing in the southwest, stopping at schools along
the way to give talks on AIDS, sexually transmitted diseases, teenage
pregnancy, and substance abuse. "Congratulation for being the 1st
Bhutanese to bike across the Kingdom," said a banner welcoming
"businessman and fitness enthusiast" Wangda Tobgyal and his
companions to Phuentsholing. How very Western, I had thought
at the time. There was another picture of Wangda in Lycra cycling
shorts, straddling his mountain bike and tickling the trunk of an
elephant.

Nadya and I also liked cycling, but we were keener runners.
While living in Montreal, we were regulars on the West Island
Running Circuit, competing most spring and fall weekends in ten-
kilometre and half-marathon road races. We trained hard to get
medals and ever-faster times. After moving to New Brunswick,
we did more events, participating in the Fredericton Fall Classic,
Clarence Bastarache 10 K, Chipman NB Road Race, and Grand
Bay–Westfield Canada Day 10 K. I trained for a while with the UNB
cross-country team. From time to time, we would take part in sponsored runs, like the annual Terry Fox Run for cancer research. In
the fall before coming to Bhutan, in the company of 12,000 runners
and walkers, we ran from New Brunswick to Prince Edward Island
and back over Confederation Bridge to commemorate the twenty-
fifth anniversary of Terry Fox's Marathon of Hope across Canada.
If my wife and I were to cross the Bhutanese Himalayas running, as
Wangda and his companions had cycling, perhaps we could do so to
raise money for a good cause. I pondered this on my early morning
jogs around campus after we had been in Kanglung four months.

My teaching by then had settled into a routine, and one reason
for Dr. Jagar taking me on had become clear. I was to help write a
new, more modern curriculum for the English Department, part

of Sherubtse's drive to cut loose from Delhi University, which still governed course content and set final exams. Out with a traditional survey of English literature of the kind probably taught in England in the 1950s and no doubt imposed on Indians by the British; in with courses like post-colonial literature, literary criticism, basic writing skills, and creative writing. Instead of end-of-year exams worth 75 per cent of the final grade, continual assessment would account for the lion's share of the marks. The style of learning would also change. Fewer lectures delivered by the professor from the front of class while students sat and took notes, more pair work, group work, and student presentations. "Student-centred learning" was the buzz-phrase around college. No longer my dependant, Nadya now had a contract and gave workshops in critical thinking and essay writing to students.

External signs of change at Sherubtse were plain to see. Workmen were fitting a brand-new lecture theatre with cushioned seats suitable for a Greyhound bus, an Indian crew was clearing a space between Dr. Jagar's office and the main gate for an IT centre, and new student residences (called hostels here) had sprouted from the hill overlooking the college. Sherubtse was not only modernizing, it was growing bigger. According to the Royal University's strategic plan, the college would accommodate 1,380 students by 2010, 1,775 by 2012.[2] Money for these projects came from the Indian government—BTN 78 million (CAD 2,080,000), apparently—and much of the work would be done by Indian companies or Bhutanese companies employing Indians. Sherubtse was pulling away from Delhi University academically, but Bhutan's southern neighbour would continue to have a large role in its future.

My jogs before work would begin with a hop, skip, and jump over cowpats decorating the grass in front of our bungalow. A mud path then took me down to the stream flowing through the village. In June the stream was little more than a trickle and clogged with reeds and rubbish. Water was scarce that month. Some mornings I turned on the faucet to wash my face, got a sneeze, a thin thread of water lasting fifteen seconds, another bigger sneeze, eight brown drips, a throat-clearing sound, and then nothing. Nadya and I had to go to the faucet in the village with a bucket, a return journey of ten minutes, and started to appreciate what it meant to have running water at the twist of a tap—especially on laundry day. A chemistry lecturer living two doors up suggested our tank might be empty. He took us five minutes up the mountain to a stone bunker the size of a mail van that had cracked walls and a cow-nibbled bamboo roof. Two thick black hoses plugged into the stream behind were spitting water into the tank in fits and starts. An armful of thinner hoses in several colours radiated optimistically from a leaky hole in the bottom. One of these, Karma Lhendup assured me, was ours. The tank was almost empty and the hoses at the bottom swimming in mud.

Crossing the stream through a horseshoe-shaped, cow-proof gate, I would run along a crumbly concrete footpath on the other side to the top gate of the college. Inside, Indian labourers, thin men in ragged dhotis with towels wound around their heads to keep out the morning chill, squatted close to a fire frying chapattis. They were building new staff quarters and lived in ramshackle plank shelters with tin roofs beside the college lhakhang. Sheltered by chir pines, cypresses, silver oaks, and junipers, the road going down from there to the teaching buildings and playing field was almost too steep to jog. I was relieved when I could peel off and descend a long flight of stairs cutting through lecturers' quarters. At the bottom, I would cross the stream for a second time over a red bridge and pause on the other side to spin the college prayer wheel. At this point, I would turn the nozzle on my pepper spray to "fire."

Seventy or eighty stray dogs called Sherubtse home. They wandered endlessly around the buildings sniffing for scraps, poked their heads enquiringly into classrooms during lessons, slept stretched out in the washrooms, and attended all outdoor functions. Many of them camped within striking distance of the college mess or the canteen next to the playing field and fought over leftovers tossed out by the cooks after each meal. Their bodies bore witness to a hard life. Most had scarred shanks, ripped ears, and mange. Some had open, dirt-filled wounds on their legs and necks, others horrible cancers swelling their genitals and behinds. There were a few with no hair at all, their blotchy pink skins making them look like members of a mutant species. A chocolate brown one with friendly eyes had a growth resembling a ruptured haggis where its bottom jaw should have been. Apparently, this dog had tried to bite a farmer who was at the college gate selling his vegetables. The farmer was carrying a machete at the time. The dog would trot around campus, trailing a glistening string of saliva, and eat with its cheek to the ground through a gap at the corner of its mouth the size of a bath plug.

What to do about the dogs was a recurring topic of conversation among my colleagues. Views ranged from "They do no harm; let them be" to "Give me the gun and I am killing aaall the stray dogs," depending on whether the speaker was a Buddhist or a Hindu (the former regarding all life as sacred, the latter privileging only people, snakes, and cows). Kill them and we will be free of their unsightly presence, said the exterminators. Kill them and others from the village will replace them, countered the preservers. Lecturers with small children, Bhutanese and Indian alike, wanted them put down. Most agreed that something had to be done—at the very least, sterilization. One Saturday, a health official from Trashigang gave a talk to Sherubtseans on German measles, avian flu, and rabies. He said that sixty-six cases of rabies had been recorded in Kanglung and warned us that the disease was incurable. We should avoid dogs we saw "running amuck" or showing "tendency to eat sticks, mud, and stones," those with "excessive salivation" or barking with "changed voice." Father Mackey's solution to the dog problem back in the 1970s was to put down poison. When that failed, he called in the army to shoot the dogs, but this didn't work either. On hearing the first shot, the dogs bolted into the bushes. The need for a solution became pressing in May when a dog suspected of having rabies ran onto the basketball court and bit five students.

I liked to do six to eight laps of the campus, following dirt footpaths beside the hostels and charging up and down flights of concrete steps in between. After the fourth loop, the sun would be up, and I got glimpses between the buildings of gleaming, snow-crested mountains on the horizon. The dogs would emerge from their nests in the bushes and begin washing themselves in patches of sunlight. There was always one in the waste pit in front of each hostel. These had been dug by students at the start of the year to deal with the increase in litter around campus and were another source of lively debate. The president of FINA, the largest student body at Sherubtse, contributed via college intranet:

Dear sirs and madams,

All the pits we had dug for ourselves are filled with unhyginic materials such as sanitary towels used by females, and the dogs pick them up and scatter them on the roads. We get jitters, and disgusted when we burn the wastes in the pit. I would like to request all our esteemed colleagues not to throw your sanitary towels in the waste pit. The solution to dispose your sanitary towels off is to bury them in the ground. We are all responsible for keeping our areas clean. The initiative should come from each one of us. By the way, I am not the authority to say all these; it is only a knock in our heads about our social responsibilities.

There was no organized collection or treatment of refuse in Kanglung. There were no rubbish bins. People either burned their litter or threw it down the mountain. From what I could gather, this appeared to be the practice everywhere in the country, with the exception of Thimphu, where a dozen trucks a day hauled solid waste up to Dochu-La and dumped it in a landfill. Fortunately, the population of Bhutan is small (about 700,000) and most of the rubbish biodegradable. Nadya and I saw very little litter when we crossed the kingdom with Dr. Jagar. However, with imports from India increasing (worth 6.9 billion rupees, roughly USD 184 million, in 2001, according to *Kuensel*, 12.8 billion rupees or USD 341 million in 2005) and with more tourists arriving each year (6,393 in 2001,

13,600 in 2005)—demanding things like camera batteries, bottled water, and sunscreen—waste disposal services nationwide would surely become urgent.[3] Sherubtse needed rubbish bins with lids and, with the increase of students over the coming years, a landfill or refuse incinerator.

The last part of my jog took me past the building where my office was located and back up the hill to the top gate. Often as not, I would hear bleeping from someone's room. Power outages were practically a daily occurrence in Kanglung. Fortunately, a computer came with an APC backup, a battery the size and weight of a cinder block that bleeped and flashed hysterically when the electricity failed, giving the user two minutes to back up his or her files before the computer died. At home, Nadya and I had to make sure there were always candles and matches at hand in case of a blackout, which happened without warning and lasted anywhere from two minutes to four hours. No one at the college could tell me why the power went. It just did—especially when it rained.

Nadya and I were still new enough to Bhutan to regard everything as novel: prayer wheels that clanged, dogs with rabies, washing clothes in a bucket, chewing doma for a high, cooking by candlelight—all part of the adventure and refreshingly different from life in Canada. However, as I jogged, I couldn't help but wonder if we might do more than just help the college advance academically. Trouble was, I knew little other than English teaching, and Nadya's background was in intercultural communications. Sherubtse needed electricians, sanitation engineers, plumbers, and veterinarians.

| "Nadya, what do you think about doing a sponsored run?"

Back from one of my morning runs and feeling peculiarly alive after a cold-water bucket-bath, I put the idea of staging a run for a good cause to my wife. For the first time, I had made it to Yonphu-La, the local pass, a round trip of twenty-six kilometres. I was not sure why, but I seemed to have more energy than I had ever had in Canada. Maybe it was the altitude...or perhaps the food. Breakfast wasn't much—an Indian version of Corn Flakes, white bread with butter

45

and jam—but lunch and dinner were solid meals: rice, beef, turnip, chili peppers, bitter gourd, dal. Maybe it was the chilies, red and fiery and fresh.

"Listen to this." Nadya was sitting at the dinner table, reading *Kuensel*. "'The present rabies outbreak is a major one and has mainly affected the three dzongkhags of Trashigang, Trashiyangtse and Mongar.'" Under the headline, "Rabies Not Yet Contained," was a picture of an infected cow with wide eyes and saliva dribbling from its mouth. "I hope Mutu doesn't get it."

Nadya was also doing more running than she used to, now that swimming and cycling, her other sports, were not possible. We didn't run together as our speeds differed, and I worried about dogs attacking her. I had had one or two nasty encounters myself, padding past people's houses before dawn. But Nadya said she wasn't bothered and refused to take the pepper spray. I liked it when the house dog we inherited accompanied her on a run. Mutu, despite being medium-sized and fox-like in build, didn't put up with any nonsense from other dogs. While we were out shopping once, we watched her fasten onto the back leg of a dog half again her size until the stricken creature squealed for mercy.

"What would we be raising money for?"

"Um, something the college needs, I thought, like an electricity generator or a garbage incinerator."

"Sounds like a good idea," Nadya said. "How about kennels for the dogs?"

She went into the kitchen and brought back a plate of toast. She scraped the milk fat off her tea and put it in a saucer. We got our milk from a neighbour with two cows, an arrangement made for us by a zoology lecturer. A boy called Sonam brought it over every other evening in an old whisky bottle: 500 millilitres for half a buck.

"How far were you thinking?"

"Um, from here to Thimphu."

My wife paused before taking a bite out of her toast.

"That's six hundred kilometres, Tony!"

"Five hundred and seventy-eight."

Do a sponsored run around here, I had decided, and we would end up with enough money to buy the college one litter bin. Students had no money, and the shops and restaurants in Kanglung were all family operations. For twenty kilometres in either direction, it was mountains, trees, chortens, and isolated farms. We would have to hit the towns, where there were dzongs, government offices, hotels, businesses, gas stations, and proper restaurants. I had no doubt that we could raise money in Bhutan. As in most developing countries, there were those who had money and those who did not. I knew it would be important to seek donations in Thimphu, where we saw Land Cruisers humming along Norzin Lam like those on the streets of Fredericton. Given that Sherubtse was the leading university college in the kingdom, it had occurred to me that many of the civil servants and hoteliers could well be alumni.

"We haven't run anything like that far before, have we?"

"No," I conceded. "Not even close."

"We'd need to do an awful lot of training."

"True," I admitted. "But it would be for a good cause, and no one has run across Bhutan before."

"There's also the matter of getting permission to do such a thing. Remember all the documents we needed to work here?"

There was a bark at the back door. Nadya took her saucer to the kitchen, opened a can of mackerel, poured the oil from the can into a plastic bowl, added two handfuls of zao, stirred, and then tossed the milk skin on top. In a few minutes, armed with a faggot of firewood, I would step outside to make sure that none of Kanglung's strays robbed Mutu of this concoction. I heard the school bell ring and turned my chair around to face the front window. A stream of children was coursing down the mountain. A teacher at the gate of the school waved them in. When I ran up the mountain, I found myself dodging these kids on my way back down. Some of the boys liked to race me around a couple of bends in the road, yelling, "Hallo, Sar! Hallo, Sar!" little legs motoring beneath their ghos, lunch tins rattling.

Nadya returned and picked up her class register.

"Can I leave you the dishes?" It was important, my wife knew, to feed Mutu just before leaving for work so the dog wouldn't tail her. "See what Dr. Jagar thinks."

| "Kuzu zangpo, Tony. Come in."

The college had adjourned for summer recess before I got chance to poke my head in Dr. Jagar's office. I found him late one morning in July, half-hidden behind a mountain of papers rising from his in-tray.

"Kuzu zangpo, Sir. How was your holiday?"

"Exhausting. I wanted to stay here and catch up on my work, but I had to go to Paro for meetings." The director of Sherubtse was also the deputy vice-chancellor academic at the National Institute of Education in Paro.

"You worked during your holiday?"

"Yes. And when I get called for a meeting in Thimphu or Paro, it always takes a full week to go and come back." He shook his head helplessly. "I need a helicopter!"

"I hope I'm not disturbing you at..."

"No, not at all. I was just going for lunch. Do you want to join me? I hear you were in India. You chose an interesting time of year to go!"

An Indian colleague had persuaded us to accompany him to his home town of Muzaffarpur in Bihar state, a hellish journey of several days in battered taxis and crowded trains. Our first taxi ride from the border to Rangia on a dusty two-lane road at dusk was indicative of what was to follow. Sadu Ali, a young man with rich curls of dark hair and an air of studied nonchalance, drove his Suzuki Alto at breakneck speed, honking his horn at the buses, trucks, bicycle rickshaws, pedestrians, and cows that got in his way. At one point, he hit a dog, catapulting it yelping into a corn field; at another, he forced a rickshaw loaded with squawking chickens off the road. Trying to overtake a bus, he nearly hit an oncoming goods truck that had blinking lights around its radiator and an illuminated Hindu god stuck to the roof. The truck flashed its lights and blared its horn at us manically. The passengers on board the bus jeered and flung litter.

"If you are growing bad habit, you will be gaining bad harvest," observed Dr. Shukla, our travel companion, a reference perhaps to the buckled BRO road signs: "Safety on the road is safe tea at home," "Drinking whisky, driving risky."

Dilapidated single-storey buildings lit by lanterns, tufts of chopped-off rebar sprouting from their roofs, flew by. People squatted in front on rugs or under bamboo shelters selling sugar cane, jackfruit, engine parts, or chapattis. I glimpsed a shadowy restaurant with wrecked rickshaws out front and a fat-bellied sow driving her snout into a mound of rubbish heaped at the side. Gods forbid that Bhutan turn out like this, I thought at the time: the east–west highway heaving with traffic, litter everywhere, Guru Rinpoche pinned to the cab of a truck.

Dr. Jagar and I walked across campus together and down a steep, stone staircase shaded by cedar trees. Two dozen dogs were sitting outside the college mess at the bottom, licking their chops. Somebody had fed them. The students eating at the trestle table nearest the door went quiet when we entered. At the counter, two cooks were ladling rice, dal, turnips, and beef curry into bowls. As brown curry smothered each heap of rice, my stomach tightened. "Slimy in, slimy out," my brother had remarked in an email when he heard about our cases of "Delhi belly." Nadya and I had returned from India sick, but we seemed to be better now. Nevertheless, I remained wary. I presented my bowl and watched the curry drain through the rice, leaving more bones and vertebrae than meat.

"I sometimes come and eat here," Dr. Jagar said, declining the curry. The cook handed him a cup of dal. "One of the problems is the students take the bones out of their bowls and put them on the table." We sat down at an empty table. "Then the cook comes, and he brushes them on the floor." I looked down and saw gnawed splinters of bone under several of the tables.

"And the dogs come in and eat them," I added. As if on cue, a particularly battered bitch with flaccid teats sidled over and collapsed under the chair next to mine. She didn't seem to have the energy to beg.

"This is very unhygienic. And it looks bad to have dogs sniffing round our legs when dignitaries come."

Twenty students bowled into the mess, chatting loudly. When they spotted Dr. Jagar, they straightened their ghos, bowed, and said, "Good afternoon, Sar." One passed out bowls to the rest, and they formed an orderly line. Some other students got up and left, rinsing their bowls under a faucet on their way out. I looked at the debris left on their table.

"Have you thought of introducing trays?"

"Yes. This is one solution, but trays are difficult to get. We'd have to get them from India." With all that was going on at the college, I was surprised that Dr. Jagar had time to think about this. "What did you want to talk to me about?"

I suddenly felt like I should not be wasting the director's time. "Um, Nadya and I were thinking of, ah, running across Bhutan to raise money for, for..."

I expected my lunch companion to choke on a turnip. As Dr. Jagar had spent several years studying abroad, I felt sure that he was familiar with the idea of a sponsored run. I wiped a dribble of curry from my chin, before continuing. I had tried to eat with my fingers in a civilized manner like the Bhutanese and Indians did, but I always managed to decorate my face and shirt.

"...a worthy cause. The question is, um, what cause that might be...and, of course...whether or not you approve of such a venture. We thought we might raise money to build kennels for the dogs at the college or buy an incinerator perhaps, given, ah, the litter problem we have."

Dr. Jagar separated some rice from the mound in his bowl, squeezed it into a ball with his fingers, placed it in his mouth, and chewed thoughtfully. He looked over at the next table. A tall lad I had seen out on the soccer field a few times was shovelling rice and curry into his mouth from a mound twice the size of mine. Another was using a splinter of bone as a toothpick.

"How about taking some of our students with you?"

"Sorry?"

"I know of one or two who might be interested."

I scratched the side of my head with my clean hand and looked down in my bowl. He had to be joking.

The first sports event on the college calendar had been the Annual Spring Marathon, a half-marathon for boys, 10 K for girls, a race to Yonphula, the next village, and back. Nadya and I had trained for several weeks to prepare for this, getting our legs ready for the steep climb, but seemed to be the only ones. Maybe few students would be taking part. On race day, however, there were some two hundred on the start line, jumping up and down and slapping their thighs, sneakers, tennis shoes, sandals, or flip-flops on their feet. When Dr. Jagar bellowed, "Five, four, three, two, one, yaaah!" and waved his flag, the students bolted for the college gate, elbowing and shoving one another. A girl running at full throttle stumbled and fell, and four others following close behind sprawled over her. I was grateful that Mr. Sangay had advised the two guest runners from Canada to begin near the back. We overtook most of the runners before leaving Kanglung and the rest by the three-kilometre marker. Some had slowed to a snail's pace and were gasping for breath; others had become walkers with their hands on their hips and their heads bowed. I passed one student with watery eyes, trying desperately to breathe around a rolled-up rag coated in glucose powder sticking out his mouth. Another was doubled over at the side of the road, relieving himself of his breakfast. About seventy runners completed the Annual Spring Marathon.

Sports Day had followed a few weeks later. Mr. Sangay had borrowed cement from the building site near the main gate to draw a race track on the playing field. The students competed in 100-, 200-, 400-, and 800-metre events. The longer the race, the fewer the finishers. In my event, the 5000, 9 of the 45 that began the race crossed the finish line, the dropouts unashamedly melting into the ring of spectators.

Finishing my curry, I wiped my mouth and looked again at Dr. Jagar.

"Well, yes...yes. That's a good idea. Yes. I suppose we *could* take some students with us, if...if, that is, any were up to the task."

In the course of her visits across the country, Her Majesty the Queen Ashi Dorji Wangmo Wangchuck has observed and interacted with people from remote and far-flung villages and communities. These interactions and observations have led her to establish the Tarayana Foundation to help disadvantaged people gain more economic independence through small and targeted assistance. One of the stark realities of those visits was the fact that there were many families who could not send their children to school because they could not afford school uniforms and other associated expenses.

—TARAYANA FOUNDATION,
"Tarayana Scholarship Endowment Fund:
Introduction," 2006

53

5 Royal Sanction

"Oh yes, Your Highness. Our runners are thoroughly committed to raising money for Tarayana, dedicated to helping disadvantaged children go to school."

His Royal Highness Prince Jigyel Ugyen Wangchuck, second son of the fourth Druk Gyalpo and Queen Ashi Dorji Wangmo Wangchuck, looks at me unsatisfied. He has a round, blemishless face and shiny, dark hair, neatly parted on one side. He is wearing a crisp, dark-grey gho, black socks, and dress shoes. Behind him is a large, black Land Cruiser with "BHUTAN 17" on the license plate. A burly bodyguard in matching black gho stares at the line of sweaty students in Tara-thon T-shirts standing to attention at the side of the road. We are halfway through our third day of running, tracking the curves of the Drangme Chhu and enjoying relatively flat conditions. Nadya and I are happy to be on the right side of the river now, Mr. Sangay having spotted us at the last minute yesterday and turned the bus around.

"No, I mean physically. Are their hearts awlright?" The prince is twenty-three years old and just back from England. Like his brother the king, he went to Oxford to study politics. I assume he has heard of our run from his mother.

"They had to pass a three-day running test before we accepted them on the team, Your Highness," Nadya offers, "and they did two months of hard training."

The prince looks down at the feet of the runner standing next to me. Raised by indigent grandparents because his divorced mother hadn't the means, Tee seems one of the most dedicated to our cause. "When a foreigner have that much interest and love to our country," he declared in his interview, "why not I, true citizen of Bhutan, have interest and love to my country, our people? And for them I should suffer to make them wear a smile."

"Those shoes are too big! And in a rotten state." The prince reaches down and presses the toe. Tee is wearing flimsy basketball shoes, the type that laces up around the ankle and has practically no tread. A kind of white skin covering the black toecaps is flaking off.

Due to the absence of toes inside them, the toecaps have turned up, making Tee look rather like a poor court jester.

I close my eyes. As project leader, I am partly to blame for this. Several months ago, Nadya gave the students each a kit list, recommending two pairs of new running shoes. We just assumed they would go out and buy them, but the shops in Kanglung have no running shoes and Trashigang shops only carry flimsy imitations, and most students can hardly cover their food bills. I look down the line, dreading that someone will be in flip-flops. I really should have checked everyone's kit before leaving. Not that I have chosen my own shoes wisely. I got the wrong ones sent over from Canada, a pair of lightweight racing shoes called Fastwitch. On the soles, it says, "Giddy Up!" the last thing I should do on Day 3 of a month-long ultramarathon. The cushioning underfoot is thin, and they weigh no more than a dessert spoon—ideal for sprinting along the smooth streets of a large Canadian city for no more than five kilometres. Fortunately, I also have a sturdier pair designed for long distance. I picture Tee limping into Thimphu, blistered toes sticking out his shoes, shocked faces on either side, the queen frowning.

Tee mutters something to the effect, "I feel comfortable in these shoes, Your Highness," and the prince proceeds down the line, inspecting footwear and looking for evidence of hard training. At the end, he finds Mr. Sangay, the driver, and the cook, all bowing low and breathing into their sleeves, and then the most recent addition to the team.

It would seem we are now the Long Distance Baker's Dozen. I remember hearing a couple of students telling a stray dog to go home as we were jogging away from the tea stop below Trashigang, but I did not pay much heed. Twenty minutes later, a barrel of brown fluff shot past me down the mountain. I found the same barrel dozing in the shade of the bus at our lunch spot beside the river. The dog was still with us when we camped for the night in an empty paddy field nineteen kilometres from town. It clearly had no intention of going home, and I wondered idly if I should get the driver to give it a ride back. The thirteenth runner now has a name and a ribbon around his neck. Yana is similar to a Japanese Akita, same cocked ears and short snout, but the legs are shorter and the tail points down as often as it curls over the back. I don't suppose he will be with us long, but for now we have Yana as well as the goddess Tara to look after us. Bhutanese popular belief says that dogs show people the way to salvation.

Satisfied that we have a chance of succeeding, the prince nods emphatically several times and wishes us tashi delek. BHUTAN 17 with army escort heads off for Mongar. We will reach Mongar in three days' time (shoes permitting). As the vehicles tear off, I imagine what Prince Jigyel will say to his mother when he gets home. "Oh, and I bumped into those chaps running for your foundation near Trashigang. Spirited bunch. Not sure I'd want to be in their shoes though."

"Now that His Royal Highness has touched these shoes," Tee says seriously as we continue our run, "I'll never throw them away."

| Thirty-eight kilometres of uphill to Kori-La, the first pass, will begin after we cross the Sheri Chhu, a tributary of the Drangme Chhu. Having already done sixteen kilometres today, we decide, after a long lunch beside the smaller river, to do only four of this climb and camp at a place Mr. Sangay knows.

The Sheri Chhu is where everyone, except Yana, unwinds. The temperature is in the mid-twenties, and no one is around. We can strip down, jump in, and wash away a couple of days of dust and sweat and several weeks of nervous anticipation. The team does laundry on rocks, the driver washes the dog, and Tiger demonstrates his angling skills, hooking two-inch, blunt-headed minnows out of the shallows with his fingers. I expect Yana to bite Kezang. I watch the dog's eyes becoming wider and more desperate with each soap-down and dunking. Clearly, this is a new and unwelcome experience. Any moment, there will be a flash of teeth, a thrashing of legs, and a headlong, howling dash for Trashigang. Gradually, the stray changes colour from oxtail soup to milky coffee; the knots of grime in his fur

Yana, the thirteenth runner (after his bath and wearing a yak-hair collar).

loosen and dissolve. He returns to land looking half his original size
and with an expression of deep insult on his face.

In the middle of the afternoon, Mr. Sangay signals that it is time
to leave, and the students get dressed and return to the road in
pairs, rubbing their leg muscles vigorously. Some moan at having
to run again. I decide to stay longer and write a journal entry on a
scrap of paper. The bus rumbles off in a cloud of dust, leaving me
alone in silence. A light breeze tugs at dead bark scrolling off eucalyptus trees near the road and ruffles the needles of chir pines,
coniferous trees I have often seen at low altitude in dry gullies. It
shakes the coarse grasses growing through the rocks and makes the

lizard-tongue leaves of an agave shiver. I listen for familiar bird calls but hear none. In September, after a training run near Trashigang, I shared the shade of a eucalypt beside the dzong with blue-throated barbets. As dressy as lorikeets with green bodies, blue heads, and red caps, they were sitting on low branches and going *pukuruk, pukuruk*, their throats bubbling out with each cry like frogs' throats. The only sound now is the slosh of the river, the water banking behind large boulders before rushing around the sides and erupting into froth.

Our royal encounter this morning makes me think about the queen's decision to support us. Maybe we have secured royal approval because Her Majesty is no stranger to toiling up mountains herself. She describes her walks to remote villages well beyond the reach of the road in her autobiography, *Treasures of the Thunder Dragon*, published in 2006. Her first expedition in 2000 was to Zhemgang and Mongar districts in central Bhutan. Arriving in Dunmang village after a gruelling thirteen-hour trek, she put off going to bed to deliver medicine, clothes, grain storage bins, spades, and packets of seeds to the twenty-seven households. But the villagers looked at the seeds and said they found broccoli and carrots unpalatable. Vermin-proof containers were not welcome either because their custom was to turn leftover maize into ara. "After this salutary lesson in the pitfalls of being a do-gooder," Her Majesty writes, more amused than annoyed, "I collapsed with aching limbs and blisters on my heels." The expedition continued to Khomshar village, where she met a jolly but penniless eighty-nine-year-old, once a herdsman for the second Druk Gyalpo, and decided to "adopt" him. The Tarayana Foundation was born with Meme Penjor its first benefici-ary of financial aid.

| "Our vision is to have 'a happy and poverty-free Bhutan,'" the secretary general of Tarayana, said, handing Nadya and me a leaflet when we visited the foundation a year ago. Dr. Jagar, who was on the board of directors, had arranged the interview. The office was in Zomlha Shopping Complex on Wogzin Lam in Thimphu, a miser-able four-storey building, once attractive, no doubt, with yellow

paintwork and orange pillars decorated with scowling Thunder Dragons at the entrance. Now the pillars were chipped and scuffed, the flared, silver eyebrows of the dragons dulled by dust. There was only one office in use on the fourth floor. Light from a lone fluorescent tube illuminated a rectangular wooden board with the words "Tarayana Foundation" printed above a picture of a white hand, delicate as a girl's, holding an exotic blue flower. The hand was clearly not human as it had an eye embedded in the palm.

"As Dr. Jagar probably told you," Aum Chime continued, "many remote communities still don't have the basics like electricity, telephones, health clinics, or schools. In its ninth five-year plan, the Royal Government has a development strategy to help the poor living in rural areas, but clinics and schools take time to build, and the villages farthest from the road are the last to get these things. That's where Tarayana comes in. We reach out to the people we think are the most in need and offer them assistance."

"What kind of assistance, Aum?" I asked. ("Address her as 'Aum' [Madam]," Dr. Jagar had instructed.) The secretary general was a graduate of Cornell University and one of the most articulate speakers of English I had met.

"Training and financial aid. Many villagers have little or no money and only the skills they need to survive. If their crops fail, if their animals fall sick, they suffer. Tarayana introduces new projects to their communities like paper making, nettle weaving, candle making, and pottery, so they can earn a living. Notebooks, clay pots, and nettle handbags are things the villagers can sell—if, that is, they can get them to market. We send instructors out to the villages to teach these new skills, or else the most able villagers come here for training. Our aim is to give remote communities ways they can raise their own living standards. By doing so, we're also, of course, preserving Bhutanese culture by promoting traditional crafts."

Our project seemed quite a different kettle of fish. How might we present it? It would be easy to sound like a nutty chilip: "That's right, Aum, we intend to run six hundred kilometres across the mountains with some of our students, asking people we meet along

the way to give us money for...for a cause we've yet to decide on."
No one had run across the kingdom before, and raising money by
running was a foreign concept. Aum Chime would ask us if our
students were up to the task. "Well," I would answer, "we are optimistic, given their spirited efforts on the football pitch at Sherubtse."
Then she would ask who we expected to donate. She would surely
remind us that most Bhutanese lived hand-to-mouth, and the few
who didn't probably supported them. I thought I might begin by
telling the secretary general about the Terry Fox Foundation and
how Westerners have a tradition of running for a cause: cancer,
cystic fibrosis, a new CAT scanner for the local hospital, multiple
sclerosis.

Nadya and I took turns describing our project, trying not to make
it sound any more difficult than making a bag out of nettles. Aum
Chime didn't bat an eyelid.

"Well, since you're in the education sector, maybe you could
contribute to the Tarayana Scholarship Endowment Fund."

She handed Nadya a booklet. On the front were these four words
and a picture of a little girl in a ripped shirt balancing schoolbooks
on her head.

"As I'm sure you know, education is free in Bhutan, but many
families are too poor to buy the things their children need for school,
like uniform and shoes, books, pens and paper, and a school dinner.
Two thousand ngultrums covers a child's expenses for a year."

About fifty bucks. I thought of the little boy who lived next door
to us in Kanglung. He was about the right age to attend the primary
school across the way, but, when the bell rang at eight in the morning,
he was always milking a cow or chopping up bamboo stalks for fodder.
His mother always seemed to have a lot of work for him to do.

"Would running for a cause work, do you think?" Nadya asked.
"Would people donate?"

"Business people and civil servants may, but the donor pool in
Bhutan is limited. I have difficulty every time I go to companies
with, how do you say it...my hat in my hands? But you have a new
idea that might catch people's interest. You should also try and get

The goddess Tara. Tarayana motto: Service from the Heart. Drawing by author.

the people you know in Canada or other countries to sponsor you."
I noticed in the leaflet that Tarayana had an office in New York.

"I have a meeting with the executive committee on Saturday. If
you like, I'll see what they think of your project. If that goes well, I'll
talk to Her Majesty. You might come up with a slogan, something
that will capture the public imagination."

Before leaving, I asked Aum Chime about the hand with the eye
in the palm. The same image was on the leaflet and the booklet she
had given us.

"That's our logo. The hand belongs to Tara, the Goddess of Wisdom and Compassion."

| The sun sinks, the air freshens, and a lone chorten like a crocodile tooth gleams on a darkening ridge over my head. I stick my notes behind my watch, clip my pen to the neck of my shirt, and get stiffly to my feet.

It takes me two kilometres to find my rhythm. I glance over my right shoulder and admire Trashigang dzong for the last time, keeping watch over the Drangme valley. Three kilometres in, a thin waterfall like a beard rolls off an ochre chin of rock above the road. Four kilometres, five. No bus and nowhere remotely feasible to camp, vertical wall to my left, ground falling away through jungle to my right. This is what Nadya and I had feared: nowhere to pull over between villages, nowhere to camp. It will be worse as we get higher. No one lives near the passes. Another tablet of stone at six kilometres. Is it possible that I have started to dream in the thinning light, hypnotized by the long shadows stretching across the road, and missed a turnoff? A twenty-seat, blue-and-white bus with banners fore and aft is a difficult thing to miss—even in Thimphu. I would appreciate some encouragement from the BRO, but there are no posted messages as we are no longer on a border road. I pound over a rusty steel bridge with splintery, wheel-unfriendly planks. Eight. At last, the bus. Tucked into a fold in the mountainside beside a stream and a derelict paddy field. I glide over another bridge and into camp in the dark, feeling the best I have felt since leaving Kanglung.

"Sorry, Mr. Tony." Mr. Sangay greets me with a smile. "Few extra kilometre!" I pretend to punch him in the gut and ask him to try and keep it to within one or two of the itinerary. I walk over to the hunched-over figures gathered around a campfire. No one is talking much.

"The students really had trouble getting going again after lunch," Nadya confides, rising awkwardly to her feet and steering me to one side. "We should have camped next to the Sheri Chhu."

Roadside camp: fuelling up before taking on the Yadi Loops.

"You think so? But that would have meant doing twenty kilometres of uphill tomorrow."

"True, but that might have been better than running so far after cooling down in the river. Mr. Sangay should have scouted out the campsite while we were bathing."

"I guess so. Did you say that to him?"

"He just said it would have been a waste of petrol going up and down and up again, that I should leave such decisions to him."

Before leaving Kanglung, Nadya and I worked out an itinerary that would see the team do no more than a half-marathon a day for the first two weeks. While tomorrow our students can look forward to a run of only twelve kilometres to Yadi, our next port of call, it would be better if they could get accustomed to running about the same distance each day.

Day 6: Kuzoo

Heavy rock thunders out of the Tara-thon support bus. It is
6 A.M. The cook hacks at fallen trees above the road so a billycan
of water the size of a baby's bathtub can be heated to make tea.
Kezang, our driver, sifts rice through his fingers looking for grit.
This will be our breakfast with some chana (fried chickpeas).
Two students peel potatoes to make a curry for lunch. Nadya
remains swaddled in her sleeping bag in our tent, warmed, until
she gets her tea, by Yana, the Tara-thon dog, who leans against
her. I sit in the front seat of the bus, listening to the radio.

"People, if you want yer dreams come true, you gotta get out
the sack and hit the track," says the DJ.

We are indebted to Kuzoo 105 FM. The radio station has
shown great interest in our fundraising venture. This is still
the first week of our run, but we have spoken to them on air
three times since setting out and two prior. Kuzoo (short for
kuzu zangpo, hello) is radio for a young audience, and we have
ten Bhutanese students who may be national heroes by the
time they reach the capital. Our camp is at the top of Kori-La
(2400 metres), the first pass on our crossing of the Himalayan
Kingdom.

"That was Timberlake and 'Apologize.' Better late than never
if you want yer love to last forever."

—*TONY ROBINSON-SMITH, Tara-thon blog entry (December 26, 2007)*

Bhutan has had radio since 1973. The service began when an
amateur radio operator and volunteers belonging to the National
Youth Association of Bhutan used a 400-watt transmitter to send
news and music to residents of Thimphu for thirty minutes each
Sunday. Realizing that radio could be a handy tool to disseminate
information, the Royal Government brought the station into the
Ministry of Communications, and in 1986 NYAB Radio became the
Bhutan Broadcasting Service. With a 10-kilowatt short-wave transmitter, BBS began broadcasting programs across the kingdom daily

for three hours. In 1992, to "encourage the professional growth of the Bhutanese media," the fourth Druk Gyalpo issued a royal kasho, freeing BBS from state control. BBS now has a 100-kilowatt transmitter and can be heard around the globe seven days a week in four languages. Initiated by the fifth Druk Gyalpo in September 2006, Kuzoo 105 FM is the first private radio station in Bhutan.

After Justin Timberlake is done, the DJ chats with a teenager on the telephone about the programs she watches on TV and about Bollywood films, and I am curious whether or not he is at liberty to ask whatever questions he pleases. I suspect that both BBS and Kuzoo have guidelines about what may be discussed on air and what may not. I know that, although it has become an independent corporation, BBS has an editorial board on which government representatives sit. The same is true of *Kuensel*, which began as an official government bulletin in the 1960s and gained autonomy at the same time as BBS. Without radio or TV in Kanglung, most of what Nadya and I have learned about Bhutan has come from conversations with our colleagues or from *Kuensel*. I had assumed before we came that the kingdom's only newspaper would be a mouthpiece for the government, but, while no journalist ever criticizes the royal family, *Kuensel* hardly promotes Shangri-La. I have read articles on corruption in business and government, reports on alcoholism, drug peddling, sex crimes, and domestic violence, and, most recently, bold criticism of the two political parties that came into existence last year for mud-slinging, coercion, and malpractice.

I listen to "Jumpin' Jack Flash" and watch Sonam Wangdi and Tiger toss the last of the potatoes in a billy. Kuzoo has told us it would like the Tara-thon to be an inspiration to Bhutan's younger generation. It is not something I had thought much about before the station contacted us. Yesterday, a dozen children ran up the mountain with us from Yadi Middle Secondary School. Three managed seven kilometres before running out of steam. I could tell by the looks on their faces that they had given their all. I thought it would be just Team Tara-thon after that, but, when I got to the pass, I found a boy of thirteen in running gear. Sharing my astonishment,

Nadya presented him with a tashi kaddah and shook his hand, and Mr. Sangay gave him a hundred ngultrums before flagging down a truck to take him back down the mountain. Maybe, in a few years' time, he will be leading the annual charge up to Yonphula from Sherubtse. Kuzoo is right. We are not only raising money to send kids to school.

Tiger groans and pulls faces as he gets to his feet and hobbles over to his tent. He is from Chungmashing in the lowland jungles of the southeast, three days' walk from the nearest road. "In my village," he told Nadya with a chuckle in his interview, "modern facilities are only dreamt." He was five when his parents packed him off to a primary school on the other side of the kingdom. He has been home only five times since.

"My older sister, she took me to Chhukha, Madam, and sponsor my schooling, but there was never enough money. I had to work in construction site, breaking stone to make pebble. I get ten ngultrums for one bag of pebble. I keep on beating and beating till I get ten bags. Then I gave money to my sister. She get necessary things for my schooling. When I was twenty, I unload stones for Tala hydro project. I suffer a lot. I want to do Tara-thon so that other children will not suffer."

When I arrived at the pass yesterday, I found Tiger flat on his back snoring, sleeping bag unrolled in the dirt, forearm serving as a pillow, spectacles adrift from his nose. A cold wind was ripping apart prayer flags hanging over the road, but it clearly was not bothering Tiger.

Damage reports have started to come in. Five runners have blisters on their feet, two Achilles tendon strain, three knee troubles, and one "Sore balls, Sar"—meaning, I think, the balls of his feet. Even Yana, I notice, is limping. Once again, we had run farther than planned, nineteen kilometres instead of fourteen or fifteen, and this after sweating up the steep staircase of switchbacks known as the Yadi Loops the day before. I was peeved when I arrived at Kori-La. Why hadn't Mr. Sangay stopped earlier? There were places for the bus to pull in.

"Not enough water for cook," he replied simply.

An advocate of applying ice to sore joints after a hard run, I went in search of water, knowing that it would be ice-cold at this altitude. I found only a trickle, feeding into a cracked and overgrown stone bath below the campsite. Not an ideal place to bathe, but I had some of the limpers go and stick their legs in for five minutes. There were some ungodly howls from the woods. Around the campfire, Mr. Sangay went over some basic stretching exercises, and Nadya distributed plasters and analgesic cream to the injured, demonstrating on her own legs how to rub it in thoroughly and massage the muscles. It is fortunate that we are only eighteen kilometres from Mongar and our first day of rest. We can also top up on medical supplies from the hospital there.

"Suja! Suja!" The students emerge stiffly from their tents and yell at a loaded truck crawling up to the pass in low gear, revving its engine and blasting plumes of dirty smoke into the clean air. They have been doing this since Day 2. The offer of tea is never taken up, but they do not miss a vehicle. I am glad to see them in fine spirits. It must be a boost to their confidence to scale the first tall wall separating us from Thimphu. I am amazed that all ten have made it. I guess they did more training runs in Kanglung than Nadya and I gave them credit for. More encouraging is their clear sense of mission. In Yadi, after conquering the Loops, they cleaned up quickly, put on their ghos, and went to the local tsechu with the donation box, returning in the evening with BTN 4,805.

Mr. Sangay is the last to emerge, which surprises me. I ask him if he got a good night's sleep. Our tents are squeezed onto a narrow lay-by just beyond the saddle. Very little traffic uses the lateral road at night, but, from time to time, bright lights burst into our tent and woke us. The roar of engine or squeal of brakes felt so close, I expected to get up in the morning and find our tent pegs flattened. The drivers probably think our bus has broken down.

"Royal Body Guard can sleep anywhere, Mr. Tony," Mr. Sangay answers with a grin. The reason he is last up, he tells me, is because he spent an hour and a half performing a puja "to subdue devils."

Kezang brings him a cup of tea. He dips his fingers in and flicks the liquid this way and that, muttering prayers.

"For the spirituals who have nothing. Make them to feel good too."

| Today, we must wear our Tara-thon jerseys with "Run for the Kids" on the chest as the district education officer for Mongar dzongkhag will greet us at the city limits and take us to Mongar High School, where we are to lodge for the night. We gather for a group photo in front of the chorten at Kori-La, an ugly, new construction in grey brick with a steel guardrail around the base. Embedded in the side is an image of an amiable, pale-faced god playing a lute. I recognize him from Sherubtse Lhakhang: Yulkhorsung, lord of celestial music and guardian of the easterly direction. On the other side is a more sinister character with a red face, a halo of fire, and a snake coiled around his hand: Chenmizang, lord of serpents and guardian of the westerly direction.

Everyone is raring to go, despite aches and pains. Mr. Sangay claps his hands, and the two Ugyens gallop off. They have been taking the lead since Day 1 and exude confidence. Ugyen Lhendup has come a long way since the college marathon of 2006. On that day, he collapsed at the finish line and curled up shivering; he had run for an hour and forty-five minutes without taking a drink. Determined to do the Tara-thon, he joined Nadya and me for long runs on Sundays during the summer, and we gave him a water bottle from Canada with belt and holster. Sometimes on my early morning jogs to Yonphula, I would meet him charging down to Kanglung, water bottle jigging on his hip. Like Tiger, Ugyen was born in an eastern village far from the road and had a tough childhood. His father took a tract of land in the forest and tried to make a living for his two wives and twelve children by making paper from daphne and selling it in Thimphu. To make ends meet, the family grew potatoes and chili peppers to sell locally. School for Ugyen was in Trashi Yangtse, a six-hour walk away, so he had to board.

"During those times, World Food Programme used to supply ration," he told us. "Fooding calculation came to only twenty-one ngultrums per month. You can imagine the quality of food at school from this amount! There were no beds. We used to sleep on the floor. The room was packed with all students together, about fifty children in a room of twelve metres by eight metres. There were many flea, bed bug, and louse."

Maybe this has something to do with Ugyen Lhendup being the shortest and skinniest runner on the team, despite being the oldest—not that this seems to bother him. Stripping down to bathe in the Sheri Chhu three days ago, he entertained the team with muscleman poses, berating his biceps for refusing to rise to the occasion. Ugyen Younten calls his running partner "Living Skeleton."

Ugyen Younten is skeletal himself, but tall. Ugyen Lhendup calls him "Kangdung" (Long Bone). I don't know much about him, except that his father was a doctor when he was alive and his brother is a monk. Perhaps influenced by the latter, he told us he wished to run for Tarayana to "show wealthy people what is dharma. It does not mean doing puja, but helping needed ones." He is the only member of our team who listens to music while running ("The Drill," Sar, and "Way I Are").

Our destination is practically visible from the pass, a cluster of white buildings glued to a green mountainside. I can imagine a monsoon downpour washing them off, a raging river rolling them down to the Indian plains. I emerge from the shade of oak trees, brown-leafed in wintertime, and descend through barren paddy fields (although one or two are bright yellow with what I assume is canola). Lower, the road becomes dusty, the vegetation sparser, the air drier. I find myself suddenly running beside rock like wafer biscuits, the layers alternating in colour from cream to choco-late. Buddhist graffiti decorates the thickest wafers. I have caught glimpses of this more than once from car or bus windows, wavy red writing on yellow panels, but it has always been a blur. I take a closer look. The Sanskrit letters appear to hang from an invisible thread and resemble unravelling knots, the loose ends spiralling down or looping back on themselves. Above the thread hover four simple shapes, one like a bird flying under a sun, two like cresting waves, the last a crescent moon cradling a sun—an image found at the top of chortens, symbolizing air. "Om mani padme hum," says the writing. Liberation from earthly concerns. The calligraphy seems to suit the mantra.

Seventeen kilometres from the pass, I find another uplifting message at the side of the road: "Mongar Welcomes Tara-thon." The banner is like the one that welcomed us to Trashigang. On the other side of the road, two men and four teenage girls are clapping and cheering. A portly man of about fifty-five with grey hair and twinkling eyes steps forward and seizes my hand with both of his.

"Hello, hello. I am DEO for Mongar, and this is statistical officer." He points to a smaller man with glasses, standing at his side. "Refreshments for runners are at school one kilometre from here."

We wait for everyone to arrive before beginning the last kilometre. Ten minutes pass, twenty minutes, thirty. Everyone has made it down from the pass except Nadya, Tharchen, and Yana. The bus rounds the final bend, and I see Yana's head poking out one of the windows. I would learn later that the driver scooped him up at six kilometres as he was limping badly. Nadya and our team leader are just behind the bus, moving very slowly. Something is up.

"You okay?" My wife limps to a halt and bends over, closing her eyes in pain. I look at her feet. The right ankle is horribly swollen.

"Follow me!" hollers the DEO, trotting off down the hill, waving his arm from side to side over his head.

"Tell you later." She straightens up and takes a deep breath.

We jog slowly into town behind the banner, causing traffic going up or down to pull over. I expect to peel off along a side road to the high school, but this does not happen. Mr. Sangay said there would be a left turn near a petrol station. After about a kilometre, we take a right off the highway and pass in front of Mongar Lower Secondary School. The place seems closed, but this does not deter the DEO from waving energetically in that direction. The road deteriorates. We are now on hardened mud, splashed with oil stains. There are ramshackle wooden huts to either side, one marked, "Wheelers,

Overhauling, Denting, Painting and Repair Centre." We thread our way around cars and trucks with their wheels off. Mechanics with black hands shout and wave. Two join us. We pass a building under construction, propped up with bamboo struts, to our left, then the Regional Referral Hospital, also under construction, to our right.

"This way, this way! Hello, everyone, hello!" The DEO waves his arms about. The statistical officer is running with his hands on his hips, his head nodding. The girls with the banner are purple-faced and panting.

We are now in the heart of town in front of the market. I see a signboard saying, "Vote for Naichu. Choose youthful dynamism, proven track record and rural touch." People drift over to see what is going on. Our numbers swell again. A woman and her two boys jog with us, a man carrying a sheaf of papers. I look up and see people hanging out of upstairs windows. The owner of a pharmacy with geraniums outside waves his broom. The school cannot be around here. I look for Nadya, expecting to see her suffering. We are a thousand metres below the pass, and the temperature has risen a good 15°C. She is bobbing up and down like Terry Fox, but I see a smile on her face. Now we are at Mongar petrol station alongside Tata goods trucks, waiting in line. We pass a taxi rank. From here, it appears we will return to the highway. Ahead I see an archway over the road marking the way out of town. So the school must be west of Mongar.

"Now up!" bellows the DEO, sweat streaming from his face and dripping down the front of his gho. He takes a hard left, and we run up the high street.

"Oh god," I groan. We are doubling back on ourselves. I look to left and right at our runners. Their glazed-over expressions are difficult to read. Sonam Wangdi's eyes are gleaming.

Ten minutes later, we are back where we started. Mongar High School is indeed a left turn off the lateral road when you come into Mongar from the east—a short distance, in fact, from where we first met the DEO. We stagger up a steep dirt road and finish the day's run on the school playing field. Refreshments are desi and suja, served by six girls in smart kiras behind folding tables. The DEO shakes

everyone's hand and then disappears. I thought he might introduce us to the school principal or to some of the teachers. The girls
stay to write stories and draw pictures for Tarayana, and then they
also disappear. We are left alone, sitting on the grass, surrounded
by empty buildings. Where are we to lodge for the night? Where can
we wash and get ice for Nadya's ankle? My gaze settles on a battered
shell with broken windows on the far side of the field.

1. *Marry the right person. This one person will determine 90% of your happiness or misery.*

2. *Work on something you enjoy and that's worthy of your time and talent.*

5. *Be forgiving of yourself and others.*

13. *Understand that happiness is not based on possessions, power or prestige, but on relationships with people you love and respect.*

17. *Be decisive even if it means you'll sometimes be wrong.*

19. *Be bold and courageous. When you look back on your life, you'll regret the things you didn't do more than the things you did.*

—From "21 Suggestions for Success,"
Mongar High School, principal's office

73

6 | The Longest Climb

"WHAT A..." I ALMOST SAY, "bloody tip," but, looking at the six bleary-eyed runners clutching their belongings in the doorway, bite my lip. "...disappointment."

The dormitory looks like it has taken a direct hit from heavy artillery. The windows are all shattered or cracked, the walls gouged and streaked with dirt, and most of the bunks reduced to steel frames. A thick layer of screwed-up study notes, masonry rubble, wood splinters, and noodle wrappers coats the floor. Judging by the shards of glass on the windowsills and on the few bunks with mattresses, the carnage appears to have happened recently. I imagine a final act of joyful destruction by kids gone berserk before vacation. I walk around, my Fastwitches crunching on broken glass, and find three serviceable bunks. Lifting the mattresses, though, I see that the wooden slats are either missing or snapped. Could there at least be a broom in this abandoned school? Team Leader Tharchen puts down his bag and starts picking up litter.

"Don't worry, Sar. We are used," Wangchuck Rabten says and does the same.

Like the others on the team, Wangchuck knows the rigours of a rural life. Raised in Nabji, a village in Trongsa dzongkhag with no electricity, no road, and no school, he had to walk over a mountain to the next valley for an education. It was too far for him to walk back at night, so he spent weekdays boarding in a "temporary hut," built beside the school, surviving on the rice and vegetables he carried from home.

"Well, at least, you can go and clean up. There are plenty of showers outside."

"None of them are working, Sar."

"What? You're kidding. But the school was supposed to..."

I go out and check. Eight faucets poke through a crumbly wall next to the dorm. Only three have handles. I spin two of them, not bothering to stand out of the way. I can see from the dead leaves and dry mud around my feet that they have not been used in some time. Next to the showers are toilet stalls. I already know what I am going to find there. The stench is appalling. Flies sail in and out, settling on the door jambs and glinting in the last of the afternoon sun.

"Where's Mr. Sangay?"

I look across the soccer pitch and spot him standing by the bus on the other side. I march over, scowling at the pain in my knees, which has returned after today's long downhill. *Why didn't he phone ahead and make sure the school was ready to receive us? Didn't he call the DEO and have him inform the school principal that we were coming? Where is the school principal? Surely someone from the school should be here.* I think of our stay at Yadi Middle Secondary two nights ago. A young economics teacher called Kinga had welcomed us at the gate, showed us around, and invited us to join him for dinner at the school. We spent the night on bunk beds set up in two swept classrooms.

"Mr. Sangay, have you seen the hostel? It's a disgrace. I wouldn't ask my dog to stay there!" The word "dog" comes out like a bark.

The director of sports looks at me, taken aback.

"The toilets too. Foul! Covered in shit. Flies everywhere. And none of the showers work."

No response.

I turn and watch Dendup toss bags and billycans off the roof of the bus to the two Ugyens, waiting with outstretched arms below. Nadya made out a chore rota for the team in Trashigang. Two students get up early to help the cook peel and slice potatoes for lunch, another two help him make dinner. Two pitch tents after the day's run, two collect firewood. When we are staying at a school, one pair must organize a writing or drawing activity with the pupils when we arrive, another lead the warm-up and stretching routine before we depart. She has mixed up the pairs so everyone gets to work with everyone else. Often I see three or four students doing the assigned chore together. The students unloading the bus were chatting loudly when I arrived. Now they are silent. I turn back to Mr. Sangay.

"You're the event coordinator." The words come out louder than I intended. Long Bone Ugyen stops what he is doing and looks over. I soften my voice. "We need to make sure this doesn't happen again."

Mr. Sangay excuses himself, saying he has letters of reference to write for some final-year students at Sherubtse. I sigh and wonder if I should have the team pitch camp for the night on the playing field. I go in search of Nadya. She must be scouring the school for a working faucet, so she can bathe her foot. She emerges from one of the buildings with a man in a grey gho.

"This is the vice-principal, Tony."

He installs us in the principal's office for the night. Mr. Sangay gets a classroom. The team must make do in the hostel. We explain about the water, and he switches it on before leaving. Nadya and I take a wash in the dark and then, exhausted, unroll our sleeping mats on the floor of the office. I have an unsettled night. There is a scratching sound in the walls and then scampering across the floor. Shrews would scoot out from under the fridge from time to time at our home in Kanglung, but this creature is bigger. Then I spot him under the principal's desk, a hairy silhouette with a long pale tail, caught in a shaft of moonlight stretching through the window. Nadya does not stir.

I lie awake and think back to when we first arrived in Kanglung two winters ago. The bungalow we were to live in hardly seemed ready for occupation. A section of the roof had come away, the bukkari in the living room (the only source of heat) refused to light, the washbasin was lying on the bathroom floor, the squatter toilet was flooded, the gas bottle for the stove in the kitchen was empty, the garden fence had fallen over, and there was a heap of loose trash blowing about outside the back door. But it only took our arrival for things to happen. A man called Penjor brought a new bracket for the washbasin the following day. The college gardener brought us a plunger for the toilet and wood for the stove the following week— eight visits with the wood, fifteen faggots strung to his back each time. A man up the road called Karma, who had fifteen-kilogram bottles of liquid gas to sell, rolled one to our doorstep. The next-door neighbour propped up the fence. Ugyen Dendup, head of English at Sherubtse, brought a team to fix the roof. For a hundred ngultrums (two and a half bucks), we would have five new sheets of "reiging" (such was the word on the bill).

"Mr. Tony, you have long wire?" Ugyen enquired while the workmen hammered away, himself up on the roof with his head down our chimney.

Perhaps there was such a thing in the garden shed. I went in search.

"You know William Blake's 'Chimney Sweep?'" Ugyen said, seizing the roll of wire Nadya had found and sniggering, his cheeks sooty and flushed from chewing doma. "I am he!"

I should go inside, he said, and take the stovepipe out of the wall while he poked the wire down the chimney. "Bird's nest might be in there."

Soot showered down into the lounge and then half-burned wads of *Kuensel*, which I tried to catch in a paper bag.

The same was true of convocation last year. Everyone knew at the start of March, when the academic year began, that His Majesty the King would be coming to Sherubtse to confer awards in April. It was all the talk when professors and students returned from their vacations. There would have to be elaborate preparations, of course, and careful planning. There was much of the first, but, it seemed, hardly any of the second. Nadya and I returned from recess to discover what looked like a bombsite. There were gaping holes in the roads with rusty water pipes sticking out, electrical wiring bursting from the walls in several classrooms, and mounds of dirt in the middle of the playing field. Approximately a quarter of the books were in a metre-high heap on the floor of the library. My class-room had lost its ceiling and was now knee-deep in rubble. During the air raid, many of the canine guardians of the college must have been casualties, for the "old familiars" outside the mess and in the waste pits had vanished (although a younger cohort, I noticed, had replaced them).

The college continued to resemble a war zone until the week before the big day, students and staff attending to their duties as usual. Then, a frenzy of activity. Everyone seemed to drop what they were doing and rally to the task. Each day I arrived at work, something had altered. Workmen replaced the old water pipes with new ones and buried them; they tucked the wiring back in the walls and sealed the holes. Library staff worked a night shift to reshelve the books students had returned before recess. The mounds of earth on the playing field disappeared over night, and a toilet in a little tent materialized. A marquee went up beside it. Workmen built a dais and a throne from scratch out of bamboo and wood in the Multi-Purpose Hall, where the ceremony would take place, and painted them in bright colours. In gangs of thirty, students lopped branches off trees and used them to sweep all the roads and steps. Another team, carrying paint pots and bamboo scaffolding, went to work on the college gate. Twenty minutes before the dignitaries arrived, students formed lines and chased all the stray dogs off the premises. The minute before BHUTAN 1 rolled in, the three students still touching up the gate chucked their paintbrushes into the bushes and straightened their ghos.

| Two days later, I look for Mr. Sangay, knowing that I owe him an apology. I find him sitting alone in the staffroom, using a computer. He looks at me with sadness in his eyes as I try to explain why I was upset.

"Intellectual should not raise voice," he says. We agree that lack of communication is also part of the problem. "Things must be clear-cut," he insists, chopping the desk with the edge of his hand.

I return to the principal's office with my hands in my pockets to find my wife in tears.

"I've failed. All that training and preparation...wasted! Mongar isn't even a, a fifth of the way to Thimphu."

Her foot looks the same as it did the day before yesterday, puffed up and discoloured, the anklebone all but swallowed. She is unable to get her running shoe on, even with the laces fully loosened. The old injury she got playing volleyball in her twenties has flared up again. She had bathed her foot repeatedly yesterday, thinking that this would return it to its normal shape. She sprawls on the floor of the vice-principal's office, where we spent our second night, arms folded, one shoe on, one shoe off, a look of defeat on her face. I stop rolling up my sleeping mat and give her a hug, remembering a cautionary question Singye Namgyel had asked us before our departure from Sherubtse: what happens if someone collapses or gets injured?

"You need to go to the hospital, honey."

"There's no time. We have to leave now."

It is 9:05 A.M. Flag off at 9:30, Mr. Sangay told the DEO. I look out the window and see the two men chatting. Sonam Wangdi and Sonam Gyalpo are strapping the last of the bags to the roof of the bus. The girls who served us desi when we arrived have formed a semicircle around Tharchen and Sherab for the warm-up. Our runners look in good shape although Tiger is limping again. I have no idea what they did around town yesterday but imagine they took advantage of the restaurants. Nadya said she saw Tharchen with a cream-filled pastry in his hand, looking happy. They also clearly enjoyed poking their heads in shops for donations and handed over BTN 14,495 to me in the evening, 10,000 of which came from the dzong.

"You go ahead," Nadya says, tight-lipped. "I'll get Kezang to give me a ride to the hospital. Don't worry. I'll catch you up."

She manages to wrestle the shoe on, but not without crying out in pain. She won't be able to run twenty-three kilometres to our next stop. She will have to take another day off and ride in the bus. I nod and finish packing up our gear, hating to leave her like this, but she must go and see a doctor. It will be hard to find one once we leave— the next town with a hospital is 266 kilometres away.

It feels like everyone is staring at me when I go outside. It is 9:35. I tell Mr. Sangay that we are ready to start. Madam will follow later. I tell Kezang to wait and see if she needs a lift. Like the vice-principal of Trashigang Middle Secondary, the DEO of Mongar dzongkhag has no idea how to signal the start. Mr. Sangay offers him no tips. He finally decides on a kind of silent, sweeping-brush gesture using both arms, and I chuckle despite feeling that things are beginning to go wrong.

There is no spring in my step as I run down the hill with the others. We are no longer the Long Distance Dozen...or the baker's dozen. God knows what happened to the dog. I jog half-heartedly for a kilometre, letting the others zoom ahead. Pine trees shade the road on both sides. I stop, look over my shoulder, start again. Stop. I coast for another kilometre before turning around.

"Have you seen a chilip with a bad foot?" I do an impersonation, staggering forward and back, dragging my foot behind me. The man leaning against the wall of the hospital laughs. His eyes peer at me from hollow sockets. His gho hangs off his stooped shoulders. I am a fool. He is a patient. *Why am I asking him? Why didn't I learn Dzongkha?* Tashi, the sickness-prone greengrocer in Kanglung, taught me some words for health and emergencies, but they have deserted me. I dash between wards, poking my head in each, calling Nadya's name. Pregnant woman laid out on a bed, boy with withered leg trying out a crutch, woman putting fresh sheets on a bed. *Should I be doing this?*

"Tony?"

I find her in a corridor, weaving her way around patients and their families.

"Nadya! You okay? What did the doctor say?"

"Nothing broken. My ankle needs a lot of rest though, and I have to keep it elevated. He gave me ibuprofen for the pain and some extra bandages." Her foot, I see, is now bandaged and sits more easily in the shoe. "And, look, massage cream for the team! He gave me three jars of it."

We walk out of the hospital and back to the highway. The bus is waiting.

"So, what do you want to do?"

Sitting by the rear wheel is a familiar barrel of brown fluff.

"Yana, Yana, sho!" calls Nadya. I see her smile for the first time today. The dog trots over, sore front paw apparently better. He is wearing a red shirt with "Please donate" painted on it.

"Let's run," Nadya says.

Chir pines, tangerine orchards, cornfields, tengma stalls. As we descend, the temperature climbs. Our run is more like a shuffle, Nadya sticking to the soft grass at the side of the road wherever possible. Below the road, women roast corn in shallow pans over log fires. Later, they will pound it with pestles to make a tough version of Corn Flakes, which they sell in bags at the side of the road. I tried eating tengma for breakfast one morning in Kanglung. After three mouthfuls, I realized that milk was not going to make it any softer, and I would be late for class if I stayed to finish my bowl.

At 6k, we run into the girls from the school, walking back to town. They cheer and yell, "Best of luck!" causing Yana to gallop over, expecting a treat. The dog is a handy distraction for Nadya today. He frequently dives into the bush, following scent trails. Nadya calls to him when he disappears. We go around two or three bends and then hear his nails clicking on the asphalt behind us. "Where have you been this time?" she asks him. I wonder what kind of life he had in Trashigang. Was he a stray like those at Sherubtse College, fighting savagely for scraps chucked out by restaurants? Somehow, I doubt it. He is too amiable and lacks scars. He is also remarkably quiet— not a murmur when he got his unforeseen bath in the Sheri Chhu, no expectant yaps at dinnertimes. Mutu, by contrast, took every opportunity to remind us of her existence in Kanglung. She barked at passers-by, barked when other dogs in the village barked, barked when she was hungry, and howled outside our bedroom window at night. Fond of sleeping right through to sunrise, especially on weekday nights, I got into the habit of keeping a bucket of cold water beside our bed.

Our progress is slow, but the kilometres keep slipping by. The Kuri Chhu draws nearer and nearer, a blue arm scratched with foam and freckled with stones. At 16k, we overtake Tiger, who complains of cramp and seems to be running on wooden legs. He grimaces every third stride but laughs when I ask him if he needs a piggyback. At 20k, we hear the shushing sound of water over rocks. A glittering white chorten with a gold pinnacle comes into view and then an iron bridge and two shops: Kurizampa, the lowest point on our journey. As we round the final bends, I see some of our hares, sprawled out beside the river, sunbathing. They have clearly been waiting for some time. It has taken us practically three hours to run the twenty-six kilometres.

Nadya collapses next to the chorten and removes her shoe and sock. Her ankle has blown up again, but she does not seem to be in pain. A quarter of an hour later, Tiger limps in and leans on the bridge, panting. Fetching my wallet from the bus, I go into one of the shops and buy bottles of Pepsi or Sprite for everyone. I have an ugly feeling in my stomach. Eighty-four kilometres of unrelenting uphill begins on the far side of the river, a climb of almost 3048 metres. Some of our runners will not make it. What should we do with the dropouts? Send them home? Let them ride in the bus? Nadya and I have been most insistent that this is a run across the kingdom and not a walk. And what of my wife?

But the longest climb of our journey will not begin today. We board the bus and bump along a dirt road tracking the river. From the window, I spot an eagle with broad shoulders and a white head eyeing us from its perch on a tall, grey rock standing up from the river.

| "And what is that?"

The tower at the side of the river reminds me of an Escher sketch: a precarious staircase, making right-angled turns as it rises, appearing to defy gravity. But the steps are actually tanks of water, each spilling its contents into the one below. Together, they form a long, gurgling chute. Water cascades down, slopping out in places and spattering the rocks below.

"Fish ladder, Sar," Dendup says.

I look for fish in the tanks nearest us, but see none. Climbing the ladder would be quite a feat for them. The height of the dam, we now know, is fifty-five metres. The fish would need to jump about a hundred times from one tank to the next and the next, and I find it hard to imagine migrating carp or trout managing it. Nevertheless, I am pleased with the idea. The ladder is further evidence of sustainable development.

The principal of Gyelpozhing High School, where we will stay tonight, has arranged a permit for us to visit the Kurichu Hydroelectric Plant. I am glad of the distraction. We have already learned a lot from the soldier showing us around. Financed entirely by grants and loans from India, the project is the first of its kind in eastern Bhutan, and, apparently, has already supplied power to 7,400 households in eight dzongkhags since 2005, the year it was commissioned. (I guess if we had arrived in Kanglung that year, we might have been cooking by kerosene lantern or candlelight.) Seventy per cent of the sixty megawatts generated is sold to India. The plant employs run-of-the-river technology, meaning that it uses the natural flow of the river to spin its turbines, rather than water gathered in a head pond. I think of the destructive alternative and recall travelling by ferry along the Yangtse in 1997, knowing that the three beautiful gorges were condemned.

It is rather odd, suddenly being surrounded by spinning turbines the diameter of grain-storage silos, water pipes large enough to stand in, banks of monitors with flickering needles, and an electrical grid resembling a monstrous spider's web. This machinery does not belong to the Bhutan we have got to know. And yet the mechanism, in essence, does not seem complex. Water flows into the barrage and gathers speed as it tumbles down a concrete ramp. At the bottom, it drives four turbines, resembling many-bladed propellers. Shafts rising from the turbines connect to generators that produce the electricity. The electricity goes to a grid beside the dam, and then transmission lines carry it over the mountains. A village in Lhuentse, Trashiyangtse, or Pemagatshel lights up. Then I remember that getting electricity to a village buried in the Himalayas is, in fact, no easy task.

One afternoon last winter, before beginning the climb to Tsebar in the southern dzongkhag of Pemagatshel, Nadya and I stopped at a river to refill our canteens and buy mandarins from a farmer. It was another sweltering day, and the village was a two- or three-hour trek from the river up a steep dirt path. We were about to go on our way when we heard yells from behind. Two files of people, about forty in all, were coming along the path carrying a metal box the size of a refrigerator lashed between two eight-metre bamboo poles. The poles were bending under the weight like archery bows. We put our packs back down and let them pass. Tough young men with ghos rolled down to their waists and sweat coursing down their necks were taking most of the weight, but there were women, too, middle-aged and matronly, one older with narrow shoulders and whitening hair. At the end of the train were three students from Sherubtse.

"Hello, Sar!"

"Where are you going?"

"To their village, Sar," one replied with a chuckle. "Dungmin."

"Is that on the way to Tsebar?"

"No, Sar, on other side. Over the pass. Six or seven hour from here, I think."

"But longer surely if you're carrying this?"

I studied the electrical transformer. Not only was it clearly heavy, but it was awkward, too. Three rocket-like bushings stuck out the top, two at 60° angles, and there was a cylindrical tank on a pair of steel arms, also rising from the top, but at a different angle. A sharp-cornered, rectangular control box projected about fifteen centimetres from one side. It had a door with a handle—good, no doubt, at snagging gho pouches and passing branches. Metal brackets that would be used to anchor the transformer at its destination protruded from the underside, and a valve or connecting rod of some sort pointed out one end.

"It will take...maybe a week, Sar."

"Hell. How much does it weigh?"

"Six hundred, twenty kilogram, Sar."

Our packs weighed no more than fifteen or sixteen. Surely there was a better way? But I knew that Bhutan had no helicopters, and donkeys, tethered to the poles, would probably not work either. The path was too narrow and twisty. Some kind of cart perhaps? I looked ahead. Soon, the path would take a sharp right turn down to the river and disintegrate into boulders and fallen branches. On the far bank, it resumed, but there it was narrower and inclining at a slant.

I looked again at the villagers. Their feet were sliding in and out of their flip-flops as they staggered forward. One man seemed to be doing most of the shouting. The rest heaved and groaned and laughed.

Our run from Kurizampa to Yongkola was tough that I felt, one thing its steep slop and hot day. It was really tough but still then I try to win the game. As I recal what Tee said to me... "Wangchuck, whenever you get tried and don't feel like running you think about those student who are not able to study and stay in village without education, be motivate yourself by thinking that you are doing good to them and remember the caption that was written on our shirt 'Run For the kids.'" This was what Tee told to me on the way and I keep running think that I am doing noble job.

—WANGCHUCK RABTEN, *Tara-thon blog entry (January 7, 2008)*

It is Day 9 of our marathon for Tarayana, and our itinerary says we must run to Yongkola, twenty-three kilometres from the Kuri Chhu. The bus disgorges us at the end of the bridge. It is another cloudless day. I look around at the team and try to gauge the mood. Last week, they were kicking a soccer ball about to warm up before starting the day's run. None are doing that today.

"No dashing up to Thrumshing-La like mountain goats, okay?" Nadya says, calling everyone around. "Ugyen and Ugyen, are you listening? We have a big climb ahead. Like running from Sherubtse to Yonphula and then doing it again on the same day. We have *four* days of that, okay? So save your strength. When you see the bus, stop and take a rest. Drink plenty—even if you don't feel thirsty. Okay, let's do a warm-up."

I look down at my wife's foot, wound in bandage. She has told me not to hang back. She will run to Yongkola, but at her own speed. Even if it takes her the entire day. I cannot say I feel especially lively myself. I did not get a good night's sleep. My body is baffled by the daily changes in temperature. In Mongar I needed my sleeping bag. Last night, I woke sweating and had to shrug it off. It is only 9:30 A.M., but it must already be 25°C. I stick my head through the rusted iron struts of the bridge and look for the eagle, but it has gone from its lookout. Minutes tick by. Now it is ten o'clock. We should really get going, but Mr. Sangay is with a reporter from BBS. 10:30. Finally, the bus roars to life, zooms over the bridge, and attacks a ferocious incline on the far side. Slowly, we give pursuit.

But after half an hour, we have stopped again. Wangchuck Rabten, Tharchen, and Ugyen Lhendup have ducked into two shops at a bend in the road called Lingmithang to ask for donations. I squat in the shade of some dusty eucalypts and watch two monks giving blessings to passers-by. On a table between them is a curious object. It resembles a chorten but is less than a metre high and much dressier in appearance, with doors that open out at the bottom. I wander over and crouch in front of it. Behind each door is a miniature Buddha, meticulously painted, sitting in a niche the size of a matchbox. Daisy chains of prayer flags hang in front of the doors.

"Tashi gomang," Mr. Sangay says. "Portable chorten for sick person or good fortune."

He goes to the bus and asks Kezang to hand him his wallet. He calls the team over and, walking down the line, presses a fifty-ngultrum note to each of our foreheads. He then takes the money over to the monks, puts it to his own head, and places it in one of the doors of the shrine. One of the monks rings a bell. The ritual is no less bizarre to me than the ceremony that launched us on this expedition nine days ago, and yet I hardly bat an eyelid. Nothing important happens here without propitiating the gods. Funny how I have not only come to accept this as reasonable but also believe it has worth. I have never been superstitious—never worried about black cats or broken mirrors or ladders—but, here in Bhutan, I would not walk around a chorten the wrong way or pass by a cairn on a hiking trail without leaving an offering for the god of the road. Tashi delek. That the god of the mountain send not boulders crashing down on our heads. Tashi delek. That our modest efforts to raise money for education be smiled upon. I look at the rearing land ahead. We are in the company of giants. It is fitting that we salute them.

"Stop at six kilometre, again after six, Mr. Tony?"

"Yes. Yes, please, Mr. Sangay." It is the first time he has checked with me about this.

"You know what we call this?" The director of sports seems to be in a good mood today. "Better communication."

I nod and smile, grateful to him for clearing the air between us.

"Okay, let's get on with it!" I yell, turning to the students and clapping my hands. Some of them, I notice, are back on the bus, swigging water and mopping their brows. We need to be out of this hot valley before midday. I will set an example. We made it up to Kori-La. We had a rest day in Mongar. Our legs are fresh after dunking them in the Kuri Chhu yesterday. We have had another blessing. The heat will diminish as we gain height and re-enter the forest. Picking up my knees and pumping my arms, I lead the way for the first time since leaving Kanglung. Time to conquer Thrumshing-La!

From Lingmithang, the lateral road rises gently at first. We pass fruit orchards on the right, many of the trees dripping with mandarins. I see darkening avocados and vines sagging with bubble-skinned bitter gourds. A foul taste collects in my mouth as I look at the gourds and recall almost gagging on them in Kanglung. High on the left, I spot an isolated stone turret, squatting alone on a wooded promontory. It is split down the middle and resembles an old man's molar. It could be the remains of a Norman castle if this were England. I will have to ask Mr. Sangay about it. I round a sharp bend and suddenly come face to face with a man standing motionlessly between two papaya trees. I wave. He does not respond. I try to make out his expression, but he is in the shade. Farmers often stop what they are doing when they see us. They look at us with incredulity or amusement. I wonder what this particular man is thinking: *Why are you in such a hurry? Is your house on fire? Have your cows run off?* Three kilometres done, now four. *Did your tour bus leave without you?*

My pace slackens involuntarily, and I feel light-headed. I should probably ease off at the bends where the road is at its steepest. I have been doing just the opposite to put the curves in the road behind me. Five kilometres, six. I see Ngawang standing by the bus with a bottle of water and a cup. I have said about three words to this man over the nine days. Mr. Sangay recruited him from the college mess the day before we set out. He has already proved invaluable. He is up before any of us in the morning and seems undaunted cooking meals for twelve ravenous runners three times a day over open fires at the side of the road. From the way he handles burning logs, I would say he comes equipped with hands made of asbestos.

"Kadrinche, Ngawang." I stay only for as long as it takes to drain the cup.

Unsheltered road continues for another four kilometres. My chest is heaving now, my vision blurry. I am fourteen clicks from the river, but the heat still feels intense. I shake my head. *What is wrong?* My legs feel like they have lead weights attached. Someone calls my name. I look back. I rub my face on my shirt and think of the training run I did from Trashigang to Kanglung in monsoon season, plodding laboriously uphill for two hours through thrashing thundershowers, water streaming down the road and washing around my ankles. The dead weight then was my saturated shoes. I look up at the sky, hoping for a darkened cloud—any cloud—but there is just the sun, desertlike in its unfiltered brilliance. *How can the weather be so like summer?* My pace deadens to a crawl. *Where are the chilling winds of winter?* My head is swimming. A Bhutanese superstition pops into my head: "If you have difficulty walking uphill, carry an arrow. If you have trouble walking downhill, then carry a ball." Today I need the arrow. Paddy field, abandoned tengma stall, cow—tail flicking from side to side, flies buzzing around its nose. *"Flies everywhere. And none of the showers work."* I look over my shoulder. Where are the Ugyens? Where is Yana? The Tara-thon bus suddenly steams past, but I do not recognize it until it is almost around the next bend. I wave half-heartedly. *"We need to make sure this doesn't happen again."* Slower, gaze fixed to the ground. Hoof print in cake of dry mud, tire-flattened mandarin skin, truck skid marks. Giddy. I slap my cheek. Black dots hover in front of my eyes.

I look up, swallow hard and take several gulps of air. I should not be running with my head down. *Turn it into a game.* I trundle onward, blinking furiously, willing the black dots to disperse. *Paint the roadside ahead with waypoints.* That stumpy concrete pillar marking the edge—*get there.* Now the flower with velvety leaves and small pink blooms—*make it.* Now the pile of fire-blackened stones, now those hairy tufts of lemon grass. Out of the corner of my eye, I catch a glint of metal a hundred metres over my head, then a searing flash of sunlight off glass. If I dash up the paddy staircase, I will be there in five minutes, but the road swings me away in the opposite direction. *"Where in the world you go in opposite directions to reach same place?"*

This time there is no one beside the bus. I collapse in its shadow and squeeze my eyes shut. My head is pounding. *Idiot.* When I open my eyes, I am looking at a boy with a cleft lip and a horribly disfigured stomach. He is smiling and offering me a mandarin. Surely not. I reach out for the fruit, claw off the peel, ram half of it in my mouth, and rest my head against the side of the bus. The mandarin is so ripe, the segments explode against the back of my throat as I chew, making me cough and splutter. I lean forward as juice runs down my chin. The boy looks at me closely. Embarrassed, I wipe my mouth with the back of my hand and snort helplessly. He smiles again and digs four more of the fruit out of his gho and drops them in my lap. His stomach shrinks.

"Kadrinche," I croak and hold up my hand, indicating that he should wait.

"Kezang?"

"Sar?"

"Give this boy some money from the kitty, would you?"

I clamber onto the bus, tear the cap off a water bottle, take a shot of glucose, eat three of the mandarins in rapid succession, rub my face with a flannel, and then slump in a seat and stare out the window. The little boy has vanished. My eyelids droop, and my body

slowly tilts forward until my forehead is resting on the seatback
in front. There is a tingling sensation in my hands. I close my eyes.
Dog, dusty, furless, watery-eyed, licking the boils on her back with a
black tongue. "Give me the gun and I am killing aaall the stray dogs."
I jerk my eyes open, lick my lips, try to focus on my hand, my watch,
the checkered pattern on the seatback. Still the dots. *Chorten, dark*
hole in the side, a howling wind, black clouds chasing across the sky,
torn prayers on parchment unravelling off a cracked wooden spool.
Should you circumambulate a desecrated chorten? I breathe out and

let my body sink back in my seat. The pounding in my head softens.

When I open my eyes again, I see a cowboy hat. Kezang is dozing
in the driver's seat, arms folded, hat tipped forward over his face.
He snores gently. I look around to see if anyone else is flaked out
on a seat. Where is Mr. Sangay? Tee comes up the stairs and goes to
his seat at the front. His face is scarlet, his cap pulled down over his
eyes, his Tara-thon T-shirt stuck to his stomach. I hear his basketball shoes flapping. He snatches up a water bottle.

"Is Sar okay?" Concern on his face. I look at his feet. One toecap
is soon to detach itself from the shoe. Then what?

"I'm fine, Tee. Just taking a rest. How about you?"

"Fine, Sar." He takes another swig from the bottle, scoops up
a handful of Britannia Good Day cookies and heads out, a look of
singular determination on his face.

I look again at my watch. I can read the display now: 2:34 P.M.
The black dots have gone. God, how long have I been sitting here?
I stare at the display. Timex Ironman. 2:35 P.M., 3 seconds, 4 seconds, 5.
Start/Split button, Stop/Reset button. 2:36 P.M. I take the watch off
and sling it into my bag. I take off my Fastwitch racing lights, too,
and put on my heavier running shoes. As I head out, I look again for
the little boy. There is an orchard above the road, but, in the dazzling
sunlight, I can see only the silhouette of a woman, his mother maybe,
picking mandarins and putting them in a sack. I start running—taking
small, deliberate steps and seeking shadow—and think of Dema.

Nadya and I would eat samosas or momos dipped in chili sauce at
our local restaurant most Saturdays in Kanglung. These, however,

would have been madness to eat after our vacation in India. I had a "running stomach," as a Nigerian travel companion once described severe diarrhea. Being within striking distance of a lavatory at all times was imperative. Nadya was also suffering but didn't seem quite so incapacitated. After staying with Dr. Shukla at Muzaffarpur, Nadya and I had travelled to see the ghats in Varanasi and the temple where Siddhartha became the Buddha in Bodhgaya. Pre-monsoon temperatures hovered around the 40°C mark, deadening our appetites. But we had to eat. Our final curry in a dirty restaurant in Bodhgaya was probably to blame.

Like Dr. Jagar's wife Zangmo, Dema had the ruddy complexion and callused hands of a woman used to working hard outdoors. When not serving samosas and momos to customers, she sat outside her restaurant weaving shoulder bags, peeling areca nuts with Tashi, and crunching raw chili peppers. Her restaurant was a cubby-hole with seating for eight and a TV in the corner showing Bollywood films or soaps in Hindi. Over the door was a photograph of the fourth king and on the wall a glossy poster of a Swiss village under snow with the words, "Count your life by smiles, not tears." Dema could tell we were ill as soon as we walked in—from our hang-dog expressions or the way, perhaps, we eased ourselves delicately onto the stools. She didn't wait for Nadya to order our usual lunch ("Momo plate tur, samosa pshee, ngaja niksin") but went off to the kitchen and returned with two big bowls of noodle soup with saag.

"Shey!" she ordered, standing over us while we ate and sweated.

Suja followed, salty tea made from rancid butter, a drink that I had taken a particular dislike to. Two cups of the bloody stuff.

We returned to Dema's restaurant the following day.

| "Long, long ago, there was beautiful lady who lived in Thriatangbi village..."

We sit on a low wall outside the only shop in Yongkola, plastic plates of curry on our knees, cups of suja at our elbows, listening to Mr. Sangay. I look around the circle of faces in the ebbing light. Everyone looks beat. Heads hang, spoons lift slowly. Even Tiger with his "paining knee" made it. I am flabbergasted. As far as I know, no one flagged down the Tara bus for a ride, no one thumbed a lift off a passing truck, and no one walked. These students must indeed be reincarnated mountain goats...or beneficiaries, perhaps, of Father Mackey's visionary emphasis on sport in education. I was impressed to see how the early finishers remained standing and cheered home the tail-end Charlies. Tonight, our runners will get a well-earned roof over their heads and comfortable beds to sleep in. Our event coordinator has arranged for them to stay in a bunkhouse across the road.

"This beautiful lady, she engage to a man who only came to her at night time. He left her before sun come up each day. Soon she became pregnant and want to find out where her lover go. So, you know what she do?"

Mr. Sangay is speaking of Zhongar Dzong, the ruined castle we passed on the way up to Yongkola.

"She tied a string to his waist. When morning come, she follow that string through forest and it lead to ruined dzong. After entering, she found string was tied to biiiig snake. He was owner that dzong, a bad spirit. We cannot go that dzong. No courage because bad spirit live there. Only big lama can go."

I had underestimated the Bhutanese. When their motivations are strong, they, too, are strong. I think of the villagers carrying electricity up the mountain. I think back to the dancers at tsechu, jumping and spinning for two hours at a stretch, weighty wooden masks strapped to their heads.

The more I see of the Bhutanese, the more
I am pleased with them. The common people
are good-humoured, downright, and, I think,
thoroughly trusty. The statesmen have some
of the art which belong to their profession.
They are the best-built race of men I ever saw;
many of them very handsome, with complexions
as fair as the French.

The simplicity of their manners, their slight
intercourse with strangers, and a strong
sense of religion, preserve the Bhutanese from
many of the vices to which more polished
nations are addicted.

—GEORGE BOGLE, journal entries, 1774

7 Clowns and Phalluses

NADYA AND I ATTENDED our first tsechu, an annual festival of masked dances honouring Guru Rinpoche, at Yonphula in the spring of 2006. Tshering Wangdi, our colleague from the English department, invited us to go with his family in their Suzuki Omni. His wife would bring along a picnic. It was a tight squeeze in a car not much larger than a mini, Dechen and their two little boys sharing the passenger seat in the front, Dechen's father, Nadya, and me in the back. I had a tub of red rice and another of emadatse on my knees, and Nadya had a wicker bag of Thermos flasks and a melon the size of a beach ball on hers.

The dirt road to the temple was jammed with people. Monks in dusty sandals trailed up and down, arm in arm, women with babies slung to their backs bought snacks from stalls, Indian soldiers in spotless green uniforms and matching turbans stood with their hands behind their backs, and Sherubtse students chucked balled-up socks at pyramids of tin cans. We walked by a man under a canvas awning surrounded by pictures of the guru, dressed in lavish robes and sitting on his lotus throne. We passed a woman on her knees selling cartons of "Jooz Mango," children's shoes, bouncing balls, balloons, and hair grips. A mud hut with a tin roof called Tashidema Hotal Bar was serving bottles of Hit beer and twenty-centimetre soya-bean tubes that resembled dried intestines. Stray dogs nosed the litter under everyone's feet, and a cow at the roadside bit chunks out of a cardboard box.

The road took us up to a gate with a yellow roof set in a wall of white chortens. Two policemen stood inside yelling at a forty-person scrum trying to ram its way into the temple. A skinny man with prayer beads around his neck pushed, his hands on the shoulders of a teenager in front. A plump woman with a mouthful of doma shoved, while two boys crawled through her legs. Horns bellowed, and, every now and then, cymbals crashed. Placing his youngest son on one shoulder, Tshering followed behind the woman, shouting in English that he was with visiting dignitaries.

On the other side of the gate was a courtyard enclosed by white buildings two storeys high with fenced balconies and recessed windows, around their frames a riot of curly and colourful flowers, clouds, and gems typical of Buddhist iconography. Dragon-headed gargoyles roared from the roof corners, and short yellow curtains skirted the doorways and hung from the eaves. The temple had been dressed up for the occasion. Four hundred or so people crammed onto the flagstones, sitting shoulder to shoulder, cross-legged, facing inwards. Their eyes were on sixteen dancers, wearing animal masks. There was a jackrabbit, pink ears sticking up; a toucan with a long, downturned bill; two stags with antlers; a bear or perhaps a dog with a broad snout; and a reptile with scaly green skin and flared nostrils. *The Island of Doctor Moreau* crossed my mind, then the image recently in *Kuensel* of a black-and-white cartoon dog wearing a yellow gho and running on its hind legs like a person. This was Male Fire Dog Year, according to the Tibetan almanac.

"Who are they?" Nadya asked.

"Deities," Tshering replied. "This is Drametse Nga Cham, I think. Dechen, which dance is this?" He turned around, but his wife was gone. She had found people in the crowd she knew. "Cham means dance, nga means drum. Drametse is name of village on other side of valley."

The dancers were dressed in red and blue silk brocade tunics with baggy sleeves, billowy skirts reaching down to their knees, and sashes—some worn as belts, others knotted to their thumbs. To the accompaniment of cymbals, they leapt and spun in the air, landed on alternate feet, and beat drums like those we had seen at the puja in Dr. Jagar's village. I watched one stag whirl like a dervish and realized I had seen the likes of it before. Before we came to Bhutan, my aunt had given us Michael Palin's book on the Himalayas. Palin was in Paro attending tsechu in 2004. I remembered seeing a photograph of him buried in a crowd of onlookers, an antlered deity in front balancing on one leg and baring its teeth. I looked around. My wife and I were the only Westerners here.

"And what's the meaning of it all?" Nadya asked Dechen who had rejoined us.

"Tsechu is like blessing. Just coming and seeing the gods dance is good for your karma. Also, the gods, they chase off evil spirits that make us to do bad things."

I had assumed the beast men *were* the evil spirits—demonic deities soon to be seen off by benign gods like Jampelyang, perhaps, with his flaming sword, who we had seen flanking Guru Rinpoche in a temple in Thimphu.

"Some of the gods are angry..." Dechen turned to Tshering for the right word but then remembered it. "...manifestations of Guru Rinpoche."

Oh, so the Precious Teacher was both the amiable Buddha we saw in Tangsibi and someone or something more fearsome.

"People also learn what will happen to them after they die," added Dechen's father, "if they are enlighten and enter nirvana."

"And who's the one in the middle with the funny mask?" I asked.

I had been watching a goggle-eyed old man with a white beard and a goofy smile standing in the middle of the circle, dressed in a plain gho with a green sash around the waist. He watched the dancers with his hands on his hips or with one hand cupping his wooden chin critically.

"Atsara," Tshering said. "He mock the one who do not do it properly."

The clown had just dashed over to the toucan and begun aping its lacklustre movements, then to the dog to straighten its skirt. I looked around to see whether the audience found this amusing. The spectators nearest eyed him warily. When the dance was running smoothly, the clown darted out of the circle and molested children, poking them in their tummies, pinching their thighs, or stealing their toys. The children cowered or squealed or ran away.

The dance ended when the deities waltzed out of the courtyard through a curtained doorway. They had been spinning in circles, swishing their heavy, wooden heads to the ground for most of the morning. The clown remained, seemingly at a loose end until another, holding a yellow sash, joined him. Both, I noticed, had erect phalluses sewn on the backs of their ghos.

Atsara: clown of the masked dance. Drawing by author.

We had seen many a phallus on our journey across the kingdom with Dr. Jagar. Some were made of wood and suspended from the eaves of people's houses; others were painted on store fronts and had sportive ribbons tied around their waists, worms of ejaculation issuing from their heads, and sometimes ferocious eyes. They were there to ward off evil spirits and promote fertility, Dr. Jagar told us, and were associated with a fifteenth-century mystic called Drukpa Kunley, who taught that sex was a route to enlightenment and once tied a holy string around his penis instead of around his neck, saying that it would bring him more luck with women. We had already met the "Divine Madman." He was on a signboard outside the takin enclosure in Motithang, a suburb of Thimphu. Apparently, he had created Bhutan's national animal, the oddly proportioned goat-antelope we could see behind the mesh. A takin had the head of a moose, the body of a wild boar, and hind legs shorter than the front (a feature helping it negotiate mountainous terrain perhaps). Devotees had wanted to see the lama perform a miracle:

> *Before complying, he demanded that he be given a whole cow*
> *and goat to eat. Having devoured both, leaving only the bones,*
> *he stuck the goat's head on the bones of the cow. To everyone's*
> *amazement, upon a command uttered by Drukpa Kunley,*
> *the animal came to life, arose, ran to the meadow and began*
> *to graze.*

People at the tsechu got up, stretched, milled about. The two clowns vanished into the crowd. Tshering and Dechen went off to talk to friends, and Nadya excused herself. I wandered around, taking photos. I photographed a knot of people sitting on a stone staircase leading up to where the monks had been playing their instruments. I took a shot of a pretty girl of about eight with an inflamed eye, crouching alone on her haunches. Two teenage monks posed for me. I was taking a picture of a man who, in a Russian fur hat, looked more Muscovite than Bhutanese when the yellow sash arrived on my shoulder. I jumped and took the camera away from my face. Two old men with wrinkled cheeks and permanent grins were standing in front of me. One of them was reciting a verse while the other pumped a large wooden phallus up and down with both hands under my nose. I took a step back. The one with the phallus was chuckling like a madman.

"Okay, good, good, yes," I said after a full minute had passed. Some children with dribbly noses had gathered around our legs. Two parties of adults had drifted over.

"Thank you, yes, kadrinche, ha!" I felt suitably enlightened. I expected the atsaras to move off, but they showed no inclination to do so. They stopped what they were doing, looked at each other, exchanged a few words, and then redoubled their efforts. The verse rattled out louder—it was like gunfire now. Up and down, up and down went the phallus, keeping pace.

"Okaaay. Well, I think we're done here, yes? Nadya?" I looked around for her. Perhaps she could take a photograph of this. The clowns fell silent. Their bulging wooden eyes glared at me unblinkingly. The phallus wilted. Clown One whispered into the big, false ear of Clown Two. They looked back at me. I could see two pairs of beady eyes staring out of the open mouths of the masks. Tshering might be able to explain all this. Where the devil was Tshering? If maybe I removed the sash, bowed deeply and returned it to them, muttering my humble thanks...offered to buy it even? Clown Two snatched the sash from my shoulder.

The clowns turned and wandered away, hollering cheerfully at the tops of their voices. I watched them pick through the crowd and select a man standing with a little boy clinging to his gho. They chucked the sash over the man's shoulder. The end flopped over the head of his son. The man smiled in a relaxed, friendly manner. As the chanting and jerking got under way, he dug into the front of his gho. Two ten-ngultrum notes. Clown One plucked them from his fingers, and the pair shuffled off.

"Did you make some new friends, Tony?" Nadya was at my side.

"Where *were* you?"

"Oh, sitting on the steps over there, watching you. I wanted to come over, but thought it rude to interrupt."

The dances went on all day. People came and went as they pleased, and we took a break at midday for our picnic. Nadya had offered to bring food, but Tshering and Dechen wouldn't hear of it. At dusk, we walked back down the dirt road, the parents carrying the boys. Some of my students were still trying to knock down cans with a rolled-up sock, Ugyen Lhendup, star of the college marathon, among them. Another stall was packed with drunk men gambling noisily. A pile of empty beer bottles had accumulated outside Tashidema Hotal Bar. The man with the Guru Rinpoche pictures was flat on his back asleep.

I thought of the image of the Divine Madman we had seen on the sign at the takin enclosure, a figure rather different from the Precious Teacher. With shaggy hair, unruly beard, and big earrings, Drukpa Kunley was shown roaming the mountains with a bow and arrows on his back and a large black dog at his side. Where Guru Rinpoche held a dorji in his hand to subdue demons, Drukpa Kunley preferred the "Flaming Thunderbolt of Wisdom" dangling between his legs.

As I hand over my responsibilities to my son,
I repose my full faith and belief in the people
of Bhutan to look after the future of our nation,
for it is the Bhutanese people who are the true
custodians of our tradition and culture
and the ultimate guardians of the security,
sovereignty and continued wellbeing of
our country.

May the blessings of Ugyen Guru Rinpoche,
the father of our nation Shabdrung Ngawang
Namgyal and our Guardian Deities continue
to guide the destiny of our country and protect
the future of the glorious Palden Drukpa!

—HIS MAJESTY
THE FOURTH DRUK GYALPO,
Royal kasho to Parliament, December 9, 2006

8

Death of
a Runner

I am running with "junior prof" Wangchuck Rabten today, spectacles perched precariously on his nose, hair standing up at odd angles. Team Tara-thon had a rough night, he informs me. They had to share their bunkhouse with a mad lady. I noticed her before I went to bed: shoeless and dressed in rags, a scarecrow of a woman in her sixties with long, straggly hair and cloth braids on her wrists. She was hooting and flinging her arms about wildly—happy, it would seem, at the prospect of spending a night with ten young athletes. Maybe this was the beautiful lady that Mr. Sangay told us about, shocked out of her wits for all eternity when she discovered that her lover was a snake. I wonder if she is a bad omen. Dark clouds have gathered around the mountaintops ahead.

Thankfully, so far today, the road is not as steep or as snarled with switchbacks. Thoughts drift into my mind, lodge there for a while, and then drift out to be replaced by others. I relive our late departure this morning, Mr. Sangay's starting clap and the chorus of groans in response, the lads creaking forth robotically, the uncomprehending shopkeeper sitting on the wall, the demon-lady at the side of the road twisting her hair into knots. My mind adds Prince Jigyel to the scene, standing with arms folded, hair neatly combed, shaking his head. What a fool I was yesterday, charging up the mountain like a student at Sherubtse doing his first Annual Spring Marathon. I failed, quite simply, to respect the mountain. I should know better, although, come to think of it, my races in Canada were all on flat land. I can't imagine what Tee thought, seeing me slumped in the bus. You don't begin an eighty-kilometre climb by bolting the first twenty.

At an altitude of 2000 metres on the road to Namling, our next destination, winter means lush deciduous jungle with ferns like fish bones cascading to the road, dripping lianas, and tall sprays of bamboo. The day is cloudless once again, but with altitude and shade come cooler temperatures. I realize as I run that one of my assumptions concerning plant and tree life here is at fault: the richest growth is often not to be found in the valleys next to the rivers, but halfway up the mountains where the air is moister, where it is easier to breathe. A sound like laughter comes from the bamboo thicket to my left. Nadya and I know this character from the treks we did last winter. Cocky and clamorous as our blue jay and of similar size, the white-crested laughingthrush flies in gangs of eight or ten and likes to verbally abuse struggling hikers.

I run my fingers through the leaves of a low-hanging branch and allow a liana to trail over my shoulder like a streamer. Looking to my right, I am struck—almost intimidated—by the sheer weight of vegetable life, cascading down the mountain, trying, it would seem, to roll over the road and reclaim it. Leaves of all shapes and shades catch the sunlight and flicker in the breeze, some almond-shaped, thick and waxy like the leaves of a tea plant, others broader, more like kitchen spatulas. Some plants have delicate, arching stems that support fans of thin, blade-like leaves, reminding me of open hands, while others have thicker pipes connecting to floppy lids that could serve as umbrellas. Few of the plants or trees are flowering, but I see dainty white bells hanging from wandering tendrils and, from time to time, flaming pink or red rhododendron blooms. Here and there are the stretched saw-tooth leaves of marijuana plants, which grow everywhere in Bhutan and are fed to swine. I think of the highways in Canada, the verges shorn like a bad haircut, fences up to stop moose, the road so wide. Nature is no more than a green smudge at 110 kilometres an hour. Here, humans seem to be short-stay tenants.

"Sar."

I turn my head. Two young bulls are on the road in front, staring down at us, ears cocked, muscles tensed, flicking their tails. I look about. Where the heck did they come from? There is no sign of a farm nearby, or of a farmer, and the mountain falls away sharply below the road. One, I see, has a rope dangling from its neck, and I remember the cows of Kanglung, dragging out the stakes they were tied to and coming to dine on our front hedge. The smaller bull, deciding we are up to no good, turns and bolts uphill, but instantly smacks into the side of the other. The pair shake themselves and snort at each other.

"They want to run away from us, Sar."

Or with us, it would seem. Each time we draw close, they sprint away, but then stop again forty or fifty metres up the road and allow us to catch up. An incongruous picture forms in my mind of Team Tara-thon jogging into Thimphu: two lecturers, ten university students, and a hundred school kids, followed by eight stray dogs, a herd of cows dragging stakes, three takins. Finally, we overtake the bulls and watch them gallop off downhill.

The jungle seems abruptly to end when we round a corner an hour and a half later and discover Namling, four empty road-workers' shacks and the shell of a guesthouse. The Ugyens are there, sitting on their haunches and looking cold with their hands shrugged into their sleeves. The temperature has certainly dipped. I tell them to clap home the runners as they come in. Ahead, I see a black cliff, cut with white lines of falling water, and the road clawing up the side diagonally. It will be another hard climb tomorrow, but, at least we won't have to do it in the heat. How labourers ever managed to carve a way for the road out of such vertical rock is a mystery. I know that many died while building this particular stretch of the highway. A chorten, looking like it was painted last week, stands at a crook in the road.

"We must not stop there, Sar," Long Bone Ugyen says seriously.

"Why not?"

"It is tsubta. Risky area."

Three years ago, he tells me, a bus careered off the road here, killing all aboard, including many school children. Apparently, the driver was drunk. The chorten was put up to mark the spot, and the Je Khenpo came and conducted a puja to rid the place of evil. I recall reading of similar accidents in *Kuensel*. Every few weeks, it seemed, there was a picture of a Tata truck, pointing head first down a cliff with its cab buried in a tree trunk, or a report of multiple deaths and broken spines after a vehicle left the road. In one incident near Trashigang the first year we were here, passengers were pushing a bus up a steep incline when it started to roll backwards. Before it left the road, it crushed the head of the co-driver, who was trying to jam rocks behind the back wheels. Miraculously, the bus only fell 150 metres, and eight of the nine passengers who had remained on board survived.

"But don't worry, Sar," Ugyen whispers in my ear. "I did some dice and prayed for that local deity to reach us to Thimphu. Good luck number came."

| After a cold night with our sleep mats unrolled on bare concrete inside the guesthouse, we enter tsubta early the next morning. A chilling mist percolates up from the valley, blurring the cliff and making it resemble a fortress. As we pass under its walls, I think of battlements and archers and boiling oil. The students run huddled together in a group and in silence. I see that most are now wearing sweat pants and woolly hats, and I have put running tights on over my shorts. Silvery beads of moisture settle on our clothes. We don't stop at the memorial chorten.

The gradient of the road is, at times, 15–20 per cent: by my reckoning, the steepest we have encountered so far. I should be concentrating on the ground just ahead of me but cannot help looking up—especially when I see rocks on the road ranging in size from a basketball to a beer barrel. In places, there are piles of shattered rock at the foot of scree-clogged ravines. If there were an earthquake here, I have the feeling the road would simply vanish. In Japan they drape heavy wire mesh over mountainsides to prevent landslides or else coat them in cement. Both solutions, though practical, are horrible eyesores. Maybe Bhutan needs avalanche sheds like those sheltering the Trans-Canada Highway in the Rockies. We shuffle along, breathing hard.

After four kilometres, the road narrows to little more than a single lane, and the rock wall leans over it. How do loaded trucks coming from opposite directions cope? Reversing here would be a daunting proposition, especially in icy conditions or during monsoon. On the narrowest section, we run beside a row of slender, waist-high concrete posts, intended to stop vehicles from shooting over the edge. Two are missing and several buckled. As runners, while it is true that a boulder may bounce down and clobber us, or a car on "run-power" may glide around a corner unexpectedly, we have a measure of control over our destiny. I listen out for the growl of an engine, the squeal of brakes.

At 6k, I see prayer flags strung up over the road, and the bus pulled over in front of a shrine. I remember stopping here with Dr. Jagar. A stream comes coursing down the mountain, disappears under the road and then pitches itself into the void on the other side. The shrine, a tiny cabin with an altar and nine cups of holy water behind a yellow curtain, sits right on the brink. It must have taken a feat of daring to build. When Nadya arrives, we climb the concrete steps to the shrine and, as there is no guardrail or wall, take turns leaning out over the abyss while holding onto each other's waistbands. I try to see the foot of the waterfall but cannot. Water separates and whitens, the finer droplets merging with the mist. I listen for the smack of water on rock below but can hear nothing.

The word "sublime" in Canada, like "awesome," has been drained of true meaning. It is more readily applied now to a new flavour of ice cream, a birdie on the golf course, or special effects in a sci-fi movie than to a landscape that both terrifies and inspires, the notion cherished by Edmund Burke and the Romantic poets. Nevertheless, "sublime" is the word that comes to mind as I watch the water tipping over the edge and feel the rush of rising air on my face, when I look down at the purple valley floor far below smudged in haze. I think of the poetry I taught to my third-year class at Sherubtse, the transcendence Wordsworth sought among "steep and lofty cliffs" above Tintern Abbey, Coleridge's "gardens bright with sinuous rills." The bond between the spiritual and the natural seems especially strong in Bhutan, the two mingling effortlessly. Christian Schicklgruber speaks of a "deified landscape" in *Bhutan: Mountain Fortress of the Gods*, a deity living in every rock, river, and ravine, wind teasing prayers from their flags on mountain passes, water driving prayer wheels straddling streams, chortens protecting the trails between villages and keeping demons in check on the road.

Barrelling around the bend: a Tata truck. Drawing by author.

The rattle and bang of a truck on its way down from Thrumshing-La interrupts my thoughts. It is the first vehicle to come our way this morning, and I sigh, resenting the mechanical intrusion. I turn and watch its progress on the far side of the valley. I can't see it clearly through the mist, but the thing seems barely under control, surging forward on the straight stretches, braking suddenly before swinging around corners. Maybe the driver is in a hurry. Every few seconds, it disappears behind a fold in the rock. The drone dies and tranquility is almost restored, but not for long. As the truck gets nearer, the sound divides into the strain of the engine, the chomping of gears, and the clatter of the wooden slats of the bed. This merchant must be on his way to the border to pick up a load. The truck rounds the final bends, and I wait to see if the driver will pull over and say a prayer at the shrine. No. He barrels past. Then something remarkable happens. The front wheels lock, there is a sickly scrurching sound, and the back wheels lift off the ground, spin in the air for a second, and then slam down. The tailgate shakes violently. One of our students must have dashed across the road, I think for a second. Or Yana. Then I see it, or I see the tail of it: much, much smaller than our thirteenth runner.

"Di-did you see that?" I turn to Nadya. The stink of burned rubber fills the air.

"Incroyable!" She shakes her head. "A mouse."

Returning to the road and resuming the run, I think about the Bhutanese folktale I read in Mongar about a mouse. One day, while tending her flock, a shepherdess dropped her lunch. As it was a circular loaf wrapped in a cloth, it rolled down the mountain. The girl gave chase, but it went into a mouse hole. You can keep the bread, the girl called to the mouse, but could she have her torrath back? The mouse invited her to step in, and, like Alice, the girl closed her eyes and was able to do so. What would she like for dinner? asked the mouse hospitably. Leftovers would do for a poor girl, replied the shepherdess. The mouse prepared a meal fit for a princess. What would she like to sleep on? A bed of rags would be adequate for a poor girl, she answered. The mouse gave her soft blankets and a pillow stuffed with cotton. Don't worry if your hair gets tugged during the night, warned the mouse. In the morning, the girl returned home with her hair strung with precious jewels and her torrath full of more. When a rich girl in the same village heard of the shepherdess's sudden good fortune, she, too, entered the mouse hole but demanded a sumptuous dinner and a good bed. Undiscouraged when she got neither, she anticipated riches when, in the night, she felt tugs on her hair. Back home the next day, she discovered not jewels in her hair but mouse droppings.

The tale comes from Kunzang Choden's *Folktales of Bhutan*, one of thirty books we have in a cardboard box on the bus. Knowing there would be hours to kill on our journey, Nadya persuaded Sherubtse Library to lend us some books for the winter. These include Daphne du Maurier's *The Birds and Other Stories*, Roald Dahl's *Kiss Kiss*, James Herriot's *All Creatures Great and Small*, T. Sangay Wangchuk's *Seeing with the Third Eye*, and Rinzin Namgay Dorji's *The Walk Across the Kingdom*. The folktales I have read seem mostly to be morality tales akin to Aesop's fables. Material wealth is gained through being humble and compassionate; greed and stupidity are punished. A poor farm boy spares the lives of sparrows that have eaten his seeds, and, in exchange, the sparrows give him a magic cup that fills with food on demand. A fox persuades a leopard who wants to eat him to try fishing in a lake with his tail. The leopard tries this for a night, but it is winter. The lake freezes over, and he loses the fur off his tail while trying to yank it out.

There is one folktale in the collection that tells of a runner. One day, in olden times, the Trongsa penlop ordered his garba ("attendant with wheels of fire") to carry a letter to Wangdi Phodrang, get a reply from the dzongpen there, and return the same day: a round trip of 129 kilometres. But garba Lung gi Korlo had grown weary of running long distances, having carried letters for his lord all his life. Passing through a dark ravine on his way, the reputed abode of a demoness, he yelled, "I am so tired that I would rather you took my life than that I do one more journey like this." There was no reply, but on his way back through the region, he met an old woman wearing a black kira washing meat in a water trough. Curious, he asked if the meat belonged to a large animal. No, said the old woman. "Garba Lung gi Korlo gave me his life this morning. These are his entrails." Shocked and no longer feeling the pain in his legs, the courier ran home, delivered the message to his lord, and was rewarded with a fine meal. He went home, told his wife about his strange encounter on the road, and went to bed. He never woke up.

| "Sar, I cannot bear any longer."

It is three hours later, and Tharchen and I are sitting in a stream at Sengor, seventeen kilometres from the shrine. Our shoes and socks are on a rock nearby. Glassy wafers of ice glitter in the shallows. I hope our team leader does not see this as a punishment for coming in last today. I should have collared Tiger, too, who was moaning about his thighs and also bringing up the rear.

"Five minutes done, five to go. C-come on, we'll do it together."

Tharchen is one of two lads on the team I would call a "hobby runner." Like Nadya and me, he jogs regularly for pleasure. When I was out at dawn doing my laps around Sherubtse, I would sometimes find Tharchen doing the same. When he heard of our plan to run to Thimphu for Tarayana, he doubled his training from an hour a day to two to prepare for his trial. For the last couple of days, he has been lagging behind the team and complaining of sore knees.

"Sar?"

"Yes, Tharchen, what is it?"

"Time, Sar?"

"Let me consult my watch."

"Saaar?"

"Three minutes to go."

I grit my teeth and keep my eye on the campfire two hundred metres away. I have taken cold baths after long runs before in Canada. After thirty seconds, your body adapts and the discomfort passes, your legs warming the static water around them. Dunking them in an icy stream at 3200 metres is a different proposition. The flowing water bites ever deeper, stealing body heat and carting it off. I turn away from Tharchen, close my eyes, and count down the seconds. The stinging sensation is particularly exquisite, I notice, around the crotch. I pause in my counting and peer down the front of my shorts. All I can see is an item resembling a dried fig. I look over at the fire again. I suppose if I were a Buddhist monk, I would be able to banish all thoughts of past or future. We surrender after nine minutes and lumber back to camp like golems. I may not need my watch for our runs, but for "blue-legging," as Ugyen Lhendup, the other hobby runner, has christened it, I certainly do.

"Look," someone says. "Sar has blue nose."

My knees refuse to bend as I try to sit down. My legs are wooden posts. Yet, this, I have discovered, is the trick to running day after day. When I get up tomorrow, the aches and pains will be gone. I collapse awkwardly beside my wife and get my legs as close to the fire as possible without singeing the hairs. As our camps each night are beside rivers or streams, Nadya and I have been pushing our runners to bathe their legs, but they don't seem terribly keen. For sure, at this altitude, we say, you must not go blue-legging before the cook has lit the fire.

"How's your ankle?" I ask Nadya, as sensation begins to return to mine. She has removed the bandage. The swelling seems to have gone down.

"I'm going to bathe it in a moment. The painkillers are definitely helping. I ran with Tiger today and gave him some."

"How's he doing?"

"He's in good spirits. I get cookies from the bus each time it stops and put them in my pocket. We munch them as we go along." Gingerly, she gets to her feet. "He'll be glad of a rest though."

It is the last day of the year, and, before mounting our assault on the pass, we have a day off. We were expecting Sengor High School to put us up, but today is Election Day for the National Council, and apparently there are no officials in town. Fortunately, Mr. Sangay knows the park ranger for Thrumshing-La National Park, and he has unlocked the Livestock Extension Centre for us. Our two nights here will be chilly with no electricity and no beds.

I watch my wife as she circles the fire, telling the boys to draw close, strip off their sweatpants, and massage analgesic cream into their legs. She even inspects Yana's paw. Like some of the lads, she now has a nickname. A farmer yelled "Za min thur!" as she ran past his paddy field a couple of days ago, "The only girl!" I have asked her whether she minds this status. She laughs and reminds me how she would fight with boys in the back alley in Montreal when she was a kid. She has assumed a maternal role in this event, and I see how readily "the boys" respond to her. While they work together naturally as a team, collecting donations and sharing camp chores, they clearly appreciate having her around, reminding them to run slowly and look after their feet, to rest rather than kick the soccer ball about. I imagine they find her more approachable than me, fearing perhaps that I will send them home if they don't measure up to the job. I was the one who laid down the rules at the start: no walking, no cadging lifts, no taking shortcuts. I look for Mr. Sangay,

Nadya's massage detail: Sonam Gyalpo, Tiger, and Sherab Jamtscho.

wondering how he feels about her involvement in the project, but he is not around. If she weren't here, would he be the one giving advice on injuries? Would he be acting more like a sports coach?

It occurs to me that I have met few women in positions of authority during my time in Bhutan. The registrar at RUB is a woman, and so is the head librarian at Sherubtse. The secretary general of Tarayana and the assistant DEO we met in Trashigang were both female. The overwhelming majority in office, however—whether district administrators or village heads, business leaders or hotel managers, doctors or police, school or college administrators—are men. I hear there are practically no women in the Royal Government, and the monastic body is 99 per cent male. When it comes to menial or manual work, though, women are highly conspicuous. It was always female students that served us refreshments at college functions, or wives when we got invited to professors' homes, and I remember lines of women with mud up to their knees in the paddy fields of Kanglung during monsoon season, thinning out rice plants. From time to time

in the newspaper, there would be an article saying how women had
made inroads into traditionally male professions, like painting
devotional images or driving commercial trucks. Bhutan's first and
only lady judge joined the Thimphu district court in the year we
arrived, and a much-teased twenty-two-year-old became the first
female taxi driver there. Buddhism says that men and women are
equal, but Bhutan would seem to have some way to go when it comes
to professional equality.

As Nadya does her rounds, my thoughts turn to today's election,
and I silently wish Dr. Jagar tashi delek. He aims to join Bhutan's
equivalent of the Senate, a body of twenty-five keeping checks and
balances on the governing party. The stakes for him are high. If he
doesn't win the seat for his district, he will be out of work, unable to
belong to the new government or return to his old job. There was an
article not long ago in the *Bhutan Observer*, one of two new newspapers that have appeared recently, telling of his candidature. I heave
myself to my feet and go over to the bus to root through the newspaper clippings I have collected. Flicking through, I suddenly find
a picture of him beaming up at me, dressed in a smart gho, but with
a bamboo pot-lid hat on his head of the kind paddy farmers wear
to keep the sun off. "Democracy is a gift from the King," the paper
reports him saying underneath the photo. "It is the responsibility
of the people to make it a success." After thirty-seven years as an
educator, Jagar Dorji felt it his duty to put his career aside and serve
king and country.

Stapled to the newspaper article is Dr. Jagar's farewell letter to
the college, sent to all staff and students via the intranet in August. I
have read it several times but still find it disarmingly sincere, more
the words of a caring parent than a director signing off.

Dear Sherubtseans,

*I certainly do not feel good to leave your learned and joyful
company, but as change comes to everybody the sense of attach-
ment has to be abandoned. So I do it with some courage.*

I have learnt a great deal while in Sherubtse and now I leave here with much learning. I have made many mistakes but these are because two and half years here have been filled with new activities. I am not sure how far these changes will impact you positively but I am sure they are all heading for the final vision of excellence.

I come from a humble farming family with no promising property. It is the Royal Government's efforts and His Majesty the King's continued commitment that I have been given this rare opportunity to work with you here at the peak of learning. Without this I would still be ploughing the field. I believe most of us have the same background. So we need to return this kindness with full commitments in body, mind and in our speeches.

Now the guard is changing, I wish my successor and all of you a very enriching stay in Sherubtse and prosperity and success in your future wherever you go and do.

Remember that complacency is a fool's theory while you must believe that without a disciplined mind nothing can be attained.

Yours now a well wisher.

So long,
JAGAR DORJI

Thawing out my legs in front of the fire, I think back to the time we spent with him last winter.

| "Do you like going home?"

Dr. Jagar, Zangmo, Nadya, and I had just emptied the college Land Cruiser. Three two-kilogram bags of sugar, four sacks of lentils, twenty bars of toilet soap, two three-litre bottles of cooking oil, six boxes of laundry powder, ten dried fish wrapped in newspaper, four dozen eggs on cardboard trays, and several large bags of Nestlé's Eclairs and Coconut Crunch candies were now strewn about our feet. Dr. Jagar chuckled at Nadya's question. Bought in

Trongsa, these provisions had to be carried to Tangsibi. I realized
I had been mistaken when we first visited. The real Tangsibi was
not the houses lining the east–west highway, but a village some way
down the mountain and only reachable by foot.

With sugar and eggs and oil and soap swinging from our arms,
balanced on our shoulders, or stuffed in the front of Dr. Jagar's gho,
the four of us staggered down a steep boulder path under oak trees
feathered with orchids, past mud-brick homes, and alongside a
bubbling brook. Twice the brook ran under stone chortens housing
water-driven prayer wheels that creaked and groaned as they turned.
We passed three women sitting cross-legged on the ground around a
bamboo mat. They were taking wads of white dough from a metal
billycan, flattening and shaping them into saucer-size discs, then
tossing these onto the mat, where they shrank and crumpled under
the sun and became rice crackers. A little farther on, we paused to
watch a boy behind two oxen turning the soil in a narrow paddy
field, the wooden plough a single claw crusty with earth.

No one seemed particularly surprised to see two chilips trailing
Dr. Jagar. A man repairing a wooden platform next to a paddy field
waved. A woman dashed inside her hut and came out with rice
wrapped in a red shawl, which she pressed into Zangmo's hands.
Zangmo refused the gift twice before accepting it. The path levelled
out, and we followed a rock-studded track skirting a paddy field.
Tangsibi came into view: six houses, a temple, and a staircase of
crescent-shaped paddy fields perched perilously on a narrow spur
of land 150 metres below the road and maybe a kilometre and a half
above the Mangde Chhu.

"Akay! Akay!" Eight infants flew out of the nearest house and
skidded to a halt in front of our leader. They had dirt-smeared,
beaming faces and shrill voices. Panting, Dr. Jagar put down his bags
and dug in the front of his gho for some Eclairs. A little girl of about
four in ripped rubber boots and a puffy mauve raincoat matted in
grime stared up at me. I broke open a bag of toffees.

Everyone who lived in Tangsibi was, apparently, related to either
Jagar Dorji or Zangmo. Jagar was the fifth of six brothers and had

one sister; his wife was the eldest sister of four and had three brothers. I understood that most of the siblings still lived here, but late morning wasn't a good time to meet them. Only two middle-aged women were in the village keeping an eye on the children, one of these being Sangye Dolma, one of Zangmo's sisters, a soft-spoken lady in a dark blue kira. We climbed concrete stairs stuck to the side of her house to the second floor (the first being traditionally a stable for cattle), entered the building, dropped the provisions, took off our shoes, and then climbed wooden stairs to reach the top floor. These were so narrow that my big Western feet had to negotiate them side-ways. We came out in a large, airy, furnitureless room with bare floorboards and tashi tagye on the walls adjoining a shrine room concealed behind a curtain. Sangye unrolled thin straw mats for us to sit on. She brought a pot of ngaja and a basket of zao before going off to prepare lunch.

A warm breeze wafted in through the glassless windows, and I got up and stuck my head out. It was a good 10°C warmer here than in Kanglung. Three cows snoozed under the sun on the grass below, mynah birds perched on their backs. A dozen glittering blue-black dragonflies circled and settled on a wooden water trough. The wind teased an escaped prayer flag snagged in a bush and swished through the needles of an old cedar, the only tree in the village. I saw a garden with cabbages and beans behind a bamboo fence, beyond it fields, and then a dead drop to the valley. On the other side of the valley, a wooded mountain rose up and behind it another and another, massive green waves turning browner and blurrier as they rolled into the distance.

"Are they going to plant rice in these fields, Dr. Jagar?" He joined me at the window, and we looked down at the empty paddies.

"Rice or wheat. Maybe barley," he replied.

As idyllic as the spot seemed, I imagined life here was hard. The farmers were bound to sleep well at nights after spending their days slogging up and down these terraces, tending to their crops or hunting for decent pasture for their cattle. And how nutrient-rich was the soil likely to be on the side of a mountain? A lot of the goodness probably got flushed out when it rained. Then there was the worry each summer that monsoon floods would carry away the entire crop and the family would have nothing to eat for the winter. At least Tangsibians lived within striking distance of the road so they could go to Trongsa to sell their produce or get supplies. Many Bhutanese, we understood, were three or four days' walk from the nearest road head, turning a shopping errand for salt or soap or cooking oil into an expedition.

"See the little house on legs next to the field?" Jagar pointed to one of the lower fields. "Before harvest, a boy lives there day and night and has to frighten off the wild pigs and monkeys."

He told us that some farmers lost as much as 80 per cent of their crops to wild boars, monkeys, and deer, and there was little they could do about it. All life was sacred to Buddhists, so killing the marauders was not an option, and fences were of no use as the boars burrowed under them and the monkeys climbed over.

"When you were a boy, did you plough these fields and chase away the monkeys?" I asked.

"My job was to look after the cows. At this time of year, I took the herd to the forest with my brothers because there wasn't enough food for them here. We lived there during the winter and some of the spring."

"What about school?"

"None of my brothers or my sister went to school. I was the only one to go."

"How come?" Nadya asked, joining us.

"When I was ten, a chipon came to our house and told my parents they should send one son to school. He said an educated son in the family would help them in the future."

"And why were you chosen?"

"The chipon wanted only one child from each family, my brothers were too old to go, and my sister was parents' pet and didn't want to go. Actually, I didn't want to go either. Luckily, the school was in Trongsa, so I could come home at weekends."

"And your family had enough money to send you?" I inquired.

"The government paid for the lessons, books, and stationeries, and my parents and brothers gave me clothes and rations. My family couldn't afford much. I had two ghos, but no long johns or shoes." Dr. Jagar smiled. "I went to school barefoot! In those days, there was no Tarayana Foundation."

| On New Year's Day, Mr. Sangay announces at breakfast that Dr. Jagar has been elected to the National Council. Team Tara-thon cheers and then sets about doing laundry. As it is a rest day, I decide to take a walk with the park ranger.

Ugyen Tenzin's job is to patrol the district (Mongar to Ura), report any illegal logging or poaching, check forestry permits, and monitor resources. The area we have just passed through is "cool broadleaf forest," he tells me, "Acer, birch, Taxus bacatta, champ, cane." Acer, I find out later, is maple, and Taxus bacatta is yew— neither of which I had noticed. Around Sengor, it is mainly hemlock interspersed with larch, giving the forest "grey spot" during winter- time as larch drops its needles.

"In old day, we use hemlock as duster for clean butter lamp," he informs me. "Also tasty food for yak."

"What is champ?"

"Tree with yellow flower like orchid. We use oil come from it in soap and perfume."

I tell him how splendid the rhododendrons are in their bold indigos, creams, crimsons, and purples. It was surprising on our hikes last winter to find a variety near the mountain passes with leaves as long as my forearm.

"There are fifty species of rhododendron in Bhutan. Rhododendron arboreum is main bush in Sengor area. Some kind of rhododendron we dry leaves and use for make incense. Eating flower is cure for dysentery."

"And what do you recommend tired runners chew to give them energy?" I ask.

Ugyen thinks for a moment and then laughs. I expect him to say doma, but he doesn't. "Yarsta goenbub!"

"What's that?"

"Cordyceps." That would be the fungus that grows out of the head of a caterpillar. I remember seeing two or three in a glass jar in one of the science laboratories at Sherubtse one open day, the caterpillar pale yellow and the length of my thumb, the fungus a twisted grey stick. I had not seen or heard of anything quite like it and thought naively at the time that it might somehow be a symbiotic relationship. But the fungus is a parasite that mummifies its host. Yarsta goenbub is highly sought after in Asian markets as an aphrodisiac and cure-all. At BTN 75,000 (CAD 2,000) a kilo, it is a little beyond the reach of the Tara-thon kitty.

I find that Ugyen is also knowledgeable about birds. I mention the laughingthrush and describe another that I could not find in our bird book, belonging to the same family but blue-black in colour. I see this bird quite often, streaking across the road in front of us, disturbed from its foraging in ditches.

"Whistling thrush," the park ranger says without hesitation. "In Bhutan, we call this one 'culvert in-charge.'" I know the suffix from Sherubtse. Ugyen Dendup was "English in-charge," Nadya was "Language Centre in-charge." It was given to those with special responsibilities. "Whistling thrush is boss of little river!"

"Tourist come to Sengor to see tragopan," he continues, pulling a book out of his bag and showing me one labelled Satyr tragopan. A kind of partridge, it would seem, plump and ungainly, with a blue and black head and a red and brown body, speckled with white dots. An extraordinary looking creature. According to the description, it bleats like a goat kid.

"Are there any about?"

"Not at this time of year. You must come back in the spring!"

Before going about his duties, he tells me that we are lucky not to be running in the snow. Sengor usually gets a foot of it in January. I think back to our trek to Gasa in the snow last winter and our efforts to fend off the chill by stripping down and taking tsachu, a form of bathing rather different to blue-legging.

Jigme Dorji National Park is the largest protected area in the country, encompassing an area of 4329 sq km. It protects the western parts of Paro, Thimphu and Punakha Dzongkhags (districts) and almost the entire area of Gasa Dzongkhag. Habitats in the park range from subtropical areas at 1400 m to alpine heights at 7000 m. The park management has to cope with the needs of both lowland farmers and seminomadic yak herders. Villagers are also allowed to harvest a wide variety of indigenous plants for use in incense and traditional medicines.

The park is the habitat of several endangered species, including the takin, snow leopard, blue sheep, tiger, musk deer, red panda, Himalayan black bear and serow...More than 300 species of birds have been catalogued within the park.

—LONELY PLANET, "National Parks and Protected Areas," *Bhutan*, 2002

9 | # Shabdrung Sheep

"O-HEY!"

For the sixth time, Nadya and I stepped off the path to let a caravan of horses and donkeys pass, bells clonking on their necks, their loads swinging from side to side. Though heavily laden with thirty-kilogram sacks of rice, boxes of tinned and packet food, packing cases, rolled-up blankets, canvas tarpaulins, steel billycans, and bottles of liquid gas, urged on by their child muleteers, they were clearly more adept than us at handling the slippery conditions. Slush flew up from their hooves and streaked our backpacks. The muleteers bowed as they passed and giggled. *Why on earth were the two chilips carrying their own bags?*

"O-hey!" cried the boy at the rear, swishing his stick.

We were on our way to Gasa (2770 metres above sea level), the largest village in Bhutan's northernmost dzongkhag, with a stop on the way at a hot spring. A taxi had taken three hours to get us from Punakha, the former capital, to Damji, the last village connected by road. From Damji, it was a three-hour trek to the baths, another hour from there to Gasa. According to Dr. Jagar, Gasa was real outback: the people lived in wood shacks and got about on horseback. Cross the Bari pass (at 3900 metres) even farther north, and we could visit the tribal village of Laya near the Tibetan border, where semi-nomadic yak herders lived.

Our path tracked the Mo Chhu, a bottle-green river coursing around rocks the size of bathtubs and garden sheds two hundred metres below. As it was January, the fir trees lining its banks were heavy with snow. Some trees upriver were so swaddled they resembled statues. As we waited for the donkeys to pass, I trained binoculars on the river and saw white-capped redstarts darting between the rocks and another bird of similar size, but blue rather than red, black, and white. Another kind of redstart presumably. This one liked to splay its red tail like a fan each time it landed. On our way up from Damji, female kalij pheasants had scurried across the path in front of us, their bodies plump and brown, their faces red. One had stood its ground and eyed us from the brush, its crest curling up like an inverted comma.

We arrived at the hot spring late in the afternoon. From above, it resembled a refugee camp: makeshift bamboo and canvas shelters crammed together, smouldering fires, towels and blankets strung up between trees, heaps of dead branches, a single faucet standing out of the dirt, crows. The shelters stood in front of four steaming bath houses with tin roofs and no windows. The path we were on wound down to the park ranger's office.

"Welcome to Jigme Dorji National Park. I am caretaker of bath. You can camp near river, but there is many people, or you can camp near office."

Dago, a fit-looking man of about sixty wearing a park ranger's jacket over his gho, recommended the latter. Although you had to go down a long flight of stairs to reach the baths, there was grass and more space for camping near the office. It was also quieter. He handed us a toilet key.

"We have two rules here. Wash before get in bath and take shoe off before get in bath."

We looked down at our mud-plastered boots and wondered whether he was kidding. Then I remembered the article I had snipped out of the newspaper before coming. It had said that, before the hot spring became part of the national park, people would come here and wash themselves with soap and do their laundry.

"When can we take a bath?" Nadya inquired.

"Any time you like. Some people sleep in bath."

The next morning, we stood shivering, towels around our shoulders, and puzzled over which bath to choose. According to a sign, each had medicinal benefits. The hottest was for people with tuberculosis or ulcers, the coolest for those with skin diseases or sexually trans-mitted infections. Take a warm bath if you suffered from rheumatism or arthritis; take a lukewarm one for sinusitis or other respiratory complaints. After two decades of distance running on asphalt, the third option seemed like the one for us, but, after a bucket wash in cold water, we decided to cure ourselves of tuberculosis or ulcers first. It was so hot in this bath that most people were reclining on the edge with just their legs in. Plunging ours into the grainy water,

I wondered whether, far from coming out miraculously healed, we would leave with some unpleasant infection.

Dago had said nothing to us about dress code. I wore the baggy shorts I used for running, and Nadya wore Lycra cycling shorts and a T-shirt. Custom seemed to say that only genitals need be covered, and, through the billowing steam, I could make out middle-aged and elderly women bathing bare-breasted. The younger women, however, clearly preferred not to do this. Sneaking looks at the older ones, I was sure I had never before beheld such deflated appendages. Their breasts resembled drained wine gourds. I imagined hard lives devoted to raising infant after infant after infant, but then realized that these women had probably never worn bras.

"This is the quiet time of day," whispered Tashi, a young, bilingual civil servant from Thimphu who came every year and was camping near us with Tshering, his girlfriend. They had already spent six days at the springs, bathing four times a day and once at night. Tsachu was busiest in the winter, he said, with most people staying for two weeks.

There were nineteen people either in the three-by-two-metre bath or sitting around it. When we went to the similarly sized warm bath in the afternoon, there were at least forty. The water was barely visible. All I could see were pink bodies pressed tightly together and some arms sticking up at odd angles. Did these people all know each other? And what if someone in the middle wished to get out? I was reminded of taking the morning train to work in Tokyo. The carriages were so packed that the doors would barely close, and platform staff wearing white gloves had to shove until they did. The secret to survival was to close your eyes, relax every muscle, breathe regularly, and put your mind in a happy place. Maybe the same was necessary here. No one appeared to be suffering. Some had fallen asleep. A woman held up her empty plastic water bottle, and a boy in the doorway went to refill it for her. A grizzled old man with a wall-eye grinned and chanted, "Om mani padme hum." There was obviously no room for us.

After a quick boil in tuberculosis or ulcers, Nadya and I went off to skin diseases and found Tashi. Remarkably, there were only seven other bathers with him. I looked them over before climbing in to see if any had rashes or open sores.

"Do you believe these baths have healing powers?" I asked him.

My newspaper article said that a thirty-six-year-old from Thimphu called Sangay had been coming to tsachu every winter since 2003, hoping to cure himself of sinusitis, "which western medicine had failed to provide any relief." After four years, Sangay could now, apparently, breathe freely. "He believes his illness was cured by the hot spring." For best results, the article said, it was necessary to come three years in a row.

"Bathing is spiritual," Tashi replied, closing his eyes. "People come here to meditate."

| On our fourth day at the baths, Dago told us a storm was on the way. If we wished to go to Gasa, we should do so right away. Continuing from there to Laya was out of the question though. The mountain pass was blocked and the Layaps stranded.

Leaving our tent where it was, with light packs and water bottles filled with tea, we climbed briskly through mainly coniferous forest as the first snowflakes spiralled down. A red-crowned jay and a pair of yellow-billed blue magpies were our company this time: welcome flashes of colour against a monochrome landscape. The jay was about the size of the North American blue jay, but, with its russet body and "moustachial band" (as our bird book described the dark bar descending from the corner of its beak), it looked more like an English jay. The magpies I also associated with England. Like their English cousins, these were raucous and bold and hopped about on the ground, hunting for insects; unlike them, these had long, arching blue and white tail feathers that wagged up and down crazily when the birds took to the air. We looked in the branches for snoozing red pandas, knowing that, although rare, they did inhabit the region. With their reddish-brown coats, stripy tails, and raccoon-like faces, they would be quite a sight. They ate bamboo, however—large quantities of it—and there did not seem much of it about.

After forty minutes, we could see the turrets of Tashi Thongoen Dzong rising from the trees on a ridge above us, blurry and bled of colour in the thickening air. It was built in 1646 by the Shabdrung Ngawang Namgyal, a saint and statesman from Tibet who came to Bhutan when it was little more than a collection of feuding tribes. Recognized as a reincarnation of renowned sixteenth-century Buddhist scholar Pema Karpo, the Shabdrung (meaning "at whose feet one submits") soon became a religious leader in the west and gained great political power. He constructed the first dzong or monastic fortress at Simtokha in the Thimphu valley, a cluster of buildings serving as an administrative centre for the governor and his men, a military headquarters, and a monastery. Dzongs were subsequently built at vantage points across the kingdom, the head of a valley, on a mountain spur, or at the confluence of two rivers. The seventeenth century was also a time when Bhutan was at war with Tibet, and strategically placed fortresses were needed to repel invaders. Its defensive role having passed, the dzong is now half monastery, half government offices and law courts.

With its inward-leaning white stone walls, banded near the top with a red khemar identifying the building as sacred, and its spreading yellow pagoda roofs, the dzong at Gasa resembled most others we had seen. Tall cypresses (the national tree) stood like sentinels at the back, and four guardian deities looked out from the walls at the entrance. Taking off our boots at the door, we visited the temples inside and paid our respects to the gods by placing ngultrum notes on the altars. A monk shadowed us, pouring holy water into our palms after we had said a prayer. We were about to leave the dzong, having bowed in front of the grey-bearded figure of the Shabdrung, when the monk beckoned to us. We followed him to a chapel we had not yet seen. Inside was a wooden box with a saffron sheet thrown over it. The monk swept it aside.

"This Shabdrung sheep! It follow him from Tibet!"

The Shabdrung had entered the country through Laya and Gasa, apparently, but nowhere had I read that he did so with a pet sheep.

But then I remembered that Guru Rinpoche was supposed to have arrived in Bhutan on the back of a flying tigress. We peered into the box. Definitely a sheep in there—or the bones of one, inexpertly wired together and clearly ancient. The skull had bits of black skin peeling off of it. Folded bills stuck out of the part of the ribcage that was still intact. I rolled up a five-ngultrum note and poked it carefully between two ribs, willing the skeleton not to disintegrate into a heap of dust. What would be my fate if that happened? Would I be haunted by the Shabdrung's pet sheep for the rest of my days, my slumbers rendered unnourishing by persistent baaing? It was easy to be skeptical.

Gasa village was two rows of plank huts lining a mud street on a shelf of land populated mainly, it seemed, by mules. To prevent flooding in springtime, the huts were jacked up on stones; more stones were on the roofs to stop the wood shingles from blowing off. Shredded prayer flags on leaning poles and snow-plastered bamboo fences bespoke vicious winds charging down from the mountain pass. A lone prayer wheel stood at the heart of the village, but no one was spinning it, and the wheel had lost much of its paint. Looking about, Nadya and I shuddered. Gasa felt like a frontier town, where life was raw and precarious, where supplies and self-sufficiency were critical. The donkeys wandered about unchecked, some with their heads buried in nosebags, others, relieved no doubt to be free of their loads, rolling on their backs in the dirt.

| "Last night, we were in here, and there was power cut," Tshering said on our return to the hot spring in the evening. "Some people they take advantage. They touch and rub you."

There were fourteen of us in rheumatism or arthritis. Through the steam, I watched a mother suckle her baby until it nodded off and the nipple slid from its mouth. It hadn't occurred to me, but one reason that people stayed so long at tsachu could be that they hoped to find partners. Hours were spent wallowing half-naked with nothing to do but chat and dream. Much might be achieved in cloudy water, bodies hot and receptive. I realized that I knew almost nothing about sexuality in Bhutan. Public displays of affection were clearly frowned upon: Nadya and I had not once seen a couple kiss on the street and only once two youngsters cuddling outside a night-club in Thimphu. In the country, men indulged in "night crawling," apparently. When a boy took a shine to a girl living on the next farm, he might in the dead of night climb through a window and crawl into her bed (an act made simpler, one would think, by the fact that the windows in Bhutan have no glass). If he was still there in the morning, tradition said, he was considered a member of the family. I wondered if there were rules for the bath. Was it the caretaker's duty to evict gropers?

The storm was upon us. Snowflakes spun in through the windows and evaporated in the steam. More people arrived, snow stuck to their hair. Wallowing in a bath had to be better than squatting under a canvas lean-to by the river. A heap of discarded flip-flops gathered near the door. Nadya, Tshering, and I began to feel the press of bodies. A slim girl with a water bottle slid into the bath, then a stout man plopped his ten-year-old boy in before getting in himself. A skinny teen squeezed in. Flattened against Nadya's back, I rested my head on her shoulder. I was on the morning train in Tokyo again. I breathed out and let my eyelids droop.

I became aware of a tapping sound to my right. A woman bent over a cane was shuffling along the side of the bath, looking like she might at any moment fall in. With the legs of a kalij pheasant, wattles under her chin, and stringy white hair hanging down to her waist, she had to be ninety. How would she ever be able to get in the bath? There were no steps. A man hoisted himself out of the water and offered her his arm. Propping her stick against the wall, she seized it with both hands, and he lowered her gently into the water while two girls guided her legs. Her eyes opened wider as she descended. Feet on the bottom, she let out a hoarse sigh of relief, and then, grinning at everyone, uttered a few words. A gap opened up in front of her. Those nearest swept her into the middle of the bath and then over to the spout from which the hot spring water flowed. The woman with the baby seized one of old lady's arms and placed her under the falling water. She sighed again as it splattered over her thin shoulders.

The manifold rise in real income in several highly industrialized countries over the last fifty years has not led to similar increases in happiness. It is evident that triumphs in the rat race to earn more, have more, and consume more do not bring true and lasting happiness. The rich, the powerful, and the glamorous, it appears, are often the ones who are more impoverished spiritually and socially and thereby are less happy. While there is certainly considerable room for improvement to what and how we measure both wealth and happiness, the lack of any correlation between the two, after meeting basic needs, clearly indicates that happiness cannot be found on the unending, rudderless journey powered by man's insatiable greed.

—JIGMI Y. THINLEY, leader of DPT,
  "Gross National Happiness," 2005

10 | Yalama!

"IF WHAT YOU DO IS SELFISH, you will not succeed," Singye Namgyel says, looking sternly into the faces of the ten shivering students gathered about him. He pauses, pulls his scarf tighter around his neck and smiles. "But your run is for a good cause. All good intention have good ending."

The new director of Sherubtse College has honoured his promise and stopped by on his way to Thimphu to check we are all right. The students are clearly happy to see him, their aches and pains temporarily forgotten. He has brought with him a large box of bananas, another of mandarins, and a third of milk drinks called "Amul Kool." He speaks to each of them in turn and writes down their shoe sizes. A box of new running shoes will be waiting for them, he promises, when they reach Jakar, a four-day run from here. I am most grateful for this gesture and wonder if Prince Jigyel had a word with him. This will help some of the strugglers to stay motivated.

The latest casualty is Sonam Gyalpo, a reserved lad of twenty-two from a village near Trashigang. Last to arrive today, he went straight to Nadya, complaining of a bad ankle. Nadya made him sit down while she hacked ice from the stream and put it in a plastic bag. Hunting for her dwindling supply of painkillers, as his was the kind of swelling she had experienced, she turned and found him foraging for firewood with Dendup. "Sit, Sonam Gyalpo," she yelled. "Sit! Take your weight off that leg." Sonam timidly obeyed and applied the icepack. He told us in his interview that his father had died five years ago and that his mother was now the most important person in his life. He may be missing her. He was in the habit of going home regularly from Sherubtse to feed the cattle and collect firewood for her. "I never noticed frustration or sadness on her face after father die," he confided. "Rather her face always decorated with smiles and laughter. Maybe she is bearing all hectic works and hiding her tears and sweats within herself to make me happy." His mother, he said, was enormously proud that he was spending his winter break running for education. I inspected Sonam's running shoe when he took it off. A poorly made imitation of a Puma with a thin sole, knobbly tread, and bright yellow zigzags down the side, it seemed more suited to a twenty-minute jog along a dirt trail (or for impressing girls?) than a month-long ultramarathon on asphalt.

The director probably finds us a bit of a motley crew, wearing every stitch of clothing we own and huddling around a fire that refuses to start. Our gear is strewn over the ground: blankets, billy-cans, sacks of lentils and chickpeas, tipped-over Thermos flasks, plastic cups. A rock prevents a flaccid tent yet to be erected from taking off and sailing back to Sengor. Tharchen is wearing charcoal-smudged army fatigues and a sweatshirt with the word "Reaky" on the front, and Sonam Gyalpo has a cloth toque on his head marked "11" and a grubby T-shirt showing through his jacket with "Good Bush" written beside a picture of a woman slipping off her panties and "Bad Bush" next to one of the current US president. The head of Sherubtse is in a burgundy gho and shiny brown shoes and looks like he just stepped out of his office for lunch. I am curious what the journalist from *Kuensel* accompanying him will say in his write-up. I like it that we are now creatures of the road, a world away from the Western obsession with tidiness and clean hands.

Yalama!

Finally, shaking Mr. Sangay's hand and giving him two vouchers for his cell phone, Singye Namgyel takes his leave.

"Tashi delek," he says. "I hope you reach safely to Thimphu."

Our itinerary says we should be at Thrumshing-La tonight, but the park ranger told us there would be no water or flat ground for our tents at the saddle. He recommended instead a road workers' camp thirteen kilometres from Sengor. Go farther than this, and we would have to make it to Gyazamchu, ten kilometres beyond Thrumshing-La. We have ignored his advice and found a windy gully four kilometres short. Thinking of democracy earlier in the day, I invited the team to vote on where to camp for the night: hands up for the ranger's suggestion, hands up those who wish to go farther. The students looked at each other, amused. One voted for the road workers' camp, nine for uncertainty.

"Sorry, Tiger," I said, "but the voice of the majority has just been heard!"

Firewood is scant here, and there is no running water, but a narrow lay-by on the other side of the road will give us just enough room to pitch our tents. If a trucker on ara happens to fly down the road in the middle of the night, however, we will be toast.

I look around the camp. Now that the director has gone, everyone except Sonam Gyalpo and Mr. Sangay is busy. Ngawang, the cook, is crouching beside the fire, trying to blow life into it while Tiger uses his body as a shield. Dendup has seized the cook's patang and is chopping away at an uprooted tree stump and tossing over kindling. Sonam Wangdi is helping Tee pour water from a jerry can into one of the billies. Long Bone Ugyen is snapping tent poles together while Sherab gets out pegs. Ugyen Lhendup and Wangchuck Rabten are dragging a dead branch down off the mountain. Tharchen is chipping ice into a bucket, and Kezang, our driver, is making a flute. While it is true that Nadya assigned chores to the students in Trashigang, it surprises me that they never need chivying to perform them, despite fatigue. They have even asked Nadya and me if we would like them to put up our tent. I realize, too, that we haven't had to teach the Bhutanese a thing about camp craft. Camping isn't a craft for them. It is a common activity, as natural as boiling rice or saying mantras, and they are handy with fires and machetes and expert at making do. I look at the tent Long Bone has now put up: no fly sheet, zips that jam, a hole in the side as large as my bottom. The day before our departure from Kanglung, one of our runners cut a panel from an umbrella to seal the hole.

Having helped gather wood, I get my journal from the bus and find a sheltered spot behind a boulder to write. The journal is actually a laboratory notebook, purchased in Kanglung, with lined pages for writing and blank ones for diagrams. The lined ones have "experiment number" at the top, the blank facing them "figure number." I sketch a picture on the figure page for a change, the first I have drawn for years. I used to enjoy drawing as a child, my favoured subjects being insects, ugly faces, pretty landscapes, and UFOs. I begin with the dying conifer over the road. Now we are above 3500 metres, all the deciduous trees are gone: no oak or maple or champ. The conifer is more a black spike than a tree, its few remaining branches bent or broken and cobwebbed in Spanish moss or the Himalayan equivalent. The moss billows out, but the tree itself seems undisturbed by the wind. It looks as if it has been there for centuries, survivor of countless blizzards and rock falls, as if it could last for centuries more, slowly eroding but never falling. Then I draw the perfectly symmetrical Christmas trees beneath it, the next generation perhaps, silvery green in lustre with beardless branches that resemble reaching hands.

"Sar can draw nice picture!" The fire is now curling up through the wood, and Tiger has wandered over.

"Just simple stuff, that's all. How's your knee?"

"Still paining, Sar, but getting better."

"The new shoes will help. My knees always tell me when I need to go shopping! Can you last till Jakar?"

"Of course!" He laughs. "When I doubt, I remember my childhood memories."

"Breaking rocks?"

"Yessar, and never losing hope and keeping up your spirits."

"'Tiger, tiger, burning bright?'"

"'In the forest of the night.'" He giggles.

"Is that how you got your nickname?"

"No, Sar, not from Blake's poem. When I was a boy, I was playing Police and Thieves with my friends. I was always thief. My friends, they gave me that name because I could run and jump and get away from police."

The Spanish moss ignites into fiery tongues in the last of the afternoon sun. Shadows stretch from the conifers. Tigers continue to roam the wilds of Bhutan, and I try to imagine one padding silently through the brush towards us, the light of our campfire in its eyes.

I ask Tiger about a song I often hear him singing while he goes about his camp chores. "Pelo, pelo, kabi na..." A Dzongkha song?

"No, Hindi one, Sar," he replies.

I have him write a translation in my journal.

Drink, drink, some time you drink
Drink some water from the drain.
I am hero, you are zero.

"Just that? What does it mean?"
He laughs. "I don't know, Sar."

| "Yalama!"

At Bhutan's highest pass on the lateral road, a vermilion flag of
a secular nature now flaps alongside the thousand multicoloured
Buddhist prayer flags. It would appear that Long Bone has artistic
skills. The flag is about the size of two table mats and, in white
paint, says "Tara-thon" at the top and "3-1-2008" at the bottom. A
stickman runner is at the centre, arms spread wide in what seems
to be a gesture of ecstasy, or perhaps of embrace. Our flag is likely
to last longer than the others as the creator has sewn the top and
bottom edges to bamboo canes and hung it from the corners to a
string of prayer flags. Instead of flapping torturously in the wind, it
hangs like a banner and waves regally back and forth.

"Yalama!" roar our runners again, all wearing their "Run for
the Kids" T-shirts today and throwing their arms in the air while
looking up at this evidence of their accomplishment. Nadya and I
laugh and take photos.

I look over at Mr. Sangay to see if he approves. We found him
waiting for us beside a smoking chorten at the pass, counting his
prayer beads. As we came in, he had us run three times around
the mani wall serving as a traffic island. There is no doubt that
Thrumshing-La is a sacred place. Only one other mountain pass on
the highway has a sangphu (literally "incense palace"), purifying the
air, and only this pass has a wall of stone tablets repeating over and
over the Buddhist mantra, "Om mani padme hum." No other mountain pass has anywhere near as many prayer flags. There are so many
swaddling the mani wall, it is barely visible. But our event coordinator made no objection when Kezang positioned the bus, and Long

Yalama! Team Tara-thon celebrates at Thrumshing-La, the highest pass.

Bone strung his flag up with the others. Raising a flag here seems to reinforce the spiritual dimension of our marathon.

I look at my wife and see tears in her eyes, and think for a while about happiness. We rejoice with our runners, but I am not sure that we feel quite as they do. Allowing for the exuberance of youth, there is no doubt that we share with them the elation of having run to the highest point on our journey. A hard climb is now behind us. Despite "paining" knees and swollen ankles, with two weeks of running and 220 kilometres done, we are proving equal to the task we have set ourselves. The road will, of course, exact further tolls, but the mood is one of optimism. But is the happiness Nadya and I feel more relief that the project we have mounted is succeeding and pride that we have turned ten Bhutanese into distance runners? I cannot speak for Nadya, but I know that my own motivation for launching the Tara-thon is questionable. I wished to be the first to run across Bhutan. It is not that I don't believe in our cause, but I also run for acknowledgement and welcome the attention of the media. Looking back into my past, I know that I have derived happiness mostly from personal achievement: fast times and medals in road races, a black belt in karate, crossing Canada by bicycle, a master's degree. Is my happiness here on Thrumshing-La more egotistic back-slapping than joy in a shared accomplishment?

This does not appear to be the case with our students. Unless I am deluding myself, they are running primarily for queen and country and wouldn't be here if our objective were merely to set a record. When the going is hard, they have told us and have written in our Tara-thon blog, they conjure up a picture in their heads of the children they are raising money to help. Several were once those kids in need themselves. They are probably also drawing strength and joy from the Buddhist notion that helping others earns them merit. Taking part in this charitable endeavour brings them a little closer to nirvana.

We remain at Thrumshing-La until our teeth start to chatter, swig a cup of suja, and then commence our descent. The morning sun disappears as we drop below the saddle. There were banks of old snow, crusty with ice, under the prayer flags. Now it is on both sides of the road and frozen to some of the hemlock branches. The streams we pass are frozen solid: long, rippling beards that smooth out into slabs of marble when they meet the road. I hear the drain-like trickle of water flowing underneath. Where the water has spilled out over the road and frozen, we must skate a little, and I think again of my winter runs in Canada. To my right through the trees, I can see Tibet, a row of ragged, glittering teeth cutting the sky.

"Yalama!" The word echoes off the fortress walls, our hares staying in touch with our tortoises.

| "I think I have latitude sickness, Sar," Tee admits when we reach Gyazamchu. I smile but look carefully at his eyes. They are, indeed, wandering about in their sockets. "My head, it feel sort of cloudy."

I remember the sensation from one of our hikes last winter. Climbing to a pass at 4200 metres, separating two Brokpa villages in the east, I began to feel giddy and nauseous. I stopped, leaned against a tree, closed my eyes, drank water, waited for my heart to stop tripping, and thought about my trip to the Chilean Andes in 1994. Suffering in the same way at a similar altitude, I chose to ignore the warnings bells and foolishly quickened my pace. An hour later at the Bolivian border, I collapsed with a splitting headache that plagued me for three days.

Should we stop at Gyazamchu then? Fourteen kilometres is hardly a full day's run and will put us behind on our schedule. I look around, recognizing this insalubrious spot. Nadya and I camped here a night with Dr. Jagar, Zangmo, and Pema. Just as before, the place is strewn with litter. Gyazamchu is a canteen where buses stop and a derelict shelter marked "Labour Camp." I remember Dr. Jagar pulling in beside the shelter in the dark, my putting our headlamp on the little boy's head, and sending him off to fetch firewood. There was so little wood, we ended up cooking over a garbage fire. The canteen is where Pema ate his ill-fated bowl of rice porridge. Tee should probably go in and have some.

I put it once again to the vote. The chef in the canteen says it is twenty-five kilometres to Ura, the first village on this side of the pass, or four to a cowshed, where there is barely any water but probably enough space for tents. Gyazamchu? No show of hands. Ura? Three hares stick their paws in the air. Cowshed? No votes. I look at Sonam Gyalpo with his limp, at Tee rubbing his eyes. Nadya tells me she had to give Tee altitude-sickness pills on the other side of Thrumshing-La.

"As project leader, um, my vote is worth five of yours!" I grin and wait for a cry of protest.

The four kilometres turn out to be four uphill kilometres, surprisingly, and it takes our tortoises over an hour to cover the

Dendup attends to personal hygiene.

distance. As we unpack our gear next to a tumbledown shack in fading light, I see several of the team blinking with exhaustion. We probably shouldn't have spent as long as we did at the pass this morning. Riding high on the moment, none of us thought to go to the bus for a jacket. Mr. Sangay pours out cups of suja, and Nadya urges the boys to change out of their sweaty running gear.

While Ngawang prepares a dinner of rice, cabbage curry, and dal, Kezang plays his "snake-charmer," a flute he made a couple of days ago out of bamboo, one end stuck in half a plastic bottle to amplify the sound. The students laugh as they go about their chores at the odd warbles the instrument produces. In cowboy hat, overly short gho (it only extends to mid-thigh), and trekking boots, our driver is a bizarre-looking fellow, a cross between a Bhutanese and a Westerner, who has picked up English through taking tourists rafting and kayaking for Lotus Tours. He has already played a role larger than his designation in this Tara-thon. He helps out around camp and clearly gets on well with the students (who call him "Atta Kezang") and with Yana (who appears to have forgiven him for the unsolicited bath in the Sheri Chhu). How avuncular Kezang truly is, I cannot tell, but imagine our students find him more approachable than Mr. Sangay, Nadya, or me.

Scant firewood means a small campfire to fend off a bitter evening chill, so we retire early, Nadya and I shrugging on our sleeping bags fully dressed. During the cold night, I toss, turn, and fart repeatedly, my stomach troubled by the curry, and Nadya snores at "excited hog volume" (or so I decide while writing in my journal the next day). If she sleeps on her side, she doesn't snore, but doctor's orders are that she must sleep on her back with her damaged ankle elevated. Unable to sleep, I look through the tent flap and see Yana, sitting by the embers of the fire staring at the moon.

A young man dressed in a dark gho and white sneakers jogs down a flight of stone steps leading from his village to a wooden bridge. He is carrying a suitcase in one hand and a ghetto-blaster in the other and sings as he goes. He crosses the bridge and runs up a path on the other side. He must now follow a narrower dirt path over a grassy ridge to another bridge. From the ridge, he can see the motor road and the bus to Thimphu pulling over to pick up three passengers. He yells, begins to sprint, stops for a moment to whistle at the bus, sprints again. The bus leaves without him.

His curses echo off the grey, snow-dusted mountains. Dondup sits despondently on his suitcase at the side of the road and lights a cigarette. A summer breeze makes moss trailing from the branch of a tree wag like a dog's tail. Three geese glide by overhead, honking.

—*from* Travellers and Magicians, *Zeitgeist Films, 2003*

The sun is out, and I feel warm for the first time in days. I can wear shorts, a T-shirt, and my lightweight running shoes. For the first forty minutes of the day's run, I am with Dendup, who now has "Tara-thon" painted in white on the side of his red baseball cap. He is a steady, middle-of-the-pack runner, who has made it this far apparently unscathed. I give him the nickname "Chapsa Dendup" as he has already dashed into the trees twice this morning to relieve himself. He laughs and says he drank too much suja at breakfast. After a couple of uphill bends in the road from the cowshed, we seem to turn a corner. I stop for a moment to drink in the new view, parading below. To our right is the mountain, the rock leaning over the road now an orange colour and blotched with black lichen. To our left is the abyss, free here of mist. I assume a river is down there somewhere, but all I can see is a procession of dark-green, interlocking knuckles of land. Ahead of us, the way is all down, the highway looping around a succession of rounded spurs. A large, brown eagle swoops low over the road, its primary feathers splayed like fingers, its shadow clear-edged on the asphalt, and vanishes into conifers below.

We set off again, and I chuckle remembering *Travellers and Magicians*, the movie Nadya and I saw before coming to Bhutan. It was about a restless government official who wished to leave his quiet village in the east and go to America, the land of his dreams. Dondup misses the one bus going across the country and has to hitchhike, but there is almost no traffic. He spends hours and then a night at the roadside, frustrated when other hitchhikers show up, angry when the batteries of his tape player die. A monk heading the same way teases him for his impatience and tells him an enchanting story about a trainee magician who gets lost in the forest and falls in love with a woodcutter's wife. It was a peaceful, slow film with shots of a rugged and apparently largely undisturbed land, and it ignited our interests in coming to the Himalayan kingdom. Like Dondup, I am keen to reach Thimphu, but I also want to bask in this landscape. Nadya said yesterday that she was so happy we had chosen a slow way of saying goodbye to Bhutan.

Buffeted by cool wind rising from the valley, Dendup and I glide down the switchbacks and let the rhythm of the run carry us. After ten minutes, I no longer hear the slap of our shoes on the road or our panting breath. I am no longer conscious of my forty-three-year-old body with its achy joints. My arms swing effortlessly, and the action seems to match the sway of the plants and trees at the roadside. It is probably the rush of endorphins or the effect of the rarified air, but, flushed with well-being, I seem more to flow down the mountain than run down it; I feel suddenly unencumbered, free of anxiety, light. In Canada, running would always calm my body, clear my mind, and improve my mood, but here in Bhutan, the activity can be positively transformative. After the strain of reaching a saddle, the legs die, the body sags, and the mind is liberated. Conscious still of winding road, rippling prayer flag, or blooming rhododendron, it rides high, questing for a larger view, some greater meaning, a spiritual insight even. A couple of the students have spoken of meditating while they run. Perhaps the activity helps them detach from earthly concerns and reside in the moment.

I am glad that our Tara-thon is not a Tara-trek. Walking does not produce these effects as readily: trekkers, loaded with packs and in heavy boots, tend to remain grounded. It is true that nature encounters are briefer for runners, but sometimes these can be more intense as they can steal up on a bird or an animal. I smile, remembering the astonished bulls two days ago, the fleeing culvert-in-charge, the deer and skunks I used to startle while out on dawn runs in the woods near Fredericton. More so than hiking, perhaps, distance running is also a test of strength and of will, an exercise of mind over body. "Everyone can run—we are built for it—but very few people do, particularly adults," an old man who had run all his life once said to me at a road race in Canada. Run far, especially over mountainous terrain, and you must silence the inevitable outcries from knees, calves, thighs, stomach, and chest, and resist the impulse to stop and walk. Your reward is the stillness and calm that forward motion at velocity begets.

Dendup ducks into the woods again, and I slow to a trot. The highway uncoils below me, twisting from left to right and wriggling finally into forest. Part of my joy, I realize, is that there are no bill-boards polluting the natural splendour, no pictures of false smiles and tooth-whitening products, no "It's the real thing. Coke," no cars with absurd names like "Escape" or "Odyssey" or "Pathfinder" seen on TV driving alone in wilderness settings, no laundry detergents and softer than soft towels. The image of a junk-food sign beside the walking trail in Fredericton enters my head. For weeks, I ran past a monster burger a metre high, beaming down at me in Technicolor: two meat patties resembling hockey pucks, a square of shiny processed cheese wilting between them, glittering onion rings, and curls of lettuce smothered in mayonnaise, the two halves of the bun as substantial as bath sponges barely containing the stack. Having ads along the highway or in towns, suggesting that material things can yield happiness, would be particularly offensive in this Buddhist land, where desire leads to suffering.

The bang of a hammer wakes me. I round a bend and suddenly find a woman squatting at the side of the road, beating a rock. She has a baby wrapped in a blanket on her back and a dirty pink scarf pulled up over her mouth.

"Kuzu zangpo!" I bellow, unthinkingly. Dendup laughs. Two other labourers are staggering towards her, holding between them a jute sack sling filled with rocks. The woman looks up from her work, and I see the fatigue in her eyes. She nods once and waves a dust-whitened hand.

I run on, feeling guilty. A book review I read last winter on *A Baby in a Backpack to Bhutan*, a travel memoir written by an Australian visitor, comes to mind. The Bhutanese reviewer was surprised that, once again, a Westerner had written a book using what he termed "the *Lost Horizon* approach," waxing lyrical about majestic scenery and monasteries perched on hilltops, an approach he slammed as a failure to understand his country. He did not elaborate on why, but his critique reminded me of Nancy Gettelman's *Bhutan: A Himalayan Cultural Diary*, a documentary video Nadya and I had seen in Fredericton. The Canadian novelist had been to Bhutan on assignment in 1969 and described her return twenty-five years later. "Back in my beloved Himalayan paradise at last, Bhutan truly is Shangri-La. The descent into the Paro valley was absolutely gorgeous. We could already tell from the air that Bhutan is clean, prosperous, vigorous, progressive, well kept. Cool, cultivated, green Paro valley lies at 7,200 feet, blessed relief after hot, humid Calcutta..."

Now that the media has tagged Druk Yul the "Last Shangri-La," and tour companies actively entice customers using the label, it is easy, I imagine, for a visitor from the West to come to Bhutan in the hope of finding a hidden sanctuary, a place of extraordinary natural beauty inhabited by peace-loving, godly people, just as many did when travelling to Tibet in the 1950s. I came myself with this expectation, and the road to Ura on this beautiful January morning shows me once again that it exists.

But to see Bhutan as simply Shangri-La is to overlook its problems. I think of diseased dogs roaming the college campus, lightless villages many days' walk from the road, garbage tossed down mountainsides, fenceless cornfields raided by monkeys and wild boars, doma-ruined mouths, and Nepali-Bhutanese refugees. I remember the hard lives of Tangsibians, perhaps wholly reliant, before Dr. Jagar became their benefactor, on the success of the harvest to survive winter. They would likely find the notion of Shangri-La incongruous, as would the woman I just passed breaking rocks, or, for that matter, Dondup, an educated government official bored to his back teeth living in a remote village. "I love the view, but I would not want the life," Jamie Zeppa, a volunteer teacher here with WUSC in the 1980s, decided towards the end of her memoir. I remember reading a column in the *Bhutan Times* last summer called People Speak. The person who wrote in was a housewife who said she got no compensation when her husband, an official courier, fell off a cliff and died while running between villages. When her hut collapsed shortly after, she failed again to get reparation though she was eligible (a government-backed scheme insuring all rural households against natural disaster). The housewife had to move into a cowshed with her eighty-year-old grandmother and two teenage daughters. Then she got in a traffic accident. Hospitalized and broke, she had to take her daughters out of school and send them to work. The title of the article was "What does GNH mean to her?"

Is Druk Yul the happy kingdom that many foreign journalists, intrigued by the concept of Gross National Happiness, the fourth king's development concept, make it out to be? Bhutan is one of the poorer nations on Earth, ranked 141st of the 187 on the United Nations' Human Development Index for 2007;[4] and yet, from what Nadya and I have witnessed on our unguided hikes around the countryside, where most Bhutanese live, that poverty is not typically grinding. Village life on a mountainside can be basic—shockingly so, by our standards—houses lit by candles, the kids shoeless and dirty, everyone drawing water from a single well; but we met no homeless people and only one beggar (a little girl who asked for a pen at a tourist spot). Most Bhutanese lead healthy, active lives and live relatively long (men, on average, to 66, women to 70) and seem, for the most part, to be high-spirited. They inhabit a protected and generally pristine land (a law saying that at least 60 per cent of the kingdom must remain forested at all times with 25 per cent put aside for national parks, reserves, and wildlife sanctuaries), they adore their king and believe he has their best interests in mind, and they are clearly proud to be who they are (decorating their houses in the traditional way, wearing the required national dress in public, gathering frequently to honour their gods). While it is difficult for a foreign visitor to really tell whether the Bhutanese are genuinely happy, it appears on the surface, at least, that most of them are.

This general state of happiness is endorsed by a pilot study conducted by the Centre for Bhutan Studies, a research body commissioned by the Royal Government to create a set of domains or indicators to measure Gross National Happiness for 2008. The centre began its study in February 2006 and took a year and a half to interview 350 Bhutanese (old and young, male and female, educated and uneducated) from nine dzongkhags across the kingdom and compile the results (each interview lasting, apparently, a full day). To the question "How much do you enjoy life?" 78.6 per cent of the respondents answered either "Quite a lot" or "An extreme amount." Asked to rate their overall quality of life, 62 per cent reported that it was "good" (the other options being very poor, poor, neither good nor poor, and very good). Fifty-six per cent said they were completely satisfied with their health and 86.6 per cent completely satisfied with their family relationships. The study focused on the psychological and spiritual well-being of the individual, but happiness clearly derives, too, from community. The Bhutanese, Nadya and I noticed from the start, seem to do virtually everything together. Farmers help each other to plant and harvest crops, dashos rub shoulders with yak herders at tsechu, students at Sherubtse complete assignments together, an entire village crams into one house to see in the New Year. Our runners seem at their happiest when in camp, helping one another do chores. Maybe this is why the Bhutanese are not naturally drawn to running; it is, in essence, a solo act.

With eleven of the twenty kilometres for the day done, I emerge from the shadow of a spur and behold, in brilliant sunshine, a galleon in full sail. For a second time today, I stop and stare. Three towering, rectangular white shrouds, bloated with wind, appear to ride conifer waves on a westerly course. I must be heading north, then, at present, as this vessel is Gangkhar Puensum, the tallest in Bhutan's flotilla, and I know it marks the border with Tibet. Sum means "three," a student once told me, puen "brother," and I imagine three deities navigating their stone ship for millennia towards the setting sun.

I run on, and, five minutes later, hear a cry behind me. "Yalama!" Someone else has seen the galleon.

| "Angay Sonam say you can retire on this bench, Mr. Tony, and Madam Nadya on bench on other side of room. Dasho is away on business."

"What about the team, Mr. Sangay?"

"There is room for them downstair."

No two nights are the same. The night before last, our tents went up beside a cowshed and an ice-choked stream near a mountain pass. Last night, we were laid out like moth pupae on the concrete floor of a furnitureless Department of Roads shelter, three kilometres short of the village of Ura. Tonight, we are on the second floor of a posh house belonging to an absent dignitary. It would seem that our event coordinator simply knocked on the door of this house and asked the owners whether they would mind putting up twelve runners, who hadn't washed in a week, and a stray dog, who may have only had one wash in his life. I have not seen Mr. Sangay look this happy since returning to his old school in Trashigang.

The room seems as though it is rarely used. Three dusty armchairs stand in front of a table supporting a vase of equally dusty plastic roses. Two thick, curly edged rugs cover the floor, the larger with a pancake-shaped hole in it. Black-and-white photographs of Bhutan's kings lean out from the walls, the most recent one being of Jigme Singye Wangchuck wearing embroidered leather boots and looking about the age he was when he took up office in 1972. I try the bench, with its richly patterned but faded cushioning, for size and find that my feet dangle over the end.

When he returns in the morning, Mr. Sangay tells me about our hosts. In traditional Bhutanese society, there are four castes, he explains, making me write them down ("Short pencil better than long memory, Mr. Tony"): "dung ju, aristocracy; chejey, middle class; khochi penchen, working class; and drapa, servants." The family living in this house is dung ju, and dung ju is rooted in "Gyalpo tshri-shung dretsum," meaning "saintly stock." Angay Sonam is the lady of the house and mother of the absent dasho, Karma Geley, who is advisor to the present king and "a renowned person in country since second king." I nod, jotting down the unfamiliar words as he spells them, and realize that we are privileged to be guests here. It surprises me to hear that Bhutan has a caste system, and I assume it belongs more to feudal times. The stratification in Bhutanese society today seems to have to do with professional status, and

THE DRAGON RUN

I recall how the maintenance staff who fixed our roof in Kanglung deferred to Ugyen Dendup and how Mr. Sangay showed great respect for Dr. Jagar. It is pleasing that a Bhutanese of humble origins, like Jagar Dorji, can rise through the ranks and become the director of a university college, even a national councillor.

Mr. Sangay takes us down to meet Angay, saying that he has told her about our project. I find her leaning on her walking stick in front of the house. I can see she is old, but I would not have guessed eighty-nine. Angay Sonam's eyes are clear and bright, her hearing good, her voice steady, and her hair more grey than white. She is obviously proud to be Bhutanese, judging by her fine quality kira, pinned at the shoulder with silver brooches. The rings on her fingers and bronze or gold bracelet on her wrist may be markers of her caste. I have not seen this much jewellery on a Bhutanese person before, but it does not seem ostentatious on this woman. The way her earrings drag down the earlobes makes me think of Lord Buddha.

"Nami samé kadrinche," I say, bowing my head, grateful to her for opening her doors to so many strangers.

Angay seizes my hand and presses it to her head. I am taken aback. No Bhutanese has ever done that before. I wonder if I should do the same with hers, but then figure that it is her way of giving us her blessing. Unsure of what to say, I ask her the secret to a long life. Mr. Sangay translates. Angay giggles and answers without hesitation.

"She say she walk up and down, day by day."

Putting my bag on the bus before we begin our run to Jakar, I dig out my journal and look for an entry from 2006. I remember scribbling down the words of a reincarnated lama who came to Sherubtse and gave a talk on the brevity of life and on happiness.

This life is short. The future life is long. We have already wasted half of our life. We all do bad karmas to get happiness, to get a nice home, more money, more pleasure. It is very stupid. We are accumulating a lot of bad karmas to have happiness. Even the animals, the ants, keeping busy jumping around, they also want

to be free from suffering. All sentient beings are busy wanting
happiness. That's how we survive in this world. From the point
of view from spiritual path, it is stupid. Life is short. Happiness
is impermanent. It is like dew on the grass.

The Four Friends shows an elephant, a monkey, a hare and a bird, perched acrobat-fashion one on top of the other, standing under a tall tree laden with fruit. The fable relates how the elephant, though strong and mighty, needs the agile monkey to help him reach the fruit on the tree. But, it continues, there would be no tree if the bird hadn't eaten a seed to begin with and then deposited it on the soil in its droppings; and the seed would not have grown into a tree had the hare not protected and nurtured its roots underground. The elephant, the monkey, the hare and the bird also symbolize, respectively, the four terrestrial habitats—the ground, the air, the underground and the sky. The fable underlines the virtue of cooperation, and the connections and interdependence between all creatures great and small, and all elements, in nature's cycle.

—QUEEN ASHI DORJI WANGMO WANGCHUCK, *Treasures of the Thunder Dragon: A Portrait of Bhutan*, 2006

11 | Cure for Our Sufferings

IN THE MID-EIGHTH CENTURY, King Sendhaka of Bumthang lost his son in the war he was waging with King Na'oche, his neighbour to the south. Sendhaka was so distressed by this that he desecrated the dwelling place of Bumthang's principal deity, Shelging Karpo. Angered, the god took revenge by stealing the king's life spirit. One of his secretaries, fearing that His Majesty would die, asked a highly revered tantric master to come to Bumthang to restore him to health by using his supernatural powers.

It was Guru Rinpoche's first visit to the region that would become known as Bhutan. He found the rock where the deity was living and meditated there before calling on the king's daughter to bring him water in a gold pitcher. While she was away, he transformed himself into his eight manifestations and performed a dance. The divinities living in the area were stunned by this spectacle and came out to watch, but not Shelging Karpo. When the princess returned, the guru tried a different tactic and changed her into five princesses. Attracted by the light flashing off their pitchers, the god turned himself into a white lion and came out of hiding. Guru Rinpoche responded by becoming a garuda. He swooped down, seized the god in his talons, and made him return the life spirit he had stolen. Promising to respect Buddhism, Shelging Karpo remained a guardian deity of Bumthang. On his recovery, King Sendhaka converted to Buddhism, as did King Na'oche, and, at the bidding of the guru, the two agreed to meet and make peace.

The Precious Teacher left more signs of his visit to Bumthang than he did in any other dzongkhag. On our first crossing of the kingdom, when we passed through Jakar, Dr. Jagar and Zangmo took Nadya and me to the site of Guru Rinpoche's epic encounter with the deity. The guru left an imprint of his body on the rock where he had meditated, and Kurjey Lhakhang has been built over it (kur meaning "body," jey "print"). Pinned to the roof of the temple is the head of a horned and hook-billed griffon above another of a white lion. On a faded mural inside the door, Shelging Karpo in human form, with gold earrings and flaming sword, rides a galloping white stallion through green clouds. We learned more about the guru's wanderings through the district while on a hike in an adjacent valley last winter.

"Here Guru Rinpoche stay for three year. No, three month," the caretaker of Tang Timochen Lhakhang informed us. "No, three... *week*. Yes, three week. He came and he subdue demon who make road not safe."

"What happened to the demon?" Nadya asked.

"He is under that stone." The monk pointed at a rock the size of a caravan next to the road. An indentation in the top shaped like a teardrop, he said, was where the guru had taken a bath.

After a week of face washes in icy streams, I fancy taking a bath myself when we pause at a beautiful river gorge on our run from Angay Sonam's house to Jakar. The water is a clear, radiant green and thoroughly inviting. But Membartsho is where Guru Rinpoche hid sacred treasures called terma and left his footprint in the rock. Strings of blue, green, red, and yellow prayer flags criss-cross over the gorge, and fist-size clay chortens resembling toadstools prickle the rocks on each side. Membartsho means "Burning Lake," and legend has it that, seven centuries after Guru Rinpoche visited Bhutan, a local saint called Pema Lingpa was told in a dream to dive into the "lake" and retrieve the treasures hidden at the bottom. This he did on two occasions. On the first, he brought to the surface a statue of Lord Buddha and several books of teachings. The second time, as some bystanders suspected him of being a demon, he went with a butter lamp, saying that only Guru Rinpoche's spiritual son, a genuine terton, would be able to return with more treasures and with the lamp still lit. The saint went on to become Bhutan's foremost treasure-finder, but I could also believe that he is still in the Burning Lake, judging from the extraordinary luminescence of the water. Watching Mr. Sangay meditate before a likeness of the saint carved into the rock and painted gold, I think again of "saintly stock." Pema Lingpa was the great, great grandfather of His Majesty Ugyen Wangchuck, the first king of Bhutan.

| "Kuzu zangpo-la. I am Jigme Wangchuck, assistant agricultural officer."

"Hello, my name is Rinzin Dorji. I am assistant forestry officer. This is Jigme Wangdi, livestock officer."

"Sangay Wangchuck, Sir, cultural officer."

"Kuzu zangpo-la. Sonam Dendup, secretary for District Development Committee."

"Kuzu zangpo-la," I reply, taking off my hat and bowing. "Thanks to all of you for coming out to welcome us."

Seven officials and one reporter from BBS are waiting for us on the outskirts of Jakar, big smiles on their faces. Like the DEO for Mongar and his statistical officer, they wish to shake our hands and run a short leg of the Tara-thon. The gesture is heartening, proof that our project is attracting public interest and has supporters. As we jog together over the Bumthang Chhu on a bridge laced with prayer flags and head up the main street, I see children scurrying around and realize I had almost forgotten that we are running for them.

I look once again at the dzong stationed on a cliff above town. It is in an ideal spot to observe all goings-on in the valley and has served as our beacon for most of the morning: first a matchstick box from fifteen kilometres, then a shoebox, a refrigerator, a minivan, finally a grand monastic fort, white with red trim. According to an article Dr. Jagar wrote on place names and their meanings, the town got its official name in the sixteenth century when the great, great grand-father of the Shabdrung Ngawang Namgyel looked up as he was laying the foundation for a monastery and saw a white bird. Believing this to be an auspicious sign, he followed the bird, abandoning the site he had chosen, and started building again at the place where it landed. Ja means "bird," kar "white."

Our run finishes at a chipped concrete traffic island with a three-way sign sprouting from it saying, "Gompa 6," "Mongar 193," and "Thimphu 260." Jakar is a traffic hub, the place where buses break their two-day journeys between Thimphu and Trashigang for the night, the usual terminus for tourist tours from the capital. As we sit on the plastic chairs the town officials have set out in a semi-circle, drink suja, and eat desi, my mood dips. We are back in the civilized world. Jambay Enterprise Internet Café and Udee Shopping Complex are behind us, and an office offering a "Toyota Coaster" service "daily (except Mondays)" to the side. There is a taxi rank and a blue truck marked "K.T. Carrier," revving its engine noisily in a space marked "PARKING FOR BUSES ONLY." Signs in windows say, "Faxes," "Xerox," "Lamination," and "Nokia 'Evolve'—Mobile's Solution." I think of the hotels here with their Western names: River Lodge, Swiss Guest House, Mountain Lodge. The driver of the truck guns his engine more vigorously.

I thought a school would put us up in Jakar, but Mr. Sangay has made other plans. Jigme, the livestock officer, escorts us to a two-storey house a kilometre from town, marked "Regional Veterinary Hospital." We can unroll our sleeping bags in the offices on the second floor, he says, and use the computer to update our blog. The livestock extension officer will attend to our needs. We are left in the company of a short Nepali man with a quivering moustache and staring eyes, who introduces himself as Jai Narayan Sharma. Our first need is a bucket: there is no running water in the hospital, but a lone faucet outside. After three weeks on the road, our clothes are beginning to stink. The bus also smells like a gym locker room and needs mucking out, a job Kezang promises to do as we will be here two nights. Does the hospital have a mop? Nadya asks Jai whether Yana could be vaccinated against rabies.

"Best thing is not to vaccinate now," Jai replies on hearing that the Tara-dog runs with the team. "Dog will be very slumberous for few days after injection. He will not be running." He puts on a pair of rubber gloves. "But I will give examination. Is your dog docile?"

Nadya walks over to Yana, who is lying on the grass, knocked out after today's twenty-five-kilometre run. She lifts a leg and drops it, lifts another and drops it, tickles his stomach. Yana does not bat an eyelid. Za min thur and the stray from Trashigang have become good friends over the last couple of weeks.

"You could do anything with this dog," she assures the vet.

Jai places his thumb and forefinger in Yana's ear, opens it wide and peeks in; he peels back the lips and inspects the teeth; he parts the fur in several places at the neck in search of fleas, he lifts the tail to inspect the anus and squeezes the testicles. Noticing blood leaking from the penis, he squirts it with disinfectant. Yana opens his eyes dreamily but does not protest.

I recall things being rather different when Nadya treated Mutu for fleas in Kanglung. She had tipped a foul-smelling chemical she got from Trashigang called deltamethrin butox ("for prevention and control of ectoparasitic infestations") into a pail of water, turning it cloudy. Then, using a Britannia Good Day cookie for bait, Nadya seized the unsuspecting patient by the scruff of the neck and slopped the mixture liberally over every furry surface. There were strangled yelps, miserable whines, the ineffectual motoring of legs on the smooth concrete behind our house, Mummy's reassuring there-theres. Smelling of paint thinners after her bath, Mutu scarpered, tail jammed between her legs, but, unfortunately for her, de-fleaing was a two-step process. Deltamethrin butox must be left on the dog's coat for an hour, said the instructions on the bottle, before being rinsed out. "If large quantities are swallowed," it warned, "gastric lavage is advised." Mutu was easy to catch. She had licked herself and was discovered staggering around the village, cross-eyed and drooling.

"Your dog is having transmissible disease," Jai decides, sucking on his moustache, his examination complete. "There is tumour growth, very likely picked up from female."

"Is it bad? Does he need surgery?" my wife asks, concerned.

"Tumour have very high supply of blood. If we cut, he will make whole house dirty! But don't worry. Tumour is not large one. You can operate when you reach to Thimphu."

While Nadya holds his head, Yana gets his willy swabbed with iodine antiseptic wash. It is this treatment that finally makes him wriggle.

I ask Jai about stray dogs in Bumthang. Are there fewer here than in other parts of the country, perhaps, given there is a veterinary hospital? No, he replies. The hospital has dog sterilization campaigns from time to time but mainly treats cattle. Besides, dogs are highly mobile. They sterilize the ones they can catch, but more keep appearing. From what I have read over the past year, it seems to me that the Bhutanese are still unsure what to do about stray dogs, the main problem being, of course, that they carry rabies. Almost BTN 6 million was spent on anti-rabies vaccines in 2006, apparently, each rabies shot (of the six necessary) costing BTN 300 (CAD 8). In the summer, the Royal Government declared stray dogs "a public nuisance" and called for a nationwide program to address the problem. There were, it was estimated, fifty thousand dogs living in the kingdom, but less than a third had been sterilized. Pounds would need to be built in all dzongkhags, where dogs could be looked after, sterilized, and vaccinated against rabies. Dog owners living in Thimphu should register their pets at the animal hospital, where they would receive a collar, marked "pet." The aim, said Works and Human Settlement Minister Lyonpo Kinzang Dorji, was to have Bhutan stray-free by December.

Yana, the stray turned Tara runner, snores gently, blissfully unaware that he is now officially considered "a public nuisance." What is his fate? Will he be scooped in a sack and put in a pound, or is he destined to join the seven thousand strays living in Thimphu, tearing at one another's flanks over food scraps? I think of Dawa, Kunzang Choden's fictional stray. Born the runt of the litter in Paro, Dawa escapes an early death when he fails to climb a garbage heap to get his share of meat tossed out by a restaurant. He watches his mother and siblings die horribly, twitching and convulsing: the meat has been laced with poison. Malnourished, he grows up with an undersized body, an overly large head, and rickets, but survives by learning Dzongkha from monks and comes to understand when people mean him harm. Further disfigured by mange, he sets out on a pilgrimage across the kingdom in search of a sacred cave in the

Tang valley in Bumthang, where a princess with leprosy once sought a cure. After many adventures, he finds the cave and sits outside, waiting for the miraculous to happen. Dawa is not transformed into the Prince of Canines, nor does he become enlightened, shed his skin, and become a bodhisattva. He sits and waits for years until his mange passes naturally and new hair grows on his body. Then he runs home and finds, looking at his reflection in a puddle, that he has grown old.

Yana twitches and licks his lips. The Bhutanese believe that dogs are one rung below human beings on the ladder of reincarnation. Maybe the Tara-dog will have earned enough merit by running in the Tara-thon to be reborn next time around as a human.

After we have updated our blog and hung our laundry out to dry on bushes beside the river, we walk into town. Nadya and I treat everyone to dinner, not only to celebrate our arrival at the halfway point on our journey but also to give our cook the evening off. Jai and Dr. Ratna Gurung, the man in charge of the veterinary hospital, are our guests. Sunny Restaurant serves us gritty, brown Bumthang buckwheat noodles called putang, then plates of beef, vegetables, and emadatse with saag soup, a welcome change from potato curry, dal, and rice.

"Oishii!" exclaims Mr. Sangay, articulating one of the half-dozen Japanese words he remembers from his trip to Fukuoka for the World Student Games in 1995. Knowing that I had spent time in Japan, he would at times greet me at Sherubtse with the words, "Konichi-wa."

Incongruously, as we wolf the food, we see ourselves arriving once again in Jakar on the television, all with windblown hair and fatuous grins. No one can hear what the reporter is saying as the restaurant is busy, but it doesn't seem to matter. There is a roar of delight—the second of the day. This afternoon, the box of new running shoes arrived.

| Day 19: January 8, 2008; destination: Zungney (at 2615 metres), sixteen kilometres from Jakar. After a day off, we return to the

New shoes for Long Bone and Living Skeleton.

town square and sit once again on plastic chairs, but this time in the company of the dzongdag and the drangpon. Mr. Sangay knows them both. The district administrator once faced him on the football pitch, and the judge started a taekwondo club when he was a student at Sherubtse. I really don't feel like eating another breakfast or giving a speech, but observing protocol is essential. The dzongdag has just handed us an envelope of money, donated by officials working at the dzong. This brings the total we have collected on the road to about BTN 115,000. Yesterday, Nadya heard from a Sherubtse student called Dodo, leading a group of students who have volunteered to collect donations on our behalf in towns not on our route. Dodo said they had raised BTN 50,000. Donations are also starting to dribble in from Canada and England. All told, we can probably sponsor 105 kids to go to school for a year. This does not seem to me like many.

It is just as well we don't have far to run today. I feel bloated. After our usual Tara-thon breakfast of chana and dal, Nadya and I joined Jai at his home for a Nepali one of suji (suja made with ghee) and basra (cream of wheat). The livestock extension officer lived with his wife and two children in a single room with the kitchen to one side, the family bed pressed against the dinner table, and pots and coats hanging from nails in the walls. A picture of Krishna, blue-skinned and baby-faced, hung on the wall. Jai told us he was from Samste, a small town on the southern border and spoke "Munglonay, a language that has developed not from the epicentre but from the periphery." He said he enjoyed his work but wished his research would be taken seriously.

"When I was in Samste, I was searching in forest for cure for HIV patients, and I have good result, but authorities, they do not appreciate. They are not considering. They call me crackpot!"

Nadya and I have not been to Samste or spent time anywhere in the south of the kingdom, where most Nepali Bhutanese live, but we are aware that this ethnic group accounts for roughly a third of the nation. Since the Royal Government tightened its citizenship laws in the late 1980s, approximately 100,000 Lhotshampas, as they are known, have either been deported or chosen to leave Bhutan because of escalating hostilities between north and south. Jamie Zeppa was here at this time and wrote of the strained atmosphere at Sherubtse and of outbreaks of violence in the south. There is never any talk in the Bhutanese newspapers about the exiles, most of whom now live in refugee camps in eastern Nepal (their native country unwilling to take them back). It is clearly a delicate issue. On the one side is the immigrant minority, welcomed to the kingdom originally by the first Druk Gyalpo to assist with development, but subsequently called on to prove their citizenship and adhere to Buddhist ways, despite being largely Hindu. On the other is the Royal Government, wishing at a time of rapid modernization and greater internationalization to maintain cultural integrity and preserve Buddhist traditions. Hostilities within the country ceased in the early 1990s, and, judging by how well the Nepali-Bhutanese students in my classes at Sherubtse interacted with the Ngalop and Sharchop majority, wounds appear to have healed. But do the Lhotshampas who have remained in Bhutan still resent the clampdown and suffer from discrimination? And what is the fate of the refugees?[5]

Running under the arch that marks the edge of town and seeing that it is decorated with the "Four Friends," Bhutan's symbol of cooperation and kinship, I wonder whether the new democratic Bhutan will be more accepting of its Lhotshampa community. Gross National Happiness, which considers in one of its nine measurement domains "equitable living standards," would seem to require it. I am reminded, too, that the Four Friends lived at Sherubtse, captured in gay colours on a floor-to-ceiling mural outside the assembly hall, the animals forming a pyramid under the tree. Maybe Dr. Jagar was the elephant there, the professors and lecturers the monkeys on his back supporting the student hares and birds (male and female?) so they might collect the fruit of knowledge. The thought amuses me. Perhaps, for the Tara-thon, we are the birds or, more fittingly, the hares, reaching into the highest branches of the tree symbolizing Bhutanese society for donations, the elephant Tarayana supporting us from below as we do so. In due course, we will plant seeds, I suppose, so more trees may grow.

The village of Zungney is only thirty-five metres higher than Jakar, yet, after four meandering flat kilometres from town, we find ourselves tackling murderously steep switchbacks reminiscent of the Yadi Loops. Despite a day off and new shoes, our runners are sluggish, but Mr. Sangay said that many of them had stayed out late drinking after our dinner at Sunny Restaurant. Though the day is bright once again, I cannot help feeling, as we begin our fourth of six blocks of running, that something is going to go wrong. Surely, we cannot run for a month through the Himalayas in winter without being pounded by a blizzard. Temperatures have been below zero every night since Namling, and there was snow at Thrumshing-La. We must cross another three passes to reach our destination. Nadya thinks that next week will be critical. Injuries have not healed, and the cumulative stress of running up and down mountains is beginning to show. Yesterday, she topped up on painkillers and analgesic cream. She also found rehydration salts. I guess if we were Buddhists, we would be able simply to live in the present and let the future look after itself.

We crest a minor pass called Kheki-La, and, on the other side, run through a new village called Namgar. A highway is under construction here that will enable traffic from Trashigang or Thimphu to bypass Jakar. Ura to Namgar is currently sixty-one kilometres; the new road will make it thirty-six. Jakar is destined either to become a ghost town or a pleasant base for tourists who wish to visit Kurjey Lhakhang or the Burning Lake. I wonder, as we run the remaining four or five kilometres to our destination, how long it will take for Bhutan to develop a domestic air service.[6]

"This shop is for tourists, Ma'am," warns Ugyen Lhendup when we arrive at Zungney, seeing Nadya with her purse.

Bumthang district is also known for its textiles. Yathra products are made from coarse sheep or yak wool and patterned distinctively and repetitively with diamonds, stars, interlocking triangles, and rudimentary representations of lotus flowers in bold colours. At Gonpo Trashi Yathra General Tshongkhang, we see shoulder bags, scarves, kiras, shawls, jackets, table runners, rugs, and wall hangings. Nadya has her eye on a bag. I am reluctant to think about souvenirs before the Tara-thon is over, and yet, waiting outside the store for her, notice in the window a miniature wooden prayer wheel like the one Kezang has stuck to the dashboard in the bus and spins before turning the ignition. Could one reside on my bedside table in Canada, perhaps, a reminder each morning of the emptiness of material concerns? I crouch over to inspect the prayer wheel and quickly see that it is overpriced and poorly painted, the gold letters of "Om Mane Padme Hum" bleeding onto the red background.

Straightening up, I find myself looking into the face of an old Sherpa porter, or my idea of one. The eyes are heavily lidded and set far apart, the nose flat and scarred as though punched, and the skin deeply wrinkled and chapped. Stiff white bristles poke out of the chin at all angles.

Taken aback, I ask after the man's health in Sharchop: "Er, kuzu zangpo-la. Hang ten cha?"

The Sherpa looks at me puzzled and then releases a torrent of language that sounds like it is probably Dzongkha, but could be a dialect. He is a short man with one arm in a cast that extends to his knuckles. With his good hand, he reaches up and touches a bag hanging on a hook outside the store and says the word "baa" and "yap." Each time he opens his mouth, I see on the lower jaw an isolated tooth that has been whittled down so severely it resembles a rusty carpet tack. Ugyen Lhendup joins us. The man is now clearly speaking about other things.

"Gonpo says you are huge, Sar," Ugyen translates, "and that you came by air, but he goes about by walking. He said he is Khampa warrior. At age twenty, he ran down from his village in Tibet. China chased him. China is no good, he says. Bhutan is good. He has Bhutanese wife."

As Gonpo Trashi is obviously the owner of the store, maybe, rather than trying to interest me in a yak-hair bag, he was saying that the lady inside is buying one. I ask about his arm.

"He says he fell down three year ago, Sar. He was drunk, and he fell down from the corridor and broke his arm and had his nerve cut."

As Ugyen translates, Gonpo makes gestures with his good hand that seem to go with his story: fingers running downhill for his escape from China, fingers running along his sleeve as he dashes along the corridor, thumb up for drinking, thumb down about falling over. He seems to understand English but not speak it. He would need to speak some, though, to do business with passing tourists.

"How old is he, Ugyen?"

"He says he is seventy-three, Sar"

"Agi shigi yoré," says Gonpo, looking down at his feet, his garrulity suddenly exhausted.

"What did he say?"

Ugyen looks baffled. "He is speaking now Tibetan language." He asks him to repeat it in Dzongkha. "He says he is going to die soon."

Nadya comes out of the tshongkhang with her bag.

I shake Gonpo's hand. "We never know our time." It is all I can think of to say. Ugyen translates, and the Tibetan outlaw smiles.

| It is twenty-four kilometres from Zungney to Yotong-La, the third high pass on our journey. The gradient is not severe as the road tracks a river, which wanders lazily down a wide valley. Life does not seem harsh in the villages we run through. In Dongkhar, Chumey, and Gaytsa, I see houses in good shape, hens and sleeping dogs, wooden platforms piled with hay, little square chortens beside the river, a temple. We pass a vocational institute of large yellow buildings with a basketball court out front and a sign saying, "Be Somebody." We run by a store with two ejaculating pink penises painted on it. The sign over the front door says, "General cum Store."

The tail-end Charlies, Sherab and Sonam Gyalpo, are running with me today. Despite switching to new shoes (or, perhaps, because of this), they are suffering. Sherab has bandaged both of his calves and has trouble managing the uphill, and Sonam says he keeps getting cramp in his right calf. His ankle is now fine. Nadya got angry with him last night. He asked her for advice on cramp, and she told him to take the rehydration salts she had bought and use the massage cream. He did neither. She also saw him walking a part of the run yesterday. I have asked Mr. Sangay to have a word with him. Our proposal to Tarayana promises that we will "Run for the Kids" from Kanglung to Thimphu, and we seek donations from the general public on this understanding. If we walk, we undermine our pledge. I remember Nadya and me um-ing and ah-ing about Sonam Gyalpo in Kanglung. Although brimming with enthusiasm, he was the only one of the ten who did not complete the three-day running trial.

We halt for a night next to a bridge five clicks short of the saddle. For once, there is plenty of water, firewood, and space for our tents. A sign informs us, very precisely, that the bridge is seventy-three feet long and we are 318.720 kilometres from Trashigang. For some reason, our event coordinator has decided that this would be an auspicious place to celebrate Losar, even though Buddhist New Year isn't for another month. So we have our largest bonfire yet, and the cook serves extra chili peppers with dinner. There are speeches. Mr. Sangay asks me to say something to the team. Caught off guard, I tell a joke.

"Three strings want to go to the pub for a beer, but a sign says that no strings are allowed in. Two try going in anyway, but are thrown out: 'Get out!' says the barman. 'You're strings!' Seeing this, the third string ties a knot in his body and messes up his hair. When challenged by the barman ('Hey, you're a string, aren't you?'), the string calmly replies, 'No, I'm a frayed knot.'"

Thirteen puzzled faces.

"It's a play on words. You know the expression, 'I'm afraid not'?"

Thirteen puzzled faces. No whispering. Just like one of my classes on eighteenth-century poetry at Sherubtse. I giggle self-consciously.

"Well, 'frayed' means, um, come apart or unravelled," I persist, unwilling to cut my losses, "...and, and a knot, well, you know what a knot is, right?"

Nadya, catching more the spirit of the occasion, leads a Québécoise version of "Head, Shoulders, Knees, and Toes" and quickly has all ten students on their feet, tapping their heads, slapping their shoulders, and doubling over repeatedly. After the rigours of the day's run, I expect protest or, at least, for Team Leader Tharchen, perhaps, to ask for an explanation. But no. They are game—even for eleven verses, each faster than the last.

"Great...way...of stretching the body!" Nadya says, sitting down abruptly, leaving the boys hanging onto each other's waists, panting.

Mr. Sangay then asks each student to come forward and say a few words, and I am touched by their expressions of gratitude.

"Without vision of Sar and Madam, we could not do." "I am privilege to run for queen and country. I will never forget until old man!" "I love all you Tara-thoners."

More surprising is when Tharchen presents Nadya and me with a gift, which the team presumably bought in Jakar. It is a diary-sized slab of stone the shape of the kingdom, carved with fabulous beasts: a Thunder Dragon, a garuda, and a howling dog with a leonine tail. Embedded in the stone is a clock and on the back the words, "Bhutan Map Watch."

"For good memory of Bhutan," he mumbles.

Nadya and I look at each other, unsure what to say. Kadrinche seems horribly lame. And why it is happening now? Then I remember Christmas Eve in Yadi. Nadya told the lads that Santa Claus had been known to visit the Himalayas. They should hang out their running socks before going to bed. They looked at her like she was mad, but played along, pretending to be asleep when a beardless Santa crept into their dorm. The following morning, when they discovered lucky charms and candy, they were jubilant.

Mr. Sangay claps his hands, and we all get up and form a big circle around the fire. It is time for a few dances. The first one is deceptively simple: three steps in a clockwise direction, turn and face the person behind, raise both arms and one foot, turn again and repeat the other way, and then take off around the circle again. The Bhutanese sing as they dance, and the moves come as naturally as breathing. For me, as usual, it takes fierce concentration and repeated apologies as I fail to move at the right time and bump into the dancer in front of me and the dancer behind. I should be better at this by now. At Sherubtse, each semester ended with dinner around a campfire and dances. I would usually try and retreat into the shadows or pretend to be engrossed in a conversation with an Indian colleague when the call to dance came. However, this did not always work. Either Dr. Jagar or Nadya would collar me. It would normally take five minutes for two gaps to appear in the circle, one in front of me, the other behind. The final dance was called Tashi Lebay, which traditionally marks the end of a festive event. For this, you had to hook pinkies with those on either side of you and swing your arms up and down while stepping forward and back. Restrained like this, I caused less disruption and was reminded of doing the Hokey Pokey with my family as a child.

As the fire dies down, I realize that the spontaneity of tonight's event is what has made it special, a contrast to all the stress attendant in the run-up to Christmas or New Year back home: the shopping frenzy, the frantic house-cleaning before the arrival of guests, the hours spent in the kitchen. We will no longer be together when the Buddhist year officially starts, so why not celebrate now?

A freezing wind dissuades us from lingering long to celebrate our arrival at Yotong-La the following morning. Waiting for the last of the team to arrive, I take a photograph of Mr. Sangay, standing by the solitary, prayer flag–wrapped chorten marking the spot, another of six children who emerge from a labourer's hut, and a third of a red sign beside a dirt path saying in yellow letters, "Health Route taken by the Move for Health Team."

On September 25, 2002, Lyonpo Sangay Ngedup, then the minister for health and education, and six other Bhutanese set out from Trashigang, carrying tents, gas stove, and rations in backpacks weighing thirty kilograms. Their aim was to walk across the kingdom to raise money for the Bhutan Health Trust Fund and spread messages about living healthily. It took them sixteen days to reach the capital, and they managed to raise BTN 30 million (CAD 800,000), the donations coming both from within the kingdom and from abroad. As a source of inspiration, Nancy Strickland gave me the seventy-five-page diary that one member of the expedition had kept, and I have now added it to the Tara book box. Soaked by monsoon rains and bitten by leeches, suffering from blistered feet, diarrhea, and altitude sickness, the walkers clearly had a tough time. One photo shows them clawing their way up a muddy gully to reach Thrumshing-La, another of them reversing down a slippery path from Samteygang, ghos peeled to their waists. "We felt like soldiers returning from battle," the author says on the final day of the trek.

Camping on the edge of the east–west highway.

Sonam Gyalpo finally arrives at the chorten with Yana at his heels and hobbles around it twice. He is now wearing an elasticized support stocking on his right leg that he got in Jakar. Beginning somewhere inside his shorts and extending to his ankle, it resembles one worn for varicose veins.

"Good work, Sonam! All downhill from here," I yell, clapping energetically. The kids from the huts look at me and then join in. Something Lyonpo Sangay said to supporters he met along the way on his trek occurs to me. "You are our petrol" or words to that effect. "With your support and warm wishes, we can walk more."

"I must expect pain on this Tara-thon!" Sonam calls out and laughs. It is a relief to see he is in high spirits. His latest injury, he says, is a pulled muscle behind the knee.

As we descend into Trongsa dzongkhag, I think more about the
minister's walk. It is good to have this precedent, especially as it was
an unqualified success and saw all seven walkers finish. The Move
for Health may have happened five years ago, but no doubt people
remember it. I am hoping more will turn out and cheer on our lads
as we approach the bigger towns of Trongsa and Wangdi Phodrang.
Our tail-end Charlies need the encouragement. We will not raise
BTN 30 million for our cause, but, now that articles on the Tara-
thon have appeared in the national newspaper and we have been on
TV, public interest might increase.

When we pitch camp for the night seventeen kilometres from the
saddle, I ask Mr. Sangay to call the officials at Trongsa and remind
them to put up the Tara-thon banners sent by Tarayana. This did
not happen at either Mongar or Jakar.

"Winter sweat very expensive one," he replies; it is not always
easy to get people motivated.

| "We thought to serve you desi," says the district administrator of
Trongsa, a relaxed, portly man about my age, dressed in a dark gho,
an alumnus of Sherubtse, "but you runners need something more!"

As in Jakar, we have run down the town's only main street,
past general stores, restaurants, guesthouses, and barking dogs,
and settled ourselves on chairs arranged in a semicircle at the
edge of town. Over our heads is a wooden arch like the one used at
Sherubtse for the annual marathon, but this one is strung with a
Tara-thon banner. Refreshments are suja and a dish I haven't had
before: shamdey, rice mixed with meat, saag, and boiled egg. The
dzongdag tells us that the town is a beneficiary of Tarayana and that
he has already arranged for shops and businesses to donate. We
will not need to go door to door, as we usually do, asking for money.
We should simply drop by the dzong and pick up the envelope.
We are "at halfway point" on our long marathon, he insists with a
broad smile, referring no doubt to the traditional idea that Bhutan's
largest dzong is the gateway between east and west and splits the

kingdom neatly in two. In terms of road kilometres, we are well beyond that.

When Tiger, Tee, Nadya, and I visit the dzong in the afternoon, we learn that the dzongdag is busy listening to a tender for construction work and can't see us right away. So we wait in a small, stone-flagged upper courtyard, the home of a plump, white rooster with a mangled leg (perhaps there to wake the monks for morning prayer) and peer over the parapet. The drop to the floor of the Mangde valley, where the Mangde Chhu slithers noiselessly, is near vertical. The old highway zigzags down into the valley and climbs the other side. This is the first time Nadya and I have been inside the dzong. The jumble of tall-walled buildings adheres to a narrow ridge of uplifted rock with equally steep sides, challenging all would-be invaders (although lightning conductors have made the walls scalable for rhesus macaques). In the seventeenth and eighteenth centuries, the old highway passed through the main courtyard of the dzong, making it a perfect stronghold for the penlop of Trongsa to control all east–west traffic. It is little surprise that the family that would come to govern this realm would do so initially from this seat.

After waiting for half an hour, I wander off to explore. Trongsa dzong houses twenty-three temples, a giant clay statue of the Buddha of the Future, and, as I noticed on my way in, some remarkable murals. A richly coloured representation of Zangdopelri, rendered in paint, is my first stop. Guru Rinpoche, decked out in robes fit for a king, rules Buddhist paradise from his lotus-leaf throne, holding a dorji in his right hand and in his left a skull cup containing the nectar of life. His consorts, two ivory-skinned females symbolizing wisdom and knowledge, are to either side of him, and, at his feet, his eight manifestations, wrathful and benign. I imagine the manifestations springing to life and performing an elaborate dance, as at tsechu, to lure Shelging Karpo out of hiding. A second, equally vivid mural nearby is of a mandala, the quadrant nearest me a depiction of Buddhist hell. Here, scowling, pot-bellied deities with animal heads seize naked people and chop them into pieces, toss them into cauldrons of boiling water, or stretch them out on wooden racks.

Pause to spin the prayer wheel! Drawing by author.

One deity, wearing a human skin as a cloak, has ripped out a woman's heart and offers it to Guru Rinpoche. I recall last winter a monk sweeping aside a curtain and showing us similar images on the walls of his temple. "If you behave badly in this life," he assured us, wagging a finger and laughing, "this will happen to you!"

I have yet to ascertain how much of this the Bhutanese truly believe. That they accept it is beyond question. Buddhism is a part of everyday life, its rituals as habitual as eating or drinking and the principal gods as familiar as family members. The students at Sherubtse College would circumambulate the campus chorten between classes or spin the prayer wheel before taking a test almost, it seemed, without thinking. They went to the lhakhang after class to say their prayers or do prostrations at the feet of Guru Rinpoche or Sakyamuni. "We do, Sar, because we are Bhutanese," they would explain, cheerfully and cryptically. Asked about boiling cauldrons and hell, "It is to scare us, Sar," they would reply, "to make us to do good deed." But could this be your fate, do you think? Laughter. "Maybe, Sar, maybe!" It only occurred to me later that Christians back home might well respond similarly.

The daily presence and practice of a belief—one that recognizes all life as sacred and encourages meritorious behaviour—is uplifting. Many Bhutanese live hand-to-mouth, but their spiritual wealth is undeniable, and they celebrate this proudly and ubiquitously in their art. I think of the painted flowers that bloom around the windows of houses, the gilded robes of dancers at tsechu, the bold primary colours of tashi tagye–adorned curtains in front of offices at college, the floral designs on the traffic policeman's kiosk at Thimphu's busiest intersection. It occurs to me that the national flag, a yellow triangle standing for the secular authority of the monarchy over an orange one symbolizing the spiritual power of Buddhism, may gesture towards this richness. The clawed feet of the Thunder Dragon occupying the centre are all in the orange triangle, each clasping a jewel. How removed from daily life, by contrast, is religious faith for believers back home, something reserved for Sundays. Bhutanese Buddhists live their faith and seem to delight in it. I remember what Buddhist monk Mynak Tulku said in *Bhutan: Mountain Fortress of the Gods* about tsechu: those attending are blessed "through their enjoyment" of the sacred dances.

I want to poke my head in one or two of the temples, but hear Tee calling my name. Tiger, he says, has requested an audience with the Lam Neten. A bold initiative. Tee and I cross to the monastic side of the dzong and climb three flights of wooden stairs. At the top, I find my wife adjusting her kira and a less-than-tigerish-looking Tiger, biting his lip. We take off our shoes.

The abbot of Trongsa is a slender, silver-haired man, wrapped in a vermilion cape. When we enter his chamber, he is sitting on a kind of dais, softened by blue carpet, a senior monk in burgundy standing at his side. Tiger and Tee bow low, and Nadya and I follow suit. The abbot smiles and invites us with a gesture to sit on the bench at a right angle to him. Before speaking, he removes the lid keeping a cup of suja at his elbow warm, and takes a sip. I see that one of the two thangka hanging on the wall behind him is of the goddess Tara.

"First of all, he say that he is very pleased to see Sar and Madam," Tee translates, "and that Sar and Madam are doing great job for the country. He say this type of work should be done by us Bhutanese, and why we don't do this one? He says like that, Sar."

I nod, imagining monks running across the kingdom in red robes and imitation Pumas.

"Lam say, 'ma didi pay tendel didi,'" Tee says, looking to left and right helplessly. "I think I have to take help from Tiger for this one."

"We people don't know, um, where we are going...in life, Sar," Tiger supplies, recovering some of his composure, "but we meet each other without knowing. I mean, we don't plan to meet, but we meet."

"Fate brings us together," offers Nadya.

"Yes, Ma'am."

The senior monk crouches down, and Lam Neten whispers something in his ear. The monk nods several times and leaves the room.

This is the second time Nadya and I have met a Buddhist abbot in private. One weekend last summer, we hiked to Trashigang from Kanglung and visited our landlord at the dzong. As the Lam Neten spoke reasonable English, we could have a conversation. Before becoming an abbot, he told us, he meditated for nine years, three of which were spent alone in the jungle. How did he survive? Nadya wanted to know. Did he beg for food? No, he answered, he wasn't allowed to. He lived on milk and cheese brought by villagers. "They came to my cabin early in morning, knock on door, and

Dressed in a kira, Nadya receives a donation from the Lam Neten of Trongsa Dzong.

then run away!" Didn't he get lonely? No, never. It was wonderful. No one ever bothered him. In fact, he wanted to go again. His life was so noisy now, and the young monks entering the dzong were demanding. They didn't seem to have the attention spans of their seniors. They were too easily distracted. And what did he regard as most important in life? I asked before we left him in peace. Prayer. If he went to Mongar, the next town, he could die on the way. Fail to pray before going, and he could be reborn as an ant or a worm.

The senior monk returns and hands the abbot an orange envelope. We all stand up. Lam Neten presents it to Nadya with a tashi kaddah while I take a photograph. He also gives her a dozen paper wallets, covered in Sanskrit letters and tied with blue or red string. They look like bookmarks.

"He say the monks will pray for our safe reach to Thimphu," says Tee. We say kadrinche, back out of the room and put our shoes on.

The envelope contains BTN 10,000 and the one we pick up from the dzongdag on our way out another 9,100. Together, about 500 Canadian dollars. Another ten kids can go to school for a year.

When I untie one of the holy wallets, peppercorns roll out.

"Not pepper, Sar, jinlap!" exclaims Tiger, laughing. "Medicinal plant prepared by big lama. We must take before eating in the morning or when we are paining. It is like a blessing. It will cure our .sufferings. It will make us to be strong for our mission."

I return the medicine to its wallet and tuck it in my pocket, a little insurance against any rough road ahead.

175

The practice of the "middle way" in daily life is manifested in two features of East Asian communication: emotional control and avoidance of aggressive behaviors. Through self-discipline and self-restraint emotional control is considered the responsibility of cultivated persons. Showing raw emotion threatens the principle of the "middle way." In addition, the emphasis on self-discipline and self-restraint leads to the avoidance of showing aggressive behaviors in the process of interaction. Showing aggressive behaviors immediately violates the principle of compassion and harmony.

—RUEYLING CHUANG AND
 GUO-MING CHEN, "Buddhist Perspectives
 and Human Communication," 2003

12 | Bumpy Road to Wangdi

BY THE TIME the district administrator, the judge, the police superintendent, a senior monk, a representative of the business community, the Telecom manager, and the Tara-thon event co-ordinator have delivered their speeches, the Long Distance Dozen, swollen with shamdey and suja and shivering in their Tara T-shirts, are ready to make a dash into the bushes. The runners perch on the edges of their seats outside the Royal Pavilion, arms folded, legs crossed, gnawing their knuckles, and nodding seriously. Heavy rain pummelled Trongsa last night, and the temperature has dipped. Slugs of grey cloud creep up from the Mangde valley and curl over the highway.

"Yo-yaah!" yells the dzongdag finally and charges off down the hill in the direction of Thimphu, much to the delight of the doma-chewing women minding their vegetables at the market nearby.

The police superintendent takes off after him, followed soon after by the Telecom manager, three giggling market vendors in flap-ping flip-flops, a Sherubtse alumna who served us kewadatse and keptang in her hotel last night, a man in his early twenties with long, wavy hair in a red gho and white sneakers, a gang of whooping chil-dren, and four barking dogs. Having irrigated the bushes, Team Tara-thon gives chase. It is Day 24 of our ultramarathon, and we must descend seven kilometres from Trongsa to the Mangde Chhu, cross a bridge, and then climb fifteen to Dr. Jagar's home village, Tangsibi, on the far side of the valley.

A kilometre from town, we discover the dzongdag doubled over, gasping for breath, gho unravelled over his knees, a big smile on his red face. I clap him on the back and congratulate him on being the first district administrator to run a stretch of the Tara-thon. He snorts and mutters something about putting on a few pounds in recent years. Like the hotelier, he was once a student at the "Peak of Learning" and has treated us, during our two-day stay in Trongsa, like visiting royalty. He unlocked the guest house beside the Royal Pavilion, birth place of the third Druk Gyalpo, and, for the first time since leaving Kanglung, we got the chance to sleep on beds with mattresses, pillows, and duvets, read under electric lights, and wash in hot water.

Leaving our new acquaintances to walk back to town, we descend farther, and I feel a rush of affection for the team as we settle into a steady pace. They might have stampeded from town, whizzed past the winded Trongsans, and made for the river. Instead, despite the chilly conditions, they slowed down, linked arms with the women, and ruffled the little boys' hair. Long Bone and Tiger stopped at the side of the road and waved everyone onward, yelling, "You can do! You can do!" Even Sonam Gyalpo with his elasticized stocking and Sherab with his bandaged calves seemed to forget their injuries and join in the fun. How much poorer this experience would have been, I think, if Nadya and I had set out from Kanglung alone.

Half an hour after crossing the Mangde Chhu, cloud engulfs us. The road narrows, and rock towers over us once again—although here, white paint splats on the bits that jut out warn loaded trucks. After the commotion of our departure, we are suddenly and eerily alone, listening to each other's slapping soles and Yana's clicking toenails. At a bend where the old highway intersects with the new, we stop to look back at the dzong. It is hard to make out and seems, leached of colour, like an old household ornament. Another half hour of running and a mustard-coloured blotch appears. For a moment, I am flummoxed. Wangchuck Rabten, ten metres ahead of me, starts skipping from side to side, and I stub my toe on something hard. Smashed rocks and lumps of earth, hairy with plant roots, litter the road. The blotch materializes into an inert excavator with a hydraulic arm and a bucket, squatting alone on a shelf of shattered rock. Road widening. It seems like a futile task. Surely dynamite would be needed here—although I recall Dr. Jagar saying that environmental laws only permit its use in exceptional circumstances.

The gradient eases, and a brisk wind shreds the cloud. Another forty-five minutes of twists and turns, and a line of houses comes into view, some looking distinctly familiar. One belongs to Dr. Jagar's sister. Our run for the day ends in front of a new temple, its woodwork yet to be enlivened by paint. This was no more than a stack of timber when Nadya and I first visited.

The students, driver, and cook will unroll their bedding in the temple, declares Mr. Sangay. Sir Tony, Madam Nadya, and he will stay with Dr. Jagar's niece in the house next door. He introduces us to a shy woman in her late twenties called Sonam Pelden. With three rambunctious kids and a baby to look after, she must be earning good karma by welcoming guests into her house while her husband is away on business. She is also clearly a resourceful woman as she has wrapped a wire cage around the bukkari to prevent her three- and four-year-olds from burning their fingers on the metal. She occupies the eight-year-old with laundry duties, the soapy clothes going into a large enamel basin on the floor, the child climbing in barefoot and stamping the dirt out of them. As the children crawl and leapfrog over our bags, shrieking ecstatically through the evening, and the mother suckles her tearful baby, I wonder at such a life. Nadya and I have decided not to have any children. We value too much our liberty, the freedom to drop everything in Canada and travel. The irony of the cause we have chosen for our run is not lost on me as I visit the bathroom and find a washbasin full of vomit. In truth, I find kids bothersome and enervating, a strain on the nerves. I think back to the ball banging on our roof in Kanglung, kicked over our fence repeatedly by kids playing soccer. I acknowledge that Bhutan needs educated kids, but weren't we going to raise money to buy Sherubtse a garbage incinerator or kennels for the strays?

After dinner, Ngawang making enough to feed Sonam and her children as well as the team, the village gup drops by. He has heard of our project and passed the hat around Tangsibi. Nadya gives him a puzzled look. Ngapcha, he said, didn't he? Five hundred. He has given her BTN 800. The three hundred extra, he explains, is a contribution from a neighbouring village. We shake his hand and thank him, once again humbled by an act of generosity.

"Trin karpo tshe la tsug; sa nagpo gom gyi jael," he says before leaving.

Mr. Sangay translates. "'Mark the distance by the cloud. Measure the distance by footstep.' In old time, they look at cloud and mark their day for walk. Then they measure it with footstep."

| Travelling by bus or by car on a long journey, you get only a vague sense of the land. You sit in your seat and doze for much of the time or stare vacantly out the window, images flashing in front of your eyes quickly replaced by others, until everything becomes a blur. Only the sudden appearance of an oddity jolts you. Here, it might be grey langurs leaping between trees, a cow on the road, or a roadside shrine. I thought the sixty-one kilometres from the Mangde Chhu, another low point on our run, to Pele-La was an unrelenting ascent. Running, I realize that the nineteen-kilometre stretch to Chendebji, our next stop, is, in fact, undulating.

Today, I am with Sonam Wangdi, who never rushes and has so far avoided injury. He has discovered fun on the Tara-thon, he says, and gives me a summary of his new life.

"We Tara-thoners must eat dal and chana every morning for breakfast, run for hours and get exhausted, then eat potato and rice for lunch, the same every time. Then we do painful blue-legging in river because Sar says it is good for us. After dinner—that is same one as lunch—we hang around camp after 7 p.m. with nothing to do. Monotonous and fun."

I ask him if he has read any of the books from the box. Yes, Daphne du Maurier's *The Birds*, he assures me.

"But it doesn't make any sense, Sar. Why do the birds attack the people?"

It seems bizarre to me, too, I tell him, imagining laughing-thrushes swooping down from the trees and giggling insanely while pecking our ears.

We pass through tiny villages, and Sonam translates their names: Sakhachew means "top of hard land," Banglapokto "dominant hill-top pass," and Serphuchen "golden place." Streams erupt from the verge and splatter down on the road, gather themselves, then gurgle under it. In a car, I probably wouldn't have paid much heed to dull cracking sounds coming from under the wheels. Running, I see that the villagers have laid bamboo canes out over the road. Flattened by passing cars, Sonam informs me, these will then be woven into fences or mats. I am curious how long the villagers must wait for the bamboo to be crushed. Only two vehicles have passed us this morning.

As we coast along, I reflect on the house call Nadya and I made after breakfast. Dr. Jagar's sister wasn't at home, just her disabled husband Kezang and their daughter Jangchub. We hadn't seen the family since the puja last year and wished to bid them farewell. Mr. Sangay decided to tag along.

"Yalama!" exclaimed Kezang, spotting Mr. Sangay. "Am I dreaming?"

The two hadn't met since the 1970s when they served together in the Royal Body Guard. It was a happy and a sad reunion. After leaving the army, Kezang had become a high-school teacher, he told us, and then a headmaster. But something was wrong. He had increasing trouble getting out of bed in the mornings and found he was losing control of parts of his body. After a year of stiffening up and stumbling around with a cane, he was diagnosed with muscular dystrophy and had to resign. He got compensation for lost earnings from the government at first, but that dried up, and he had to look to his son-in-law for support. Paralyzed now from the neck down, but alert mentally, Kezang was fully able to reflect on his lamentable situation.

"Look at me, stuck here in this corner. What an awful life! Can't get a proper night's sleep, relying on my family to feed and dress me, unable to do anything for them in return. Horrible!"

Mr. Sangay seemed close to tears and stuffed a five-hundred-ngultrum note in his old friend's gho. Just one organization assists people with disabilities in Bhutan and this only gives vocational training to youngsters so they can enter the workforce. It is up to the family and the community to look after those with physical or mental disabilities, belief in karma helping the Bhutanese to do so with compassion. We spent half an hour drinking tea with Kezang, Jangchub sitting on her knees at his side, tipping the liquid into his mouth and wiping his chin. From time to time, at his bidding, she seized him under the armpits, hoisted him off the floor, and unwound his wasted legs.

"We are so lucky," I muttered to Mr. Sangay as we walked down the dirt path back to the road. It was the only thing I could think of to say.

At Chendebji, Mr. Sangay runs into another one-time army buddy and, fortunately, this is a happier encounter for him. Jamba is a cheery, wrinkle-eyed seventy-year-old who served in the guard for the third and fourth kings. His job now is to look after one of the three most sacred Nepali-style chortens in the kingdom. Gomchen Drub Zhidhe, a renowned drupthop, or master meditator, vanquished here two demonesses in the habit of snatching travellers from the road and devouring them, he tells us. A great Buddhist lama then built a twenty-metre-high chorten to mark the spot, taking the model from Bepo in Nepal. A Nepali chorten differs from a Bhutanese one in that it is dome-shaped rather than square and has a stepped spire decorated with a pair of eyes. Jamba gives us permission to sleep in the Royal Pavilion facing the chorten, which, with its missing fourth wall, is more like a stage in a theatre. The pinched, gold-and-black eyes of the Buddha will watch over us while we sleep.

Before dinner, I go blue-legging with Tharchen. As our team leader is still inclined to run at the back of the pack, I ask him how the tail-end Charlies are doing. Are they going to make it to Thimphu? Should they take a day or two off and ride in the bus? What about Sonam Gyalpo with his pulled muscle? With two mountain passes still to cross, Nadya and I think that the cumulative strains of three and a half weeks of running may get the better of our weakest runners.

Things are fine at the moment, Tharchen assures me, in his thoughtful, deliberate manner. "They can bear. Better if Sar leave

Tail-end Charlies: Sonam Gyalpo, Tiger, and Nadya.

them be right now as they are worry to be sent home. We take turn to run with Sonam. When he suffer, we say, 'Khemi, atsi chira in, betshu!' Just a few more minute, you can do!"

I nod. While it would be wonderful for the entire team to run all the way to the capital, it would be irresponsible of Nadya, Mr. Sangay, and me to let our students soldier on in pain until they drop and then have to spend three months after the Tara-thon recuperating. Sherubtse College has placed ten students in our charge. Singye Namgyel would be less than impressed if we returned damaged goods. I resolve to keep an eye on our slowest runners in the new day. The severest section of the climb to Pele-La begins, no doubt, around the next corner.

Judging by the lively chatter around camp, team morale remains high. Mr. Sangay wanders off, counting his prayer beads, and Nadya and I sit with the students, she encouraging those with "paining" legs to draw close to the fire and knead their muscles. "Look, like this," she demonstrates once again, squeezing analgesic cream into the palm of her hand and working it into her own left thigh. She has become the Tara nurse, the boys coming to her for help with all manner of complaints ("Not just knee and foot problems," she tells me, "but headaches, altitude sickness, stomach aches, even mouth ulcers"). She hands out ibuprofen for headaches and tells them to stop sneaking extra chili peppers into their meals. Conversation around the fire is generally in Dzongkha, but this evening, out of deference to us, or, perhaps, because we have become more intimate after twenty-five days on the road together, it is in English.

"How much training did you really do for this event?" Nadya asks, shaking her head and clucking as those massaging their legs whimper and moan.

"I ran ten kilometres in the morning and ten again in the evenings." Tee is the first to answer. "Then, after a few weeks, I increase morning run to twenty kilometre."

"I did some training runs in the mornings," offers Sonam Wangdi quietly, "and I took eggs and chickpea and milk every evening."

"I didn't do *any* training for this Tara-thon!" Tiger says, rocking forward and back and laughing.

I rub my eyes. Nadya and I should have done more in Kanglung to whip our team into shape. After the three-day trial in September, some of the selected showed up for our pre-dawn training runs, but most did not. We might have established a training routine before classes ended and the students went home to revise for their exams and insisted they stick to it.

"But," adds Tiger, serious now, "when I was young boy, I run ten kilometres every day to school and back." Like Haile Gebrselassie, the boy who became a running legend because he didn't want to be late for school.

Tharchen admits to loathing running at school but says he happily got in the habit of doing two hours a day to train for the Tara-thon. Ugyen Lhendup recollects how he used to chase after his father's cows when he was a boy and so, by default, became a runner. He also didn't like running much at school. He recalls how he helped a friend in his class to finish a race.

"...he was twentieth in line at halfway and completely exhausted, so I switch between pushing him and pulling him. With my help, he finish in fifth position."

I imagine him dragging his pal along by the waistband of his shorts. Nadya, noticing how Ugyen Lhendup likes to zip away ahead of the pack each morning, has thought of a nickname for him: "Road Runner." He had never heard of the bird or the cartoon but seems to like this better than "Living Skeleton." Tharchen also has a nickname now. He is "Coco," meaning egg, the team has decided. Our team leader is the only one to have put on weight since leaving Kanglung.

As dusk darkens the mountains and the stars freckle the sky, conversation flicks from Bollywood movies to life on other planets to our arrival in Thimphu to wildlife programs on television. Wangchuck Rabten asks us about our travels, and Nadya describes the visit we made in 1997 to Emeishan, one of China's most sacred mountains.

"We had to climb three thousand steps to reach the summit, and our thighs hurt a lot on the second and third days, but we made it to the top. We stayed in temples on the way, washed in streams, and had tea with the monks. Oh, and on the first day, a monkey tried to steal Tony's lunch."

"That's right, a hairy baboon with a pink bottom, an ugly brute," I say, picking up the story. "He was on the stairs above, snarling, so I took off my daypack and held it in front of me for protection. But the baboon grabbed it, and, well, we had a tug-of-war! I carried a big stick with me after that."

Laughter. The students appreciate this anecdote far more than the joke I told at camp three nights ago.

"China is more development country, isn't it, Ma'am?" Sherab asks. Nadya has got to know Sherab better than me as he continues to have trouble with his calves and heels and is on her daily leg-massage detail.

"We were there when China was modernizing," she replies, after thinking for a bit. "There was a lot of construction and tall cranes and dust. The air was very dirty. Some parts of China, the big cities, were changing fast, but life in the countryside was still primitive. I think China still has a long way to go to raise the living standards of the villagers."

"It is the same like in India," Dendup says.

"What do you think about the way Bhutan is changing now His Majesty is stepping down?" I ask. "Are you worried about the future?"

"We are worry that there will be strikes, revolts, corruptions, and demonstrations, like we can see on television in India," Ugyen Lhendup offers, after a short silence.

"I felt sorry to hear His Majesty is stepping down," says Wangchuck Rabten. "We were happy and enjoy peace and prosperity under his reign."

"If His Majesty decide that it is time for Bhutan to become democracy, then it is time," Tharchen says philosophically. "Gross National Happiness is the guiding principle for our development. It is like while we fly higher, yet we are mindful keeping our shadow grounded."

In the twenty-two months Nadya and I have been in Bhutan, I have not once heard criticism of the king. "Do you think His Majesty is right to pass the crown to his son?" "Do you think the Bhutanese should go to the polls and elect their own government?" we asked our Bhutanese colleagues at Sherubtse. "We were all very surprise when His Majesty announce he is stepping down," Ugyen Dendup admitted, "but he know what is best for us." "We repose faith in fourth king and fifth king," Mr. Sangay said levelly. "The farmer in country don't know what to do. When they vote, they just choose favourite colour!" remarked Tshering Wangdi. Dr. Jagar said he found the fourth king's abdication hard to accept but thought his son mature enough to take over. "He will be on the throne at the prime of life and able to display his leadership at this time of starting a new era."

| Ten kilometres west of Chendebji, the highway dips to a bridge crossing the Chendebji Chhu and a cluster of roadside shops and restaurants called Chazam. Buses from Thimphu or from Jakar like to stop here, the drivers giving their passengers twenty minutes to gulp down noodles and suja or purchase dried river weed, for which the spot is known. We also pause on our day's run before attacking a seventeen-kilometre climb to Pele-La on the far bank. Noticing that the Tara biscuit box is practically empty, I buy every packet the shops have, and Nadya searches for river weed so Ngawang can make soup at the pass. The word is it has snowed up there.

We shuffle off in a tight pack, no one wishing to forge ahead, and I enjoy the slow pace and sense of camaraderie, the twelve of us breathing roughly in time, our feet pattering on the asphalt in near-unison. I look to my left and right to see if the students are following the advice I gave in Trongsa: when running uphill, keep your eyes on the road about six metres ahead; do not look at the horizon or you will never get there. Sonam Wangdi, I see, is on the shoulder of Tharchen, Wangchuck Rabten beside Tee. Dendup shadows the two Ugyens. Their eyes are less on the road than on their partners. They appear to be tuning into each other's movements, harmonizing. I haven't mentioned this as a technique, and, as far as I know, neither has Nadya. I think of drafting during a cycle race, letting the leader cut the air and do the hard work, then switching places.

We pass a solitary general store to our left with an ejaculating phallus painted in bright colours on the front. Arriving from the west on his peregrinations in the fifteenth century, the Divine Madman stopped to ask an old man what villages lay in the valley east of Pele-La. "First Rukhubji, then Chendibji, and then Tangsbji," answered the man. As every village appeared to be home to a bji or demon, the tantric master turned around and went back the way he had come. Around another bend, and to our right we pass a shallow cave adorned with a Buddha and some text in English. I have time to read the first three lines: "May all sentient beings be free from wanting to be praised, not wanting to be criticised, wanting to be happy, not wanting to be unhappy, wanting to gain..." In *Travellers and Magicians*, unable to find an onward ride to Thimphu, Dondup spends a night here, his determination to escape Bhutan beginning to waver, given that a fellow hitchhiker happens to be an attractive young woman from his home village.

The road creeps upwards, twisting torturously, and the team strings out, each pair of runners finding their own pace. At 6k from Chazam, I stop to catch my breath. Above, a line of conifers, crusted with snow and ice, gleams in the afternoon sun, and eight vultures draw figure eights over the pass. Below is Rukhubji, a dozen houses stuck to the mountainside with silver tin roofs, a yellow roof on the temple, a red one on the school. In the far distance, the chorten at Chendebji sticks up like a cat's tooth. On the switchbacks, Dendup is coming my way, Nadya following just behind, and Wangchuck Rabten and Tee are heading the opposite way on the loop below. I smile, remembering Dr. Jagar's words: "Where in the world you go in opposite directions to reach same place?" Sonam Gyalpo and Sherab bring up the rear several loops lower, trundling along behind Tiger, Tharchen, and Yana. I fill my lungs and cup my hands around my mouth.

"Go, go, you Tara-thoners!"

The night stop is at Longte, a clearing just below the snowline, six kilometres from Rukhubji, five from Pele-La. Gyalpo arrives last on wobbly legs, drains a cup of suja and then, as Tiger did at Kori-La, promptly flakes out. Ugyen Lhendup takes the cook's patang, hacks off some live rhododendron branches, and tosses them on the camp fire, a puja to petition the gods of the pass not to send snow. A band of swarthy cow herders with sculpted calves and firewood strapped to their backs joins us in the early evening, and we serve them tea— a chance visit, it would seem, until Mr. Sangay informs me that the gup of Rukhubji bade them bring us the wood. Maybe the Divine Madman would have enjoyed a hospitable welcome after all.

| No vultures swoop down and carry off our stragglers on our ascent through grassy barrens and dwarf bamboo to Pele-La the next day. Ten smiling students gather for a photograph by the chorten

marking the saddle while a sangphu Mr. Sangay has lit spews forth smoke. Luck remains with us. There are no signs of fresh snow on the ground, after all, and the sky remains clear. Peering through a gap in the moss-draped hemlocks, I see a row of shark's teeth to the west, Jumolhari being the most incisor-like, and a pleated land below. The forest from this perspective resembles lichen. There is no sign of the lateral road, but, about fifty kilometres away as the crow flies, tucked away in one of the folds, is the capital city. If everything goes according to plan, we will arrive there in nine days.

Team Tara-thon strings out once again, and I position myself somewhere between the hares and tortoises. Running alone, I try to recover the rhythm I had coming down from Thrumshing-La, transcend my body, and let my thoughts drift, making the seventeen kilometres to Nobding Lower Secondary School, our destination for the day, sail by unnoticed. The highway prevents this, though; I keep stumbling. The west side of the pass would appear to see worse weather than the east. The asphalt is rutted, pot-holed, and, in some places, absent. We run over bare sections of gravel and stones, and sharp rocks pressing through the thin soles of my Fastwitches make me grimace. When I reach the bus at 6k, I hop aboard and switch to my sturdier shoes. The temperature steadily rises as we descend, and hemlock, yew, cypress, and juniper give way to oak, maple, birch, and alder.

"Up here now! Welcome. This my restaurant."

A young man in a blue-and-red checked gho is suddenly at the side of the highway, waving his arms. He wants me to divert up a side road to a building decorated with phalluses. I slow down, opening my mouth to protest, say kadrinche, and explain that we are bound for Nobding, but then notice the name of the village written on a sign to one side of the building and four Tara-hares drinking tea. Three minutes later, I am with them, holding a china cup in one hand and a plate of desi in the other. Our host is Kinley, the village chief. The refreshments, he says, are courtesy of the Wangdi DEO, part of an official welcome to the dzongkhag. If this is the official reception, then where is Mr. Sangay? The bus, I know, is ahead of us.

Forty-five minutes later, when everyone has arrived, we jog down into the village and meet it on its way up.

"What happen? We wait at the school for you," splutters the event coordinator from the passenger seat, his arms folded over his chest. He orders Kezang to turn around.

We follow the bus for about half a kilometre until it pulls in through a gate in a dismantled perimeter wall. Nobding Lower Secondary is clearly undergoing repairs, although no workmen are visible. Smashed concrete slabs and piles of masonry rubble sit on a ringless basketball court in front of the entrance. There are deep pits in the ground and exposed water pipes. The dormitory resembles the one at Mongar High School. Nadya asks Mr. Sangay if the kitchen functions and whether there is running water.

"Just you...I will arrange all," he replies. "Mr. Tony, your living quarter is this way."

He leads us to an office with a sheet of blue canvas for a ceiling. The furniture inside is in disarray and covered in dust. We can unroll our sleeping mats on the floor, he suggests, between the filing cabinet and the desk.

"Tonight, Mr. Sangay, we've been invited by the gup to eat at the restaurant up the road," I say, relaying an invitation from Kinley. He nods silently and marches off.

An hour later, Kezang knocks on the door. Mr. Sangay has got angry with him, he says, about taking the team up to the restaurant this evening by bus.

"He say it waste of petrol, Sar."

I sigh. "The students ran twenty-two kilometres today, and they have twenty-six to do tomorrow," I reply. "Let's drive up."

| "I could *kill* that Mr. Sangay!" Nadya hisses, bursting in through the door the following day, face red, tears streaming down her cheeks.

I stop packing my bag and look at her, stunned.

"Why? What happened? What did he say to you?"

She opens her mouth to answer, then changes her mind and shakes her head.

"I, I…Just give me five minutes, okay?"

She closes her eyes and sighs, then reaches down and scoops her sleeping bag off the floor and stuffs it viciously into its compression sack, pulling hard on the straps. She pauses for a moment to mutter something obscene in French, then starts rolling up her sleeping mat, but stops again and tosses it aside. She stands up and looks about the room, sees the savaged chip packet on the desk, the cause of last night's disturbance, walks over and smacks it to the floor. Nibbled potato chips fly in all directions. I should have known not to leave food out. Once the rats had ripped open the packet in the early hours of the morning and scattered the contents, there was no point in getting up. The school has no electricity, and, in darkness, we would never have been able to clear up the mess. "If the food is on the desk," my wife reasoned from her sleeping bag, "that probably means they won't be chewing on our faces." This observation made me think of Winston Smith's torture in *1984*.

I thought we had made our peace with the event coordinator last night. Though he refused to ride with us in the bus to the restaurant, he clearly enjoyed the company of the gup and the fine dinner of red rice, potato curry, and beef. "The RBG doesn't mind going on foot, hey, Mr. Sangay?" I said at the end of the evening with a chuckle. He rode back to the school with us in the bus.

Nadya tells me about the conversation she had with him this morning. One of the students had recommended a suitable place to camp near Khelakha, another village on the road to Wangdi Phodrang, so she mentioned this to Mr. Sangay.

"'Student should come to me,'" he said. "'If ten people give opinion, then nothing arrange.'" Nadya manages a passable impersonation of the coach, with the same gravelly, aphoristic delivery. "I said to him, I said, 'Can't we at least discuss it?' No. He would arrange our night stops, he replied. That was that. I should concern myself with my own affairs. Well, I just lost it. I said, 'Why can't you communicate with me?'"

I pick up the chip packet and scrunch it up into a ball.

"Let's go and talk to him."

Day 28 of the Tara-thon is overcast and surprisingly muggy, given that we were above the snowline yesterday. The students are on the basketball court, packing their bags and loading the billycans onto the roof of the bus. The fifteen stray dogs that hung around at breakfast time are sitting watching them, noses twitching. Judging by the way they competed for scraps earlier, they are famished now the school mess is closed for winter recess.

"Mr. Sangay, may I have a word with you?" I steer him to one side. "Nadya is pretty upset. Did you have an argument with..."

"I am just old man," he yells. "No one listen to me!"

"Listen, we need to..." My own temper flares, but I bite my lip, remembering what happened in Mongar. I indicate that we should move farther off. "Look, we are all under a lot of stress at present, but we have a job to do here, and we need to do it together." I look over my shoulder at the students. They are pretending not to notice. "Could you apologize to Nadya, please?"

Mr. Sangay pouts and folds his arms. I can tell without looking at the team that all activity has come to a standstill.

"Gather round for a minute, would you?" I say, walking over to the bus.

Looking around the circle of faces, I realize that we are at a critical point in our run. Our destination appears to be within striking distance, yet we still have over a hundred kilometres left and one tall pass to conquer. I have no idea what to say beyond obvious things to boost morale, so I dig into my past and tell a story about crossing the Indian Ocean on a sailing yacht.

"...in the sixth month of our seven at sea, quarrels broke out among the crew. We were all tired and starting to get on each other's nerves. But we had a job to do. We had to deliver the boat to its owner in Europe. He was counting on us to complete our voyage, you see."

Mr. Sangay follows with a speech on sports psychology. Nadya decides that enough has been said for one morning and goes in search of Yana.

The day's run is long, the tortoises taking forever to get down the mountain. At the end of the final leg, the bus stopping, for some reason, after ten kilometres rather than the usual six, the team has to wait an hour and a quarter for Sonam Gyalpo to catch up. Concerned, Nadya suggests Kezang backtrack and find him. I put this to Mr. Sangay, who reluctantly agrees. When Sonam finally appears, bus trundling along at walking pace behind him, I see I was mistaken. Our slowest runner was not alone. One taller-than-average hare had hung back to run with him: Long Bone, with water bottle on a strap slung over his shoulder.

Our camp for the night is not at the village of Khelakha but beside a steel bridge built by the Japanese to carry the lateral road over the Dang Chhu. Nadya has the lads go blue-legging ("Come on, no excuses! There's no ice in the water here!"). Despite the tensions of the morning and the hours of running, they seem to be in good spirits, she reports back, now that we are just thirteen kilometres from Wangdi Phodrang. On our day off there, she would like half the team to collect donations around town while the other half does the same in Punakha, home to one of the kingdom's largest dzongs. The second group will need Kezang to take them as Punakha is twenty-one kilometres from Wangdi. I try to patch things up with Mr. Sangay as he should really approve of such an initiative.

"Well, Mr. Tony, what to do?" he says morosely. "Madam, she have her own mind."

| Wangdi seems to me less like a town than a refuelling depot. Buses, Tata trucks, and yellow taxi cabs hover around two battered Bharat Petroleum pumps that look like one-armed robots holding guns to their heads. More taxis circle the petrol station, revving their engines and waiting for a turn. Like Jakar and Trongsa, Wangdi Phodrang is a junctural town: go north for Punakha, the former capital; go north a bit and then west to get to Thimphu; head south for Sarpang and the Indian border; head east for Mongar and Trashigang. The name means "the palace where the four directions are gathered." Legend has it that, in the seventeenth century, Yeshe Goenpo, the guardian spirit of Bhutan, told the Shabdrung to go to a rocky spur over-

looking two rivers and build a fortress where he saw ravens fly off in four directions.

Apart from the dzong, there are, apparently, some 230 businesses crammed onto this narrow promontory overlooking the meeting point of the Dang Chhu and Puna Tsang Chhu. There have been efforts to relocate the town to a fifteen-hectare area of flatter ground to the side, where street lights, a two-lane road, and parking spaces have been constructed in readiness. Unfortunately, only 138 plots of land are available there. Allocating these has caused dispute and complaints to the Ministry of Works and Human Settlement, and Bajothang, as the new town is called, has been waiting for occupancy since October 2005. With its rectangles of wild flowers, it resembles an elaborate ornamental garden.

Shabby stores line the oil-streaked dirt road, each with a tin roof weighed down by stones and an overflowing garbage pail out front. A sign on one store says, "Tharpa Lhamo's Gift Shop and Bar"; another reads, "Deki General Cum Bar Shop." As the vehicles shunt this way and that, dust and fumes mingle, and I start coughing. With the heat, it feels like being back in India. Once again, we have switched climates. Three days ago, we were listening to the creak of ice-crusty pines and blowing on our fingers; now, sun-baked cacti border the road and sweat darkens our armpits. Blissfully, we did not have to jog around the town twice with the dzongdag and his administrative assistant when we arrived yesterday, waving at everyone and smiling, like in Mongar. Mr. Sangay stopped us at Wangdi Middle Secondary on the edge of town, where the dzongdag and his staff were waiting.

Five Tara-thoners, dressed in their ghos but smelling of sweat, disperse to collect donations. I head back to the school to see if I can do laundry but find, once again, that there is no water. The assistant DEO said yesterday that the pipes were being repaired but assured us the water would be back "after some time." Twenty-four hours have passed. I consider hiking down to one of the rivers to do the chore but decide instead to explore the school. Like others we have stayed at, there are philosophical messages on wooden signs around the grounds and on posters taped to the walls indoors ("A man educated yesterday stops learning today will be uneducated tomorrow," "He who learns and makes no use of his learning is a beast of burden with a load of books"), and, as at Sherubtse, labels on the trees: Prunus persica (peach), Magnifira indica (mango), and Punica granatum (pomegranate). In one of the classrooms, I come across some dog-eared textbooks, tossed on the floor. On the front of one, there is a picture of a family outside their house, the father hanging washing out on the line, the mother sitting under a tree making a basket, their kids playing on the grass. "Gross National Happiness" is written above the picture, "Small is Beautiful" below it. I open the book:

> *Every society has evolved its own ways of preparing its younger*
> *members for adulthood primarily through an education process,*
> *now generally known as family life education. Traditionally,*
> *most elements of family life education have been informal,*
> *taking place in the home...*

When I go back outside, I see Mr. Sangay snoozing in a plastic chair in the shade, head slumped on his chest, prayer beads dangling from his hand. I haven't seen him like this before. Maybe the heat got to him. Maybe he is feeling his age. It can't be easy, retiring last month from Sherubtse after nearly two decades of service. I fear that Nadya and I have estranged this man, have failed to give him the sort of respect he clearly commands among his countrymen. A story he told me one afternoon at Sherubtse comes to mind. In 1994 he went to Hungary to take a soccer-coaching course and met a young Israeli doing the same.

"Every morning when he see me, he say, 'Hey, Bhutan!' in loud voice. Every morning, same: 'Hey, Bhutan!' Like that. After few time, I say to him, 'How old do you think I am?' and he say nothing. He look at his feet. After that, he say, 'Good morning, Mr. Sangay, how are you today?'"

Before we set out on our run, I had assumed that Team Tara-thon would be one big happy family, united in its mission, Mr. Sangay acting as a father figure, fixing problems and giving practical advice, drawing on his army training and his years as a sports coach. We are indebted to him for arranging our night stops and hooking us up with dignitaries, but he has not been involved with the students as much as I expected. He must have plenty to say on keeping a pair of legs in good running order. Perhaps he feels that Nadya has ousted him in that duty. I guess event coordinator and project leaders should have sat down together in Kanglung and discussed our respective roles. I realize, too, that I have spent too much time in my own head to pay heed to any signs of discord. And I really shouldn't have barked at him in front of the students in Mongar. Like in Japan, shaming an elder in public here is unforgivable.

A dark side of my self emerges when I turn on the faucet in the school yard for the eighth time of the day and see water finally dribble out. Since breakfast, half a dozen boys have been hanging about the school, yelling "Hi!" and "What's your name?" incessantly, performing break-dancing moves around our legs, and snatching things from our hands. They are nine or ten years old—too young for middle secondary—and, filthy and shoeless, look like the kind of children we are running for. The team has been tolerant. "They are very naughty boys," Tharchen, the model of good behaviour, conceded when the urchins were climbing on his back and trying to steal his plate at lunchtime. As I fill my bucket with soapy water and put the clothes in, a boy with snot running down his face thrusts his hands in. I swat him away, but he is undeterred. In again go his hands. I seize him this time by the shirtfront, lift him off the ground, and toss him across the yard. He lands hard on his behind and falls backwards, but is almost instantly on his feet again. His friends stop dashing about. The boy doesn't cry, but there is shock in his face.

"Don't. Do. That," I say, wagging my finger.

He walks off, rubbing his bum, trailed by his gang, and I wonder again about our chosen cause. While it seems right to send town kids to school so that, in due course, they can take over their parents' businesses and run them efficiently, is it such a good idea to educate village children? I think of the little boy with the cleft lip selling mandarins at the roadside near Lingmithang. Maybe he shouldn't walk five hours to attend elementary school in Mongar. His parents own an orchard and probably rely on him to sell their crop to passers-by. If he learns to add and subtract, read and write, his family will lose him. He will go to Thimphu, buy fancy shoes, a TV, a car. Educating village children will also mean more derelict paddy fields. I remember Dr. Jagar pointing these out in Tangsibi. Literate teenagers don't want to do back-breaking work in the fields. Maybe what we are doing helps erode traditional ways and encourages migration to the towns. If kids go to school and learn their ABCs, will it be the old men who round up the yaks from the mountainsides?

And what of this charity marathon, this piece of transported Western culture we have imposed on the Bhutanese? Isn't it ludicrously out of context? The perception in the West is that the runner should be lauded for giving up his or her time and embracing hardship on behalf of the sick or less fortunate. Such willingness to suffer would appear to prove that the cause is just, the champion of it a worthy hero, and so people donate. But, for most Bhutanese, hardship is a daily reality. Far from seeing noble suffering, they may look on a supported run across the kingdom as a peculiar form of indulgence, a kind of holiday: instead of working, we have the time and money to run. While it is true that Lyonpo Sangay Ngedup on his Move for Health demonstrated that a nation can get behind such a venture, the Bhutanese would probably have recognized how tough it was for a government minister with a pack on his shoulders to walk across the country. Isn't what we are doing more of a lark, a stunt?

Wringing my clothes out, I sense that I am no longer alone. Expecting to see a Tara-thoner back from collecting donations, I turn and find the urchin looking up at me. I shouldn't have lost my temper. He holds out his hand. In it is a cracked, white brick with rounded edges.

"Soap for Sar."

| In the evening, Nadya and the other half of the team return from Punakha with BTN 10,000 from the dzongkhag administration and BTN 15,000 from the monk body. This goes with nearly BTN 50,000 received from the dzong, army, banks, post office, and police in Wangdi. Another thirty-seven village kids get to go to school.

More than the run, it was to do with the
climate and the mental preparations...
To adapt with the cleanliness, my own
cleanliness, I had to wash in the ice-cold
waters. Blue my legs, blue my nose! And
Sar Tony has been always saying to me,
"The thing that doesn't kill you, but it's hard
to bear, makes you stronger," so I believe in
that strength. I have come a long way in
adapting to all the coldness, and now I am
stronger compared to what I was thirty-five
days ago.

—UGYEN LHENDUP,
BBS interview, January 22, 2008

13 | Tea with Her Majesty

OUR SECOND DAY on the lateral road from Wangdi, with its sheltering oaks and cascading ferns, its rattly bridges and phallus-adorned bar-cum-restaurants, would be a joy if it weren't for the traffic. Taxi-vans and tourist Land Rovers sweep by us, but more obnoxious are the Tata or Eicher dumper trucks, grinding their way laboriously up to Dochu-La. These are hauling sand from the Puna Tsang Chhu to Thimphu, where a frenzy of building is taking place. The newspaper reported last year that there were 192 separate construction sites. Male Earth Rat Year will see the Bhutanese not only go to the polls for the first time and elect a government but also celebrate a hundred years of monarchy and crown their fifth king. Changlimithang Stadium alone, where most of the festivities will take place, apparently requires two thousand truckloads of sand for its makeover.

The trucks overtake us in threes or fours, spilling sand on the road and fouling the air with their exhaust fumes, making us cough and spit. Their racket causes spotted forktails feeding next to the streams to flee. The leaves on the trees nearest the road have turned black. I begin to dread the sound of a straining engine, echoing up from the valley. When the trucks are on the switchback below mine, I slow to barely a jog, pull my baseball cap down over my eyes, and practise breathing shallowly. As they pass, I run as close as possible to the edge of the road and either focus on the play of light and shadow on the asphalt ahead or look over my shoulder for glimpses of the Puna Tsang Chhu and its beaches.

"Ahhh! You...piece...of frigging..." Suddenly, I am in the bushes, snatching at plants, tripping over rocks. "What the hell...?"

I look up and get a glimpse of a grinning brown head, a red bandana, a hand holding a cigarette, then a blur of metal stanchions, sandy planks, and spinning rear wheels. Smoke engulfs me, and I hold my breath. Caught off guard at a bend in the road. I turn around and stare stupidly as the truck clatters down the mountain, speed unchecked, tailgate clapping, wheels chucking up dust. Did the driver have the engine switched off? Then another truck comes, and another: Eicher, Tata, Eicher, Tata, returning from the capital to load up with more sand. The only thing slowing them down is the loaded trucks coming up from the river. I hope the other runners are watching out. There is no escaping this. Only one road goes to the capital, and we can't simply take the day off. We need to do twenty kilometres today to remain on schedule. It is January 21. We have to be in Thimphu on January 24 to meet Her Majesty the Queen.

"Hang in there, lads! You're doing fine."

Forced off the road a second time when two trucks coming from opposite directions block the way, I turn and see that Sonam Wangdi, Tee, and Dendup are not far behind. Like me, they have slowed to a crawl, their arms barely swinging. I really couldn't blame any of the team for walking today. I expect to see tension on their faces as they pass by me. Instead, I see resignation. Laughingthrushes, cows, stray dogs, blizzards, trucks: let them come, say their expressions. I recall Dr. Shukla's cryptic remark when we were in the taxi in northern India: "Anything can come if you can expect." Then I remember that, as a twenty-year-old, I used to run alongside the busy A5 in England for miles, oblivious to the four lanes of traffic roaring by. The three runners pad past me, each nodding once and mouthing "Sar."

There are no cries of "Suja! Suja!" from the team when we reach Menchhunang, our roadside camp for the night. Everyone is tired and thirsty. At breakfast this morning, the cook forgot to boil water to refill our jerry cans. I shook one of the empties at Mr. Sangay when the bus halted at 6k in the hope that he would drive ahead and stock up at the next village. He nodded, acknowledging the problem, but, on our arrival at Thinleygang, had done nothing about it. I found him standing outside a shop-cum-bar with bottled water in the window, engaged in a lively conversation with the owner. Gravel-mouthed from breathing motor exhaust and dust, I snatched the kitty out of the glove compartment on the bus and promptly bought ten bottles of mineral water from the shopkeeper's wife. Fortunately, Menchhunang, which is just a grassy lay-by with a chorten below the highway and a truckers' canteen above it, has a water source.

Having put up our tent and helped with chores, I sit down behind the chorten and try to gather my thoughts. I think about our stay last night at the newly erected Natural Resources Training Institute in Lobesa. Karma Lhendup, a former colleague of ours at Sherubtse but now a researcher at the institute, kindly unlocked the dormitories for us. Nadya and I suddenly found ourselves in the company of Western pop idols: a snarling, muscular African-American man with heavily tattooed arms called 50 Cent; five boyish faces bathed in a golden light labelled "West Life"; a perfectly barbered Ronan Keating. I felt like ripping the posters from the walls or else sticking over them pictures of the red-necked cranes we beheld at Phobjika last winter, yaks with handlebar horns and bells on their necks, teenage monks in burgundy gowns playing soccer. I adjust my position, feeling the rough stones of the chorten pressing into my back. Has Druk Yul changed us in any lasting ways, or will we quickly revert to our old ways once back in Canada? A familiar cry comes from one of the trees, a monotonous *piao, piao, piao* that I used to loathe when sitting in my office at Sherubtse, trying to mark essays. I search the branches for a parrotlike bird with a yellowy-green body, an outsized ebony head, and a bright yellow beak. After Bhutan, will different things please or disturb us?

A vehicle grinds to an abrupt halt in the lay-by, worn-out brakes whining, folding passenger door clattering open. Yana starts barking. I glimpse a flash of colour as the great barbet shoots off. Suddenly, people are on either side of me, dashing through our campsite and into the bushes beyond. They jump in recklessly, snapping branches, hiking up their ghos or kiras. There is a pause and then deep sighs of relief. A child squats on the grass behind Mr. Sangay's tent. I rub my eyes and rise to my feet. A bus marked Pelyab Transport from Thimphu has pulled in behind ours and disgorged its passengers. The driver puts his feet up on the steering wheel and lights a cigarette. A window near the back opens and an instant noodle packet flutters out. After a few minutes, brushing themselves down, the passengers emerge from the bushes and make their way back to the road, sticking their heads in our tents as they go. A teenage boy with oiled hair reaches down and presses his thumb into my foam sleeping mat. An Indian mother with a stud in her nose snatches a baseball cap from her infant daughter and returns it to Ngawang. After ten minutes, a horn sounds, the passengers climb back on the bus, and it thunders off to Wangdi. Before dusk, five more buses and three dumper trucks pause on their journeys.

I have a fitful night's sleep. A dog howling at the moon wakes me around midnight. I try burying my head in my sleeping bag, but it is no good. The doleful wail goes on and on and on. I unzip my sleeping bag, unzip the tent flap, and scramble out into the night in my under-pants. A cold wind blowing down the mountain from the pass makes the flap thrash about. The howler is sitting on a rock outside the canteen, a large beast, but featureless in the dark. I dash to the road barefoot, pick up a stone and throw it hard. The dog doesn't budge, and I don't hear the stone land. So I pick up a handful of stones and fling them. Two smack the front of the building. The dog bolts.

"Tony? What's up?" I have woken Nadya. "What was that noise?"

"Fucking dog. Didn't you hear it?"

"Yana?"

"No, no, not Yana. One over the road outside the hut. Think I nailed it."

"Come to bed. You'll wake everyone up."

I stand by the chorten, fists balled, reluctant to move, staring at the rock beside the canteen, willing the creature to reappear.

"Tony?"

I crawl back in the tent and into my sleeping bag, heart thumping. I massage my temples and count to a hundred, trying to get my breathing under control. It takes me a good hour to fall asleep. I am in a road race with a thousand others, wearing a white bib with a number on it, waiting for the starter's gun. Bang. The lead pack shoots off, all knocking elbows and flicking heels, and I follow. Every second counts. But, after five hundred metres, the route takes an unexpected turn and heads into a shopping mall. Suddenly, we are dodging people carrying bulging plastic bags and drinking coffee from disposable cups. Which way now? There should be arrows.

Where are the race marshals? Flustered, I look to left and right, then dash up a flight of stairs. More stores: Walmart, Tim Hortons, a hair salon, a dollar store. Which way? Alone now, sprinting down a corridor, sharp right turn, down another corridor. Which way do I go? The clock is ticking. Up a down escalator, panting hard, shoving aside shoppers. Hey, buddy, watch what you're doing! There must be a fire exit in this building somefuckingwhere. Another turn. Another corridor.

I wake up, shivering. It is still dark. I put on a T-shirt and stick my head out the tent. The dog is back on the rock, baying at the moon.

| "Sonam Gyalpo?"

"Here, Sar."

"Let the others load the bus. You and Sherab start running now. Take a bottle of water with you, okay?"

"Yessar!"

"Ugyen Lhendup?"

"Sar?"

"It's 6:15. You start at 6:45, okay, fifteen minutes before everyone else."

"Sar."

"Mr. Sangay, let's be out of here by 7:00 to beat the traffic. Can you make sure we have enough boiled water?"

Eighteen kilometres separate us from the final mountain pass. I should have thought before of having the slower runners begin the day's run ahead of everyone else, especially when we are at high altitude and it is cold. It would have saved the hares having to wait around in shorts and T-shirts for the bus. It is ironic to find Road Runner now among the limpers. Jumping up and down to restore circulation after a lengthy bout of blue-legging in the Dang Chhu a few days ago, he pulled a hamstring. Yesterday, he made the mistake of wearing an old pair of running shoes, which made the injury worse. Nadya will have to find a new nickname for him.

I take off for Dochu-La, feeling stiff. In Wangdi, Mr. Sangay told Tharchen, Nadya, and me that we would have to give speeches

at the reception in Thimphu. What am I to say to the queen of
Bhutan and representatives of her government? Something mean-
ingful about the value of education, no doubt, but I cannot think
of anything that doesn't sound contrived or insincere: "The new
democratic Bhutan needs bright young minds..." "Education is the
way forward..." I have yet to set anything down on paper. Invading
my head are ugly images of home. Where has development got us?
Old-growth forests clear-cut, leaving eroded wastelands or "replacement" conifers planted for profit; thousands of square kilometres
of open-pit mining in Alberta, the earth disfigured by monstrous
shovels, Brobdingnagian trucks carting off tons of oil-rich sand, tail-
ings ponds leaking toxins into rivers; town-edge shopping malls,
promoting consumerism (and driving) with year-round "bargain
sales"; fast-food restaurants serving unhealthy meals on single-use
polystyrene plates and oversized, sugar-saturated sodas; violent
video games; auto companies, subsidized by the government,
turning out ever-larger polluters...is this what we mean by progress? I think back to sitting by the window in a restaurant on Queen
Street in Fredericton and watching the Dodge Rams and Nissan
Titans growl by.

I speed up, but, after half a kilometre, begin to feel giddy. My
arms are flapping about uselessly, no longer coordinating with my
legs; I am lurching from side to side. *Ease up, for Chrissake!* I remember
the mistake I made running up to Yongkola. I slow down and focus
on taking regular breaths. *You're leaning too far forward.* I straighten
up, shake the stiffness out of my fingers, windmill my arms. *And stop
listening for bloody trucks!* I look about. Fewer oaks and ferns now.
More pine trees with intricate moss-crusty trunks, the branches
dipping to the ground and curling up like ladles. Flashes of pink:
rhododendron flowers bursting into bloom. Near the streams, clumps
of primroses with delicate violet flowers. I think of the flowerless
shrub that grew outside my office at Sherubtse and released a
perfume each evening as heady as lilac. I think of the flowerless
parasitic orchids, spilling from a mossy branch, that Dr. Jagar
pointed out to us on our hike with him last winter, of the crude,

water-driven prayer wheels straddling streams that clunked and creaked as they turned.

"Do you want to see where I was born?" Dr. Jagar had asked us in Tangsibi.

He led Nadya and me for two hours along steep trails and through dense forest to a clearing, where there were three cows and a stone hut under a fig tree. His parents used to spend winters here with their cows, feeding them on fig leaves. Jagar was born in a stone-walled paddock to one side. His older brother Norbu, who continued to look after the cows, was supposed to be there, but the hut was empty. Instead, we met one of Bhutan's rare primates. Slender-limbed and long-tailed, it leapt from branch to branch at the edge of the clearing and then onto one ten metres above the hut, sending down a shower of leaves. There it squatted, resting an elbow on one knee, and looked down at us. While the golden fur covering its body and the halo of paler hair around its wrinkled black face were striking, it was the expression on that face that was more so. The golden langur trained its red eyes on each of us in turn, then raised its head, wrinkled its nose, and looked to the other side of the clearing.

The memory makes me think of a book in the bus book box written by T. Sangay Wangchuk, a Bhutanese raised by his grand-mother in the countryside. *Seeing with the Third Eye* tells of the intimacy villagers have with their natural surroundings, of nature as a teacher. When barbets sing in the morning, young Sangay learned from Angay, it was time to take the cattle to the forest for grazing; rain would come soon when laughingthrushes descended to lower altitudes; following the example of dogs and cats, the villagers would eat grass to cure themselves of stomach ache. "Through the Third Eye, one may see the symbiotic nature of human beings with other partners on this planet," says Sangay. I think of the Tarayana emblem, a white hand holding a delicate, thin-stemmed flower. The hand might easily crush the flower, if it were to close, but there is an eye embedded in the palm, watching what is going on. "The time has come to see things through the Third Eye," warns Sangay, speaking more broadly of humankind's destructive tendencies, "so that its wisdom could also protect the other living beings," and I am reminded of a line in an article written by Canadian environmentalist David Suzuki, which I used in my writing classes in Fredericton: "It is folly to forget our dependence on an intact ecosystem."

A solitary figure is on the road ahead, running like he has a pebble in his shoe. I close in on a skinny man with head bent, punching the air. Ugyen Lhendup is proving that he is still the Road Runner. None of his comrades have caught up with him, and he is only two kilometres from the saddle.

"Hello, Sar."

Together we jog around the final bends and under parabolas of prayer flags, suspended from the trees, and I begin to recover my rhythm. Miraculously, no sweating sand trucks have passed by this morning. January 22 must be an inauspicious day for transporting construction materials. Our destination becomes visible: an island of 108 red-and-white chortens.

"Try not to look wasted," I urge Ugyen. "There may be a crowd up there."

Mr. Sangay said the mayor of Thimphu and a reporter from BBS would be at Dochu-La to greet us. We should, perhaps, appear to be conquerors of mountains rather than limpers and groaners. I think back to my conversation with Ugyen in Chendebji. "Have you done long distance run before, Sar?" he had asked. I told him how I had once run alone for several days from the north of England to my home village in the Midlands, a knapsack on my back with a leaky water bladder inside. Dehydrated and with bad shin splints, I suffered in the final miles, but made sure that I arrived at my parents' house with a smile on my face. "I would love to do, Sar." He liked the idea that as a distraction I had taken a sci-fi novel with me to read, tearing out and tossing the pages along the way. For once, project leader from the West and college student from the East, a world apart culturally, seemed on a level, united in a common passion.

Road Runner and I dash up the final ramp to the chortens just after midday. No mayor, no reporter. Instead: five cheering

women—two matronly, three teenage—clasping Thermos flasks
and packets of biscuits. They introduce themselves as Long Bone's
adopted mother, his aunt, and his sisters, up here from the city to
welcome home the hero of the family. The suja is highly appreciated
as the temperature is close now to zero, Ugyen and I are in T-shirts
and shorts, and our bus has yet to arrive. We jog around the chortens
and clap home the other runners to keep warm: Dendup, then Long
Bone (to loud hoots from the women), Wangchuk Rabten, Sonam
Wangdi, Tiger, Tharchen, Nadya, Yana, Sherab, Tee, finally Sonam
Gyalpo, who arrives at 1:20 P.M. looking shattered, but cracks a smile
when the rest slap him on the back. All for one.

We spend the entire afternoon at the pass. At 2 P.M., the mayor
appears and presents us with tashi kaddahs, then the reporter takes
six of us aside for interviews. BBS has decided to make a documentary on the Tara-thon, and Chimi Rinzin and his cameraman wish to
shadow us to the capital.

"I remember when we were climbing up to Thrumshing-La, I
was with our Tiger, and he was limping and I was limping, and we
were wondering, 'Are we going to make it?'" Nadya tells Chimi when
asked to describe a particularly hard day. "And Tiger said, 'Well,
you know, Ma'am, when we reach Thimphu, we'll have to do this
and we'll have to do that, and make sure of this and make sure of
that. Oh, and we must stay together for an extra day to collect donations...' Well, it just blew me away! I was so impressed that he wasn't
thinking about his pain."

"It was hard on my part because it used to be very early for me
to wake and jog before class, and I thought maybe I shouldn't do
it," Sonam Wangdi says, recalling his training in Kanglung. "But my
conscience, it kept bugging me from inside. You are going to run for
good cause. It is service from the heart. So I had to do it. I asked my
friends to come and wake me, and we did it together in the dark."

In the evening, we have two surprise visits. After the television
interviews, we jog about a kilometre down from the pass and camp
in a lay-by out of the wind. With a towel under my arm, I walk to the
nearest water source, a stream beside the road with a wooden gutter,

making the water accessible to motorists. Getting a wash proves to be a slow business as the gutter is clogged with ice and there is only a dribble falling on my soapy head. A Land Cruiser passes. I turn my head and see brake lights. Someone is stopping at our campsite for suja. Having removed my shoes and socks and washed my legs, I return to camp, stamping my feet to get the blood going again.

"You missed Lyonpo, Mr. Tony Sar," says Tharchen.

"Lyonpo?"

"Lyonpo Jigme Y. Thinley, leader of DPT, maybe next prime minister of Bhutan. He gave donation of 5,000."

I nod, happy about this, but disappointed that I didn't get to shake his hand.

"Lyonpo say he saw crazy man taking bath in icy stream," chips in Mr. Sangay.

The second visitor is Nancy Strickland from the Canadian Cooperation Office. We have kept in touch with her via email, reporting on our progress, but we didn't expect to see her before arriving in Thimphu. We needn't cook tonight, she says; we are to get in our bus and follow her car. Ten minutes later, we are in a plush tourist restaurant near Dochu-La, tucking into phagshapa, kewadatse, shamudatse, dal, and mountains of rice. In a speech after dinner, Nancy says how proud she is of our runners: they are a credit to the kingdom and role models for the younger generation. While I take photographs, she rewards each runner with a reference letter from her office to present to future employers. She then calls on our team leader to accept a small white cardboard box tied with a blue ribbon, which might previously have held a cake. Tharchen unties the ribbon carefully and opens the box. Inside is a wad of money, the notes kept together with elastic bands: one lac or BTN 100,000 for Project Tara-thon (CAD 2,666). We are flabbergasted. This is the largest donation we have received by far. Wide-eyed, the runners take turns holding the wad.

| There is another surprise waiting for us when we get up the following morning. The weather has finally turned. Snow patters

Snow for breakfast? Ngawang, the Tara-thon cook.

the sides of our tents and coats the bus. During breakfast, the wind picks up. It becomes a race to get the pots clean and the tent pegs up before they disappear under a white blanket. The students run about in ecstasy, shrieking, chucking snowballs, and dumping snow over one another's heads. Yana looks stupefied. Trashigang, his home town, would never have known snow.

We return to Dochu-La, run a lap around the chortens for luck, kicking the snow, and then begin our eighteen-kilometre descent into the Thimphu valley. For Nadya and me, it is like being back in Canada on a late-November day during the first snowstorm of the season: dripping noses, numb fingers, wet feet. Nadya warns the boys to take it easy as they seem inclined to sprint downhill, hollering; the last thing we want is for someone to fall and crack his skull. The highway twists through snow-laden firs, and, save for the

Tara bus, there is no traffic. But then, at about four kilometres from the saddle, we spot the mayor's four-wheel-drive struggling up the road towards us, wheels skidding on icy patches. Concerned for our welfare, he has turned out once again from Thimphu to check we have not been snowed in. Touched, I thank him profusely, shake his hand, and assure him all is well.

We remain for the day's run in a close pack, the Long Distance (Baker's) Dozen, so BBS can film us. As we lose altitude, the wind dies and the snowflakes fatten, disintegrating when they hit the wet road. Our pace is slow, and the team sings. I am pleased to see them so exhilarated, the tense atmosphere of a few days ago forgotten, Tharchen wearing a baseball cap back to front, Tiger swinging his gloved hands across his body, Long Bone loping along, Road Runner beetling, Gyalpo limping. Yana in "Please donate" bib, nails clicking, snow on his nose, weaves through our legs.

"Yana has been more than just a runner," Nadya told Chimi Rinzin yesterday. "He has been the spirit of our team. Yana was the first to limp. When we had leg problems, we looked at Yana, and Yana was no longer limping, so we knew that we would recover, too!"

"Are you the ones on television?" hollers the old policeman from his cabin at Hongtscho, seven kilometres from Simtokha, our destination for the day. "I saw you last night!"

Nadya and I have met this man before, a happy fellow with long, grey hairs cascading from his chin. In the past, we have had to show him our road permits, but not today.

The day's run ends at a T-junction, where traffic can either turn south for Paro and the airport or Phuentsholing and the border, or else head north to Thimphu. The spot is marked by a scuffed prayer wheel serving as a traffic island, a police kiosk, and idling Maruti taxi-vans and Tata merchant trucks. My mood sinks as it did in Jakar and Wangdi. Is this the end then of fresh air and eagle days?

"No words can explain what we are feeling at the moment!" exclaims Ugyen Lhendup to the camera. "We are on top of the world!"

"The snow has come to celebrate with us," adds Sonam Wangdi gleefully.

| The thirty-fifth and final day of our ultramarathon begins in chaos. On the menu at RUB headquarters in Simtokha for January 24, 2008, is fried rice and puri sabji, tea and coffee. Bowls, plates, spoons, and cups clatter onto and off plastic trays, and the sound of excited chatter fills the mess hall. Once breakfast is done, the students fly about, digging in their bags for their Tarayana T-shirts, tying and re-tying their shoelaces, limbering up, bumping into one another. There are more of us now. Twenty-one students taking part in the "Para-thon," a seventy-two-kilometre run from Paro to Thimphu, have joined us. A few weeks before our departure from Kanglung, a second-year geography student came to see us. As the Tara-thon itinerary didn't include Paro dzongkhag, could he gather together some runners and organize a second sponsored run that would hook up with ours on the last day? Knowing that no member of staff would be supervising and that Tenzin was unlikely to put his runners through a three-day trial to see if they were up to the job, Nadya and I were skeptical but too busy at the time to object. The Para-thoners managed to raise BTN 62,911 (CAD 1,678).

Nadya stayed up late last night, totting up the cash and checking the ledger, as she knew time would be short in the morning. Her Majesty expects us in Thimphu town square at 11:10 A.M. We must hand over the money to Tarayana at that time and declare the amount we have collected. Nadya and I rapidly bundle it into wads of like denomination, tie each with string, and toss them in our battered cardboard donations box. Carrying it between us, we sprint for the Tara bus, parked now beside the traffic-island prayer wheel, and dump it on board. Mr. Sangay is standing on the island, briefing the students in the way he would for the Annual Spring Marathon at Sherubtse. The students take turns spinning the prayer wheel. I grin. With snow around, thirty-one bare-legged runners dressed in white T-shirts and shorts are a curious spectacle for the Indian truckers in dhotis and overcoats waiting to get their documents stamped at the police kiosk.

"Five, four, three, two, one!" our event coordinator bellows and claps his hands for the last time. Four hares streak off—with strict instructions to wait at the end of Lungten Zampa, the bridge that carries the highway over the Wang Chhu into the city. We must all enter the town square together.

The five kilometres to Thimphu are on undulating, wheel-worn highway tracking the river. The morning is cool but bright, the sun prying loaves of snow off tall branches and sending them crashing to the ground. After the third kilometre, I expect to hear sounds of construction and notice a change in air quality but detect neither. The first houses come into view, and I see the snow is gone from the streets but continues to stick to the rooftops and coat bamboo scaffolding wrapped around half-made buildings. There is some movement in the market area, some taxis travelling up and down the streets; otherwise, all is still. The sonnet Wordsworth composed on Westminster Bridge comes to mind, the beauty he was surprised to discover in the city in early morning, the buildings glittering, the air smokeless, the houses asleep. I would later learn that Thimphu hadn't seen this much snow in three years.

The BBS car, the Tara bus, and two police motorcycles are waiting for us at the bridge. We are to form a double-file and follow the bikes to the town square. We jog slowly over the bridge and along Norzin Lam, the main thoroughfare, waving at the people lining the way, cheering and clapping.

Her Majesty Ashi Dorji Wangmo Wangchuck is waiting for us beside the clock tower, a banner behind her saying "Tara-thon 2008—Education for All." The queen is dressed in a mauve kira and vermilion waistcoat and is flanked by Her Royal Highness Princess Ashi Sonam Dechen; the minister of education, Thinley Jamtsho; the minister of information and communications, Lyonpo Leki Dorji; the secretary of finance, Dasho Yanki; the vice-chancellor of RUB, Pema Thinley; the director of Sherubtse College, Singye Namgyel; the Indian ambassador; the deputy head of UNDP; and Nancy Strickland. She takes rolled-up tashi kaddahs from a tray held by Tshering Yangzom from Tarayana, shakes them out and drapes them over the wrists of each runner bowing low before her. BBS films her doing this, and *Kuensel* takes photos. Her Majesty

Team Tara-thon and dignitaries at Thimphu Clock Tower. Back row, from left: Kezang (driver), Ngawang (cook), Sherab Jamtscho, Singye Namgyel (director of Sherubtse), Nancy Strickland (manager of CCO), Dr. Shivaraj Bhattarai (Sherubtse), Dasho Pema Thinley (vice-chancellor of RUB), Wangchuck Rabten, Karma Tshering (CCO), Dendup Tshering, author, Sonam Gyalpo. Front row, from left: Sonam Wangdi, Ugyen Lhendup (Road Runner), Nadya, Tharchen, Tshering Dorji (Tee), Yenten Jamtscho (Tiger), Ugyen Younten (Long Bone).

then leads the way into the five-star Druk Hotel and to the conference room.

"Today, I stand before you, my heart...bursting with joy and pride," my wife begins, after Tharchen has said how thankful the students are to Sir and Madam for letting them run to "help disadvantaged children avail education."

The author and Nadya with Her Majesty the Queen (now Queen Mother) and Her Royal Highness Princess Sonam Dechan Wangchuck.

Nadya wipes tears from her eyes before continuing, and I feel my own eyes prickling. I think of a message I received from my mother in the third week of our run. "Make the most of this experience," she had said. I look around the room. Nadya and I are unlikely to be in this situation again, addressing government ministers and two members of the Bhutanese royal family, runners sitting in rows with ceremonial scarves draped around their necks, TV cameraman filming, journalists furiously scribbling notes.

"We are grateful to Her Majesty and the Tarayana Foundation for believing in our project and for giving us their approval and support..." I say when it is my turn. Much of my speech is a list of thank-yous: "...to His Royal Highness Prince Jigyel for pulling over near Trashigang and offering us his wise words, to Lam Neten of Trongsa for granting us an audience, to the director of Sherubtse College for providing us with new running shoes, to Aum Nancy for selflessly donating one lac..." I realize as I speak just how indebted we are beyond my list. What of Angay Sonam, the grandmother who opened her doors to twelve sweaty strangers near Jakar, the villagers who brought us firewood from Rukhubji, the little boy who gave me mandarins near Lingmithang? "My wife and I are soon to leave the Land of the Thunder Dragon, but its charming roars will echo in our heads for many years to come," I conclude, leaving the lectern, then remember that I haven't said how much money Project Tara-thon made. I return with the box of donations.

"There are 618,916 ngultrums in here."

About 16,500 Canadian dollars. I am pleased with our efforts. More will come from donors in Thimphu and from overseas. I make my way to the queen, but, fortunately, am intercepted by Tshering Yangzom. Her Majesty does not need to grapple with a large cardboard box.

"You have done a wonderful thing for Bhutan," the queen says when we adjourn for tea in the hotel lobby.

"It was really the students, Your Majesty, who made it a success," Nadya responds.

"We hope our project spawns others like it," I add.

"I hope so, too. Come. Let's have our photo taken next to our Dragon," the queen suggests. "I imagine you would like that. Sonam?"

A gold-bodied, silver-bearded, red-tongued Thunder Dragon scales a black marble wall in the lobby of the Druk Hotel. Her Majesty positions herself beneath it, and Nadya and I stand on either side of her. Princess Sonam comes and stands to my right. I feel decidedly odd, dressed in T-shirt, tights, and running shoes, standing between a princess and a queen. After a month on the road, washing mainly in streams and having done my laundry only twice, I imagine parts of me are ripe. If either of the Ashis notice, they are too polite to remark.

| "Through thick and thin, we made it through." Sonam Gyalpo.

"We have been together long durations. Tara-thon was tough job, but I enjoyed." Wangchuck Rabten.

"Misunderstanding help us to know each other better. In the team, there is less 'I' and more 'we.'" Sonam Wangdi.

"The love of animal kept us together!" Tee.

Day 36. Thimphu. No kilometres to run. Our farewell dinner with the team is at Tandin, the hotel Nadya and I first stayed at when we arrived in Bhutan. We have shoved several tables together in the middle of the dining room and are making quite a racket. The waiters don't seem to mind, though, and keep bringing in more red rice, shamu-datse, fish curry, vegetable curry, naan bread, and beer. Everyone is here, except Mr. Sangay, and the students take it in turns to stand up and say a few words.

"He said like this, Sar," Tharchen translates for Ngawang, the cook, who, remarkably, managed to run the final week of the Tara-thon with us. "'Though we are not from single parent, Sar and Madam are like our parent.'" I look across the table at Nadya and see she is again close to tears. I feel like we owe more to Ngawang than he to us.

We spent the morning together with "the boys" at Tango Goemba higher up the Thimphu valley, a quiet monastery built by the Divine Madman in the fifteenth century. Nadya wore her kira, me my teaching clothes, and our students, driver, and cook their ghos. A black-capped sibia sat in a bare tree and watched us struggle up the icy path to the monastery in our dress shoes. The lama, a spectacled teenager, tapped each of us in turn on the head with his sacred baton and gave us orange strings to tie around our necks to guard against evil spirits. Mr. Sangay didn't join us for that, either. The last anyone saw of him was yesterday in the Druk Hotel. He chatted briefly with one or two of the dignitaries and then disappeared.

"Sorry that we didn't always see eye to eye," I said to him before he made for the door. The Tara-thon event coordinator nodded, looked at the floor, and thanked me for acknowledging him in my speech.

"There have been misunderstanding, Mr. Tony," he replied sadly, managing a smile, "but all misunderstanding left in forest. My job is done. I hand over to director now."

"Mr. Sangay Sar was keeping grudge from Mongar," Long Bone would later comment when Nadya and I visited his house and I asked him why Mr. Sangay hadn't stuck around in Thimphu the extra day. "If we Buddhist get angry once, it snatch away all our good deed. If you chant mantra for billion time and you said bad word, then all mantra is in vain."

I wonder if Nadya and I will ever hear again from the former Royal Bodyguard. I realize that I failed to give this deeply spiritual man the credit he deserves. Apart from arranging our night halts, he prayed for us daily, sharing his morning tea with the gods of the road and wandering off each evening to count his prayer beads. Our Tara-thon began with a benediction that he insisted we have, and I remember him pressing ngultrum notes to our foreheads and making an offering to the tashi gomang on Day 9. Perhaps these acts were more important than coaching our team or helping out with camp chores. Our slow crossing of the Himalayas at this time of year might have been hell, all blizzards and biting winds at the mountain passes and lashing rain at lower altitudes. Who is to say that his spiritual ministrations didn't smooth the way for us? And then there was the effect of Mr. Sangay's presence on the team, his military bearing, his reputation as a soccer player, his association with the fourth king. This must have made our runners feel that the mission they were on was a serious affair.

There is talk around the table of the behaviour of the Para-thoners. Apparently, many of the team hadn't run from Paro to Thimphu after all, including Tenzin himself. They had admitted as much in Simtokha. When they got tired, they had flagged down their bus. Two girls couldn't even manage the last five kilometres to Thimphu and took the bus. Nadya and I look at each other guiltily; we should have arranged for a Mr. Sangay to supervise them. After the Tara-thoners had gritted their teeth, accepted days of pain, and run the distance, why should the Para-thoners share in the glory? I should, at least, have had the Tara-thoners collect their tashi kaddahs from Her Majesty before the Para-thoners. But then I think, while this must annoy our runners, it matters less in the larger scheme of things. The short-distance twenty-one also raised money for our cause and extended the reach of our project. In the years to come, our ten runners will remember that they ran right across the kingdom for Her Majesty.

I think back to the Kuzoo FM interview Nadya and I had that afternoon.

"What will you remember about the Tara-thon twenty years from now?" Dorji, the shaven-headed host with earring, had wondered.

"The looks of determination on the faces of our young runners as they scaled the mountains," I replied, conscious that our runners may be heroes for Kuzoo listeners.

What *will* I recall of the Tara-thon at the age of sixty-three? The emerald waters of the Burning Lake? The rat caught in a beam of moonlight in the principal's office in Mongar High School? Yana the stray getting his first-ever bath in the Sheri Chhu? Gonpo Trashi, the Tibetan renegade? Blue-legging? I look around the dinner table at the twelve Bhutanese that Nadya and I have been with for the past thirty-five days. Perhaps the hoots and cheers of our runners as a little vermilion Tara-thon banner joined a thousand prayer flags at Bhutan's highest pass on the lateral road crossing the Land of the Thunder Dragon.

Bhutan has wandered without a map into that psychological territory where a magical innocence is lost and there are no signposts to what lies ahead. In Buddhist terms, the Bhutanese are collectively in some kind of bardo, the place between cycles of death and rebirth, waiting to see if they will enter the next life as a nation selectively modernized for the common good but otherwise unaltered, or as another small third-world country rent with social and ethnic divisions and vulnerable to corruption, violence, and political opportunism. One way or another, change is coming. This is not Brigadoon.

223

—BARBARA CROSSETTE,

So Close to Heaven: The Vanishing Buddhist Kingdoms of the Himalayas, 1995

Epilogue

"SO, TONY, how were your treks with Tarayana?"

Nadya and I spend our final weekend in Bhutan hiking with Dr. Jagar and Zangmo. Our destination is Jili Dzong, a windblown monastic retreat a thousand metres above Paro. Today, I am tail-end Charlie, slogging up the steep dirt path, the straps of my pack digging into my shoulders. I must have been extraordinarily evil in my past life as Dr. Jagar has loaded me with five half-kilogram bricks of solidified butter to give to the monks for their lamps and one five-kilogram tent that he and his wife will use once we are up there.

"Gruelling," I reply, chest heaving, "but also an eye-opener."

In the last week of February (having gained visa extensions to stay for an extra month), Nadya and I accompanied two Tarayana field officers to village schools in Zhemgang dzongkhag, a poorer district in the south. It was Pasang and Roselene's responsibility to visit the schools there periodically to deliver cash from the Scholarship Endowment Fund to beneficiaries. Shingkhar village was a two-and-a-half-day trek from the road along mud trails rising and falling through dense forest inhabited by hornbills, sunbirds, and drongos. At the primary school, we found 150 children sitting cross-legged on the floor in two furnitureless classrooms, which they swept daily using bushes for brooms. The assembly hall for morning prayers was an area of packed dirt to the side. In Digala, six days from the road, we met a twenty-three-year-old called Lobzang, the sole teacher in charge of sixty-four children, reliant for feeding them on sporadic parcels sent by the World Food Programme. Seeing the fascination of two little girls in Shingkhar, poring over an inflatable globe and trying to find Canada, and hearing from Lobzang about the determination of another beneficiary, a boy of eight from a broken home, I had to think again about whether educating village kids was a good idea.

"Some village children should have the chance for education," says Dr. Jagar when I speak of this, "the ones who have talent for studies. Tarayana tries to choose those with most potential. In the future, they may help their villages in bigger ways than ploughing earth."

Those like little Jagar Dorji perhaps. I remember "Tangsibi and Beyond," the article he wrote describing his own path from village cow herder to deputy vice-chancellor academic at the National Institute of Education in Paro. Without schooling, he "would have been limited to being a semi-literate farmer or a gomchen," he admitted and expressed immense gratitude to those who taught him: "I prostrate to my teacher and all the subsequent teachers..."

"And, of course, students with good potential learn far more from teacher than two-plus-two or how to memorize facts," he reminds me. "They learn right attitude, right value, how to communicate better, how to look after environment, about civic responsibility, about their own country, and about the wider world."

His words make me think of Father Mackey, who defined education as "not merely memorizing information, but learning to relate to one's environment in particular and the world in general in a creative and intelligent manner." Father Mackey, the teacher who believed that sports in school were as important as academic subjects, would, I think, have approved of our sponsored run.

We look up and see our wives waiting for us at the mani wall marking the halfway point to the dzong. It is a day of brilliant sunshine but little warmth. A brisk wind makes the needles of blue pines shake and their pendulous cones wag. Nadya may not know much Dzongkha, but somehow she is managing to share a joke with Zangmo. Maybe they are laughing at the two slowcoaches. Dr. Jagar tells me that he tried to persuade his wife to attend school when she was younger, but she refused. Now she is reliant on him for a living and spends all her time at home. It is a wonder to me that their relationship works, given that one partner is educated to a high level and the other not at all. Their interests, I would have thought, must be quite divergent.

"Sorry I couldn't be at your arrival ceremony with Her Majesty," Dr. Jagar says when we catch up. "This transition has been a busy time for me. You did well. You must be happy."

"The timing was off, sadly," Nadya replies. "All the schools were closed for winter recess. We had hoped to collect stories and drawings on our theme for Tarayana."

"But you raised a lot of money, didn't you?"

"Enough to send 330 kids to school," I say. "We couldn't have done it without your help."

We find a sunny patch to sit, and Nadya breaks out the stale chocolate and peanuts she bought in Paro. I look closely at the former director of Sherubtse. Nadya and I won't forget this man. Today, in his gho, hiking boots, trekking pants, and baseball cap, he looks a curious mixture of cultures, and it occurs to me that he has managed to assimilate wisdom from the West while remaining thoroughly Bhutanese. If people like him are to govern, the Dragon Kingdom is in safe hands.

"Any thoughts, National Councillor, on who will win the election?" I ask.

He smiles, punctures a peanut shell with his thumbnail and shakes his head.

"I don't know. Both parties are promising new roads, more employment, better health care, better education quality. They both say they are going to honour GNH, that they will boost the economy while, at the same time, preserving our cultural heritage and look after the forest. Their manifestos are very similar. I don't think it really matters which one wins."

"Are you satisfied with the way the electoral process has been conducted?" Nadya inquires.

"I am worried that the right people may not get into office. In the old system, the seniors get high position after many years of service—maybe twenty or thirty years. Now, the minimum requirement for a candidate is a bachelor's degree. Many of the older, more experienced ones don't have this and so get screened out. The young graduates apply, their heads full of high hopes of leading the nation, but they don't have the respect of the people."

"So you are not optimistic about the future then?"

Prayer flags and snow: the author with Dr. Jagar Dorji and Zangmo.

"I cannot say this, but it is all very hurried. I am worried that the people are not ready for democracy. Too many are still illiterate and uneducated. They don't understand that the enticements they are being fed by the parties may not come true."

I recall an editorial from last year's *Kuensel*, entitled "Hurrying Slowly." In the past, said the writer, Bhutan developed slowly and learned from the mistakes other countries made. Now, feeling pressured by globalization and fearing that it might get left behind, it was forgetting the cautiousness that had always been its strength. "We are building not just roads but networks of highways, not just pipelines but urban infrastructure, not just houses but towns..."

Everything is happening too fast, the writer worried. Yes, we must hurry to catch up with the world, but we must hurry slowly...or expect calamity. The expression makes me think of our Tara-thon tortoises.

We walk on silently, and the way is steep. Fallen pinecones, their seeds dry and brittle, crackle underfoot. The trees thin out. After forty-five minutes, we emerge onto a grassy meadow, dusted with snow, a place for yaks or even takins to graze—in our two years here, Nadya and I have not seen a single takin out of captivity. It takes us another forty minutes to reach the saddle and Jili Dzong, a white and red turret stationed on a bare promontory of rock, defying the elements.

Dr. Jagar removes his cap and straightens his gho before knocking on the door. I get the bricks of butter out of my pack. The door creaks open, and an old monk invites us in. He must have seen us coming.

| "DPT will dedicate itself to building on the firm foundation for a peaceful and prosperous nation that is the legacy of the fourth Druk Gyalpo and of all the great kings before him. As we look to the future, we do so with the confidence and the knowledge that we'll have the benefit of the guidance and the wisdom of His Majesty the King," Lyonpo Jigme Y. Thinley declares to the nation on March 24 as Druk Phuensum Tshogpa becomes Bhutan's first democratically elected government.

Nadya and I are eating scones in the conservatory of my mother's cottage when the news comes on the radio. Instead of returning home to Canada directly, we have stopped off in England for a couple of weeks. My mother chops vegetables for a ratatouille in the kitchen, and my stepfather mows the lawn while listening to Beethoven through headphones. Their two cats lie stretched out on the sofa asleep. Suddenly, Nadya and I have comfort: flowing water, unfailing electricity, central heating, every imaginable food-stuff at the supermarket (Nadya even found Bhutanese red rice at Sainsbury's), our sizes in footwear, fifty channels to choose from on the television. I had looked forward to all this on the flight here, feeling somehow that we deserved it after living for two years in a developing country, but the joys are short-lived. The overriding feeling is of loss.

Now that Druk Phuensum Tshogpa is in charge, I wonder what is in store for Bhutan. Is it destined to embrace capitalism and modernize like its neighbours? Will those with wealth—fed by TV and internet images of cars and washing machines and body lotions and life insurance—want more of it? Will private corporations dive into international markets and seek to maximize their profits, paying only lip service to their social and environmental responsibilities? Is Bhutan going to develop at the expense of its traditional ways? Perhaps not. Lyonpo Thinley I know to be a strong advocate of Gross National Happiness, calling it "the guiding philosophy of Bhutan's development process." The policies and programs that the new government will put in place, according to the party manifesto, are intended to strike a balance between material gains and people's welfare. At a time when industrialized nations are realizing that economic growth at any cost is destructive, maybe Bhutan, putting "equitable and sustainable socio-economic development," the first pillar of the Druk Gyalpo's visionary concept, into practice, will turn out to be a leader—or, at least, proof of a better way. I go and dig out the newspaper clippings I brought back with me, remembering an article written by the Honorary Consul of the Netherlands to Bhutan in December, expressing similar thoughts.

Leaders all over the world are searching for alternative approaches to development in light of the recognition that economic development and GDP in and of themselves do not necessarily make people happy. For quite some time there has been talk of "a paradigm shift," an "alternative worldview"— something more holistic and human, capable of transforming the world. The concept of GNH is a possible answer to this transformation...

Or will Gross National Happiness be viewed by the world as a quaint but impractical Shangri-larian notion, feasible only in a backwards Buddhist country (if at all) and hardly to be taken seriously? It is probably true that government policies that call on businesses to channel a percentage of their profits towards the welfare of their employees (or society at large) and conservation of the natural environment are more likely to gain purchase in a Buddhist setting, where compassion for others earns spiritual merit and all life is sacred. However, while Bhutan has challenges to meet regarding Nepali-Bhutanese refugees, disposal of litter, and treatment of stray dogs (to name but three), it surely has valuable lessons to teach us: that relationships and community involvement are more important than accumulating wealth; that close contact with and reverence for nature helps us live healthier, less wasteful lives; that a vibrant religious philosophy and colourful folktales can instruct and enrich; that we can often walk to where we need to go; that slowing down is a good thing...

I wonder, while staring out the window at a rhododendron in bloom in the corner of the garden, whether I truly opened myself up to the experience of the past two years. Full of my Western ways and eager to make my mark, I quickly established my workaday routine on arrival and then became consumed with a pet project. As trite as it sounds, did I really stop and smell the roses? Did I feel at all a spiritual connection with bird and plant and human being in a land where gods are said to inhabit every mountain pass and every bend in the road, where winds tear prayer flags apart and streams drive prayer wheels? It will take Nadya and me time, no doubt, to appreciate more deeply the ways in which this small Himalayan kingdom has touched us and fully acknowledge what a privilege it was to go there. In my mind, too, is the question of our impact on the country. Though we went to help out, have we, in a sense, hastened its Westernization and so been instrumental in eroding its traditions? Will our student runners, for instance, aspire to lead lives like ours: earning money enough to buy digital cameras and fancy camping gear, having no obligations to family or state, travelling widely?

"Let's go for a run," Nadya suggests.

"It'll have to be across the fields," I reply, putting an elastic band around my newspaper clippings. "There are no quiet roads around here anymore."

We head out across the village green and join an overgrown path crossing a farmer's field. Butterflies pick up from dandelions and mill about our legs. In the hedgerows lining the field are yellowhammers with brilliant yellow heads and chestnut backs, their beaks stuffed with nesting material. One settles on a hawthorn twig and observes us, head twitching, before shooting off across the rows of canola plants in the direction of a solitary oak tree.

Acknowledgements

A HEARTFELT KADRINCHE-LA to Her Majesty the Queen
Mother Ashi Dorji Wangmo Wangchuck, without whose blessing
Project Tara-thon would never have gotten off the ground. I offer
my thanks to Aum Chime Paden Wangdi and her hard-working staff
at the Tarayana Foundation, and to the Royal Government of Bhutan
(especially the Ministry of Education) for their support. Special thanks
also go to Nancy Strickland and those at the Canadian Cooperation
Office for believing in us, and to our mentor and friend Dr. Jagar Dorji,
who risked taking on two lecturers from Canada at Shrubtse College
and introducing them to Tarayana. A warm kadrinche to all those at
the Royal University of Bhutan and at Sherubtse who supported
our project, especially former director Singye Namgyel who endorsed
our project and supplied running shoes to the team and to Mr.
Rongthung Sangay who served as our event coordinator, but also to
Tshering Wangdi, Karma Wangchuk, and Karma Lhendup. I commend
the ten Tara-thoners for their determination and dedication to our
cause: Ugyen Lhendup, Sherab Jamtscho, Tharchen, Tshering Dorji,
Dendup Tshering, Sonam Wangdi, Yenten Jamtscho, Ugyen Younten,
Wangchuck Rabten, and Sonam Gyalpo. Kadrinche to Ngawang,
our hardy cook, and to Cowboy Kezang, our driver and flute player.
Kadrinche to Lam Neten of Trashigang Dzong and Khenpo of
Kanglung Shedra for their blessings, and to the villagers of Kanglung
(especially Tashi, Jurmi, and Dema) for their friendship.

I am particularly indebted to my wife Nadya, the za min thur who
not only looked after "the boys" on the Tara-thon but also acted as a
tireless editor of my write-up of *The Dragon Run*.

Many people in Canada helped me prepare this book for publication, offering their suggestions for improvement and editorial assistance. I wish to thank the University of Alberta Press, in particular Linda Cameron, Kimmy Beach, Alan Brownoff, Mary Lou Roy, Meaghan Craven, and Monika Igali, for their input. Thanks go to the New Brunswick Arts Board for the creation grant and to Laurel Boone for her advice on the manuscript. Credit goes to Dr. John Ball, Mark Jarman, Dr. Ross Leckie, and Emeritus Professor Robert Cockburn at the University of New Brunswick for their support. I am indebted to Khurram and Naushaba Khurshid, Ken Keirstead and Lynne Tompkins, and Micheal Lockett for their timely advice and assistance.

I owe gratitude to the UNB Bhutan Project (especially to the late Shirley-Dale Easley, Bill Buggie, and Kathy Aubin) for inspiring Nadya and me to go to Bhutan, and to Renaissance College, UNB, for its recognition of the Tara-thon project via an "Unsung Leader" award on our return.

In England, I am indebted to Professor Tim Youngs, Dr. Anna Ball, Dr. Rory Waterman, Professor Gregory Woods, and Dr. Sarah Jackson, all at Nottingham Trent University, for guiding my writing of *The Dragon Run* in its doctoral form, and to my mother Norah Robinson-Smith and her partner Patrick Wright, my brother David Robinson-Smith and his partner Samantha Cunningham, my aunt and uncle Pauline and Ian Pentland, and my classmate Sam Wilson for their encouragement.

Finally, nami samé kadrinche to all those who donated or contributed to Project Tara-thon. The Tarayana Foundation continues to seek support for its work helping "the vulnerable and the disadvantaged help themselves." www.tarayanafoundation.org

Notes

1. According to Annual Education Statistics for 2016, Bhutan 235
    has 522 primary and secondary schools and 169,560 students.
    There are 59 middle secondary schools and 25 colleges and
    institutes.
2. According to Annual Education Statistics for 2016, Sherubtse
    College has 1,782 students, of which 912 are male and 870
    female.
3. Bhutan Tourism Monitor reports that 62,773 tourists visited
    Bhutan in 2016 (this figure is for "international tourists" and
    does not include those from the "regional market").
4. At the time of print, Bhutan ranks 132nd of 188 countries on the
    Human Development Index and is classified by the World Bank
    as a "Lower Middle Income" country.
5. Most Nepali refugees have now been resettled in foreign
    countries, most notably the United States, but also Australia,
    Canada, New Zealand, Norway, the United Kingdom, the
    Netherlands, and Denmark.
6. As of 2011, Bhutan has three domestic airports: Gelephu,
    Yonphula, and Bathpalathang (near Jakar).

Glossary

Dzongkha unless otherwise specified.

akay: grand-uncle

angay: grandmother

ara: homemade liquor made from rice, wheat, or barley

atsara: clown at tsechu

atta: uncle

Aum: Madam

bukkari: wood-burning stove

cham: religious dance

chana: chickpeas

chapsa: toilet

chhu: river

chilip: foreigner

chipon: a government official

Choekey: classical Tibetan language

chorten: Bhutanese stupa

dal: lentil soup

damaru: hand drum used by monks

dasho: an official title given by the king

datho: Buddhist astrological calendar

desi: tinted rice with raisins and coconut shavings

dharma: teachings of Buddha

doma: areca nut wrapped in betel leaf with lime

dorji: instrument used by lama to subdue demons

drangpon: judge

Druk Gyalpo: Precious Ruler of the Dragon People

Druk Yul: Land of the Thunder Dragon

drupthop: master meditator

dzong: fortress monastery, seat of religious and civic power

dzongdag: district administrator

Dzongkha: the national language of Bhutan

dzongkhag: district

dzongpen: lord of the dzong

emadatse: chili peppers in melted cheese

garuda: holy griffon

ghee: clarified butter (Hindi)

gho: traditional dress for men

goemba: Buddhist monastery

gomchen: lay-priest

gup: village chief

hang ten cha: how are you? (Sharchop)

incroyable: incredible (French)

Je Khenpo: chief abbot of the kingdom

jinlap: herbal medicine prepared by monks

kadrinche: thank you

kasho: decree

keptang: Tibetan bread

kewadatse: emadatse with potatoes

khemar: red band around a building, marking it as holy

Khenpo: abbot

kira: traditional dress for women

konichi-wa: hello (Japanese)

kuzu zangpo: hello, greetings

la: mountain pass

lac: hundred thousand

Lam Neten: chief abbot

lhakhang: Buddhist temple

Lhotshampas: Bhutanese of Nepali origin

Losar: Bhutanese New Year

lyonpo: government minister

mandala: circular cosmic diagram

mani: stone inscribed with Buddhist prayers

meme: grandfather

momo: Tibetan steamed dumpling

nami samé kadrinche: thank you "beyond the sky and the earth"

nga: drum

ngaja: sweet milk tea

Ngalops: Bhutanese of Tibetan ancestry

ngultrum: Bhutanese currency

niksin: two (Sharchop)

oishii: tasty (Japanese)

Om mani padme hum: Hail to the jewel in the lotus

patang: machete

penlop: provincial governor

phagshapa: pork with radishes and chilies

pshee: four (Sharchop)

puja: purification ceremony

puri sabji: vegetables in spicy sauce with deep-fried bread (Hindi)

putang: Bumthang buckwheat noodles

saag: leafy vegetable like spinach

sangphu: chorten incense burner

shamdey: rice with meat, vegetables, and egg

shamudatse: emadatse with mushrooms

Sharchop: "language of the east" (also known as Tshangla)

Sharchops: original inhabitants of Bhutan

shedra: monastic school

shey!: bon appétit!

sho!: come!

sokshing: a carved holy stick put in a chorten

suja: butter tea

tashi delek: good luck

tashi gomang: portable chorten

tashi kaddah: ceremonial silk scarf

tashi tagye: eight auspicious signs of Buddhism

tengma: beaten maize

239

terma: sacred treasure

terton: finder of sacred treasure

thangka: painted and embroidered Buddhist tapestry

thruesel: Buddhist benediction

torrath: cloth for wrapping lunch in

tsachu: hot spring bath

tsechu: festival of dances honouring Guru Rinpoche

tshongkhang: store

tsubta: a dangerous place

tur: one (Sharchop)

yalama: splendid, remarkable

yathra: sheep or yak wool products from Bumthang

yosha: yak cheese

za min thur: the only girl

Zangdopelri: celestial paradise of Guru Rinpoche

zao: toasted rice

Other Titles from The University of Alberta Press

Under the Holy Lake

A Memoir of Eastern Bhutan

KEN HAIGH

Experience a Canadian teacher's transformative years teaching in the remote Himalayan village of Khaling, Bhutan

Weaving a Malawi Sunrise

A Woman, A School, A People

ROBERTA LAURIE

One woman's determination to educate Malawian girls and change the future of a nation

Winter in Fireland

A Patagonian Sailing Adventure

NICHOLAS COGHLAN

British-Canadian diplomat and wife sail from Cape Town to Cape Horn in their 27-foot boat

More information at www.uap.ualberta.ca